Wong Kiew Kit has practised and taught Shaolin arts for more than 30 years and has over 2,000 students. He is the fourth generation successor of Monk Jiang Nan of the Shaolin Monastery and Grandmaster of Shaolin Wahnam Kung Fu Institute. In 1997 he was made *Qigong Master of the Year* at the Second World Congress in San Francisco. He is the author of several books on oriental wisdom including *The Art of Chi Kung, The Art of Shaolin Kung Fu, The Complete Book of Tai Chi Chuan* and *Chi Kung for Health and Vitality.*

by the same author

The Art of Chi Kung
The Art of Shaolin Kung Fu
The Complete Book of Tai Chi Chuan
Chi Kung for Health and Vitality

THE COMPLETE
BOOK OF
ZEN

Wong Kiew Kit

ELEMENT

Shaftesbury, Dorset • Boston, Massachusetts
Melbourne, Victoria

© Element Books Limited 1998
Text © Wong Kiew Kit 1998

First published in Great Britain in 1998 by
Element Books Limited
Shaftesbury, Dorset SP7 8BP

Published in the USA in 1998 by
Element Books Inc.
160 North Washington St
Boston MA 02114

Published in Australia in 1998 by
Element Books and distributed
by Penguin Books Australia Ltd
487 Maroondah Highway, Ringwood,
Victoria 3134

Cover design by Slatter-Anderson
Design by Roger Lightfoot
Phototypeset by Intype London Ltd
Printed and bound in Great Britain by
Biddles Limited, Guildford & King's Lynn

British Library Cataloguing in Publication
data available

Library of Congress Cataloging in Publication
data available

ISBN 1 86204 255 1

CONTENTS

ILLUSTRATIONS

1

WHAT IS ZEN?

Meditation, a Cosmic Glimpse, Cosmic Reality

The aspirant may have a glimpse of cosmic reality
in an inspiring moment of spiritual awakening.

PUZZLING STORIES

Let us start with some stories to illustrate interesting instances
of Zen.

One day Lin Ji, who later founded the Lin Ji or Rinzai sect
of Zen, was asleep on a bench in a corner of his monastery.
His teacher, Huang Bo, knocked on the bench to wake him
up. Lin Ji opened his eyes, took one look at his teacher then
continued to sleep. Walking away, Huang Bo found the
head monk meditating in the meditation hall. The master
reproached the head monk, saying 'That fellow over there
is practising Zen; what nonsense are you thinking of?'

When a student asked Zhao Zhou, another famous Zen
master, how to find the true self, the master answered,
'Have you eaten your porridge?' 'Yes,' the student replied.
'Go and wash your bowl!' the master ordered. The student
suddenly attained his awakening.

Dao Xin (Tao Hsin), the Fourth Patriarch, visited Fa Rong
at the Bull Head Mountain. Fa Rong was so holy that
his cottage was protected by tigers and wolves, and birds
brought him flowers every day. When Dao Xin saw these
wild animals, he pretended to be frightened and mockingly
raised his hands to protect himself. Seeing this, the holy

sage said, 'You still have that!' Later, when Fa Rong went into his house, Dao Xin wrote the word 'Buddha' on his stone seat. When Fa Rong came out and was about to sit on it, he saw the sacred word and did not sit down. 'You still have that!' Dao Xin retorted. At that instance Fa Rong was awakened and attained his enlightenment. After that he did not see the wild animals coming to protect his house nor the birds bringing him flowers.

Many people are often puzzled by such stories when reading books on Zen. But it must be pointed out that they are not just foolish games or a play on words. Although a healthy sense of humour is always present in Zen, all the characters in the stories were serious about what they said. Why was it, then, that the head monk was thinking nonsense, but Lin Ji was practising Zen? What had washing one's bowl after eating porridge to do with Zen awakening? What was the 'that' referred to by Dao Xin and Fa Rong, and why didn't the wild animals and birds come after Fa Rong's enlightenment? Unlike many Zen books which often leave you bewildered by such tantalizing questions, this book, I hope, will enable you to understand and even experience Zen yourself.

THREE MEANINGS OF ZEN

Why do people have difficulty understanding Zen? One reason is that they may not realize the word 'Zen' has at least three different, though related, meanings as Christmas Humphreys points out.[1] First, it means meditation. Zen is the Japanese term for the Chinese *chan*, which in turn is transcribed from the Sanskrit *dhyana*. In Pali it is *jhana*. 'This is the lowest meaning of the term,' Humphreys explains. In its highest meaning, it is the name for the Ultimate Absolute or Supreme Reality, 'which is beyond all names'. The middle meaning is a mystical experience of this Absolute – 'a flash of awareness, out of time and beyond the limitations of personal consciousness, of the Ultimate from which all the world we know has derived'. This mystical experience is usually called awakening, or *wu* in Chinese, and *satori* or *kensho* in Japanese.

It is interesting to note that the Chinese word wu can be

pronounced in four different tones with more than 50 meanings! Wu meaning 'awakening' is pronounced in the fourth tone. Another meaning of wu often found in Buddhism is 'emptiness', pronounced in the second tone.

These three meanings of Zen are intimately related. Meditation, the 'lowest' meaning, is the essential way to attain a direct experience of the Supreme Reality, the 'highest' meaning. During this process of cultivating meditation to attain the Supreme Reality, the aspirant may have a glimpse of this cosmic reality in an inspiring moment of spiritual awakening, and this constitutes the 'middle' meaning of Zen.

We will study all three meanings of Zen in this book. The above Zen stories or *gong-ans* (*koans* in Japanese) – public records of Zen masters' awakenings – illustrate respectively the lowest, middle and highest meanings of Zen. Zen is also used as a short form for Zen Buddhism, which forms the principal part of this book.

There are other ways of classifying Zen too. A modern Chinese Zen master, the Venerable Hui Guang, mentions 19 types of Zen.[2] But do not be overwhelmed by this number: the difference between some of these types is merely technical in nature, and a few of them are debased forms. For our present purpose, Humphreys' threefold definition of Zen as meditation, cosmic glimpse and Supreme Reality is probably the best guide.

Keeping Humphreys' guidance in mind, we can arbitrarily classify Zen (in all its three meanings) into the following categories:

1 Zen of Zen Buddhism (or Zen of Sudden Enlightenment)
2 Zen of Hinayana (or Theravada) Buddhism
3 Zen of Mahayana and Vajrayana Buddhism
4 Non-Buddhist Zen
5 Debased Zen

The first three categories constituting Buddhist Zen are described in this chapter, non-Buddhist and debased Zen in the next. Within these categories, various esoteric methods illustrating how certain masters practise and experience Zen are described. It must be emphasized that these advanced meditation techniques are included here for information only and not for self-practice. Unless readers are initiated or under the supervision of a master, they are strongly advised not to attempt on their own the techniques mentioned in Chapters 1 and 2 – faulty practice can result in serious and harmful effects. However, other techniques described elsewhere, unless warning is given, are quite safe.

THE THREE CATEGORIES OF BUDDIST ZEN

Zen of Sudden Enlightenment

Of the various kinds of Buddhist Zen, that of Zen Buddhism is noted for being the quickest means of achieving a glimpse of cosmic reality. There are three main types of Buddhism: Mahayana, Hinayana and Vajrayana. Zen Buddhism is one of the major schools of Mahayana Buddhism. Nowadays Hinayana Buddhism is usually called Theravada Buddhism, although historically Theravada was only one of many Hinayana schools. Vajrayana Buddhism developed from Mahayana.

In Zen Buddhism itself, there are many ways to catch a glimpse of cosmic reality, or, in Zen terms, to experience wu or satori. For convenience of study, these many ways can be categorized into either Tathagata Zen or Patriarch Zen, the two main approaches in meditation to achieve enlightenment.

The term 'Tathagata' is a Sanskrit term meaning 'Thusness', or *Ju Rai* in Chinese (*Ru Lai* in romanized Mandarin). Western readers will probably be more at home with the term 'Supreme Reality'. 'Tathagata' is conventionally used to refer to the Buddha too. Hence, Tathagata Zen means the type of meditation traditionally taught by the Buddha to most of the Buddhist schools.

Patriarch Zen, on the other hand, is the type of meditation transmitted by Bodhidharma, the First Patriarch of (Chinese) Zen Buddhism. Readers who may have a soft spot for the Buddha, but who would like to practise Patriarch rather than Tathagata Zen, will be pleased to learn that this too originated from the Buddha. As you will read in a later chapter, the Buddha transmitted Zen to Mahakasyapa, who in turn passed it down through 28 Indian patriarchs to Bodhidharma, who eventually took it to China.

In Tathagata Zen, the emphasis is on attaining a one-pointed mind, through the process of concentration and contemplation.

It is the kind of meditation commonly described in Buddhist sutras, and is sometimes called 'meditation inside the tradition'. In Patriarch Zen, the emphasis is on uniting with the void, through the process of keeping the mind empty. It is not usually described in the sutras, hence is often called 'meditation outside the tradition'. It is referred to by poetic terms such as dharma-eye and mind-seal. Patriarch Zen (in this case the meaning is that of an inspired flash of awareness) is transmitted from heart to heart.

The following gong-an, illustrates some interesting features of both Tathagata and Patriarch Zen.

Yang Shan asked his junior classmate Zhi Xian how he was progressing in his spiritual cultivation. 'Last year I was poor, but not poor; this year I am poor, and have nothing,' he replied.

Yang Shan was happy with the answer. He was not, of course, rejoicing at his classmate's poverty, as indicated in the surface meaning of Zhi Xian's reply. He understood its deeper meaning, and exclaimed, 'Congratulations junior classmate, you have attained Tathagata Zen, but you have not dreamt of Patriarch Zen.'

Zhi Xian replied, 'I have an organ which I use to look constantly at a pretty girl; if others do not know, please don't call me from my dream.'

Yang Shan was overjoyed and reported to their master Wei Shan that Zhi Xian had attained Patriarch Zen too.

Were they really talking about a pretty girl? When Zhi Xian said that the previous year he was poor but not poor, he meant that he was empty but not completely empty, that he had attained detachment from self but not from phenomena. In other words, he understood that his self, or ego, was an illusion, but still believed that phenomena were real, though they existed only momentarily. When Zhi Xian said that he was poor and had nothing, he meant he was emptied of everything, liberated from the attachment of both self and phenomena. In other words, he realized the illusion of both the self and the phenomenal world. Such an attainment is gradual, won by means of the kind of meditations taught by the Buddha. Zhi Xian had attained Tathagata Zen.

While Tathagata Zen emphasizes the body of the Supreme Reality, Patriarch Zen emphasizes its application. When Zhi Xian said he had an organ, he was referring to his mind or consciousness, which he could use to manifest his organic integration with the Supreme Reality. By the pretty girl he meant his own Buddha nature, which is cosmic reality. Hence, by using the organ to look constantly at the pretty girl, he meant that his consciousness and cosmic reality – which represent the application and the body of the same Ultimate Absolute – are an integrated organic whole. This is Patriarch Zen, and its attainment is sudden.

In Patriarch Zen itself, there are two major kinds of Zen cultivation, namely 'silent-illuminating-Zen' (*mo-zhao-chan*) and 'public-case-Zen' (*gong-an-chan*). In silent-illuminating-Zen the aspirant strives for the Zen experience by means of meditation during which his total personality shines forth in celestial illumination and merges into cosmic reality. In public-case-Zen the aspirant, after being pushed to the extreme by a seemingly illogical question or story, is suddenly awakened to a cosmic experience.

Both these kinds of Zen cultivation enable the aspirant to attain enlightenment – or at least an awakening – here and now; they are therefore regarded as rapid or instantaneous methods, compared to methods in Hinayana and other Mahayana schools which may take many lifetimes to accomplish. These two Zen cultivation methods will be explained in detail in later chapters so that interested readers may also experience Zen.

In the spiritual cultivation of Zen Buddhism, in both the silent-illuminating-Zen approach and the public-case-Zen approach, the objective is to attain no-mind (*wu-xin* in Chinese), where there is non-thought (*wu-nian*). Hence, in the Zen story mentioned at the start of the chapter, when Lin Ji opened his eyes to look at his teacher then went straight back to sleep, he demonstrated that there was no thought in his mind. His teacher, therefore, said he was practising Zen. The head monk, on the other hand, did not practise Zen (according to the doctrine of no-mind) because he tried to use his mind to stop thoughts. In other words, because he was using his mind, and there had been thoughts in his mind which he tried to stop, he had not attained the state of no-mind.

This no-mind aspect is what makes Zen Buddhist meditation

different from the other types of Buddhist meditation transmitted from India, where the objective is to attain a one-pointed
mind. It also constitutes one of the major differences between
Chinese and Indian Buddhism and is one of the reasons why
many scholars regard Zen, rightly or wrongly, as a product of
the Chinese mind. We shall examine this question later when
we study the development of Zen in China.

Zen of Theravada Buddhism

Meditation is the essential path to enlightenment, not only in
Zen Buddhism but in all other schools – a fact that many aspir-
ants may not be aware of. The Theravada master Sri
Dhammananda says:

> No one can attain Nibbana without developing his mind through
> the practice of meditation. Any amount of meritorious deeds alone
> would not lead a person to attain the final goal without training
> the mind.[3]

In Pali, the prominent language of Theravada Buddhism, Zen
is called jhana, or meditation, which includes mental concentration and contemplation that raises the consciousness from
normal sensuous experience to a higher form of purity for
enlightenment. This purification of the mind is hampered by
five *nirvaranas* ('hindrances to progress'): sensual desires, ill-
will, sloth, doubt, distraction. When these five hindrances are
overcome, the aspirant attains *samadhi*, or one-pointedness of
mind, and is ready for contemplation.

In Theravada meditation, the fundamental topics for contemplation are derived from the three characteristic marks of
Theravada Buddhism: *anicca* ('impermanence'), *dukkha*
('suffering') and *anatta* ('non-soul'). Hence, Zen, or jhana in
Theravada Buddhism, is of two major types: *samatha-yana*
('tranquillity meditation') and *vipassana-yana* ('insight
meditation'). These two types are also applicable to Mahayana
and Vajrayana meditation.

As the Theravada aspirant meditates, he passes through four
characteristic stages of jhana. At the first stage, the meditator
experiences transition from a consciousness of sensuous desire
to an inward serenity unshaken by external stimuli. At the

second stage, he experiences zest, bliss and one-pointedness. At the third stage, he transcends zest and abides at the most blissful state available to human beings, a state of mindfulness without even the slightest trace of disturbance. At the fourth and highest stage, the aspirant attains liberation from attachment to the sensual world, acquires vision into and control over his body, maintains perfect mindfulness and equanimity, and usually attains supernormal powers like telepathy and clairvoyance.[4] Most Theravada masters, however, regard these supernormal powers as deterrents and ignore them because their use creates karma, which inevitably leads to future rebirth. The ultimate goal of Theravada is the eradication of all karma so as to attain nirvana, known in Pali as *nibbana*, a state which transcends life and death.

Zen of Mahayana Buddhism

The extent and depth of Buddhist meditation are reflected in the variety of approaches commonly used in the three main types of Buddhism. This is because the Buddha and other Buddhist masters were aware that although people may believe in the same philosophy and strive for the same aim, they have different needs and abilities.

During insight meditation, instead of contemplating on the three Theravada doctrines of impermanence, suffering and non-soul, Mahayanists often reflect on the emptiness of cosmic reality, on the suffering of other sentient beings, on the compassion to save them, and on the determination to attain universal salvation. While Theravadin contemplation leads only to detachment from self, Mahayanist contemplation leads to detachment from both self and phenomena. Mahayanists go beyond these four meditation states to four higher states, known as *si chan pa ding* in Chinese, or the four dhyana and eight samadha states. (There are altogether eight, not twelve, meditation states, because the four dhyana states include the first four samadha states.)

At the fifth state, the Mahayana aspirant reflects on the emptiness of boundless space (*akasanantyayatana*); at the sixth state, on the infinite sphere of boundless consciousness (*vijnanantyatana*); at the seventh, on the infinite sphere of nothingness (*akincanyayatana*); and at eighth and highest Zen state, on the infinite sphere of neither thought nor non-thought (*naivasanjnanasanjnayatana*). Hence, according to Mahayanists, Hinayana Buddhism is a preparatory stage for Mahayana wisdom, because, among other reasons, Hinayana Buddhism aims only at liberation from the illusory self, neglecting liberation from the illusory phenomenal world.

Zen of Vajrayana Buddhism

While Zen in Mahayana stresses compassion and wisdom, with the Bodhisattva or the selfless saviour as an ideal, Zen in Vajrayana stresses development of supernormal powers and mysticism, with the *siddha* or spiritual magician as the perfect model. Some of the well-known powers attained through Vajrayana meditation include *tumo* (the production of mystic heat so as to withstand bitter cold with only little clothing) and *lung-gom* (whereby the meditator can travel over great distances apparently effortlessly and at tremendous speed).

Vajrayana meditation, which is much influenced by Tantricism, frequently employs aids such as mantras, mudras and mandalas. A mantra is a mystical combination of sounds, the most famous of which is *Om mani padme hum* meaning 'Hail to the Jewel in the Lotus'. A mudra is a mystical formation and positioning of the meditator's fingers, making what is known as a 'hand-seal'. A mandala is a mystical design, generally of geometrical shapes, representing the cosmos. Usually a student has to be ritualistically initiated by a master, who will provide him with his special mantra.

Hence, Buddhist meditation which is an expression of Zen and which will ultimately lead to a direct experience of the Supreme Reality is exceedingly rich. Generally speaking, though there can be many exceptions or qualifications, Theravada meditation is characterized by focusing the mind on one point, Mahayana meditation by focusing the mind on the void, and Vajrayana meditation by visualization.

Although many people associate 'Zen' with Buddhism, it is not exclusively a Buddhist practice. While Zen is spiritual, because it transcends the physical, it is not religious. Many non-Buddhists, religious and non-religious, have achieved very high levels of Zen accomplishment. There are also some Zen practices which are debased. We shall study these in the next chapter.

2

NON-BUDDHIST AND DEBASED FORMS OF ZEN

Zen in Religion, Poetry and Deviated Practice

All the greatest spiritual experiences of various religious teachers were achieved in moments of deep meditation – though they might have called it something else.

CHRISTIAN AND MUSLIM MEDITATION

Zen has contributed tremendously to life and civilization. All great human achievements, for example the timeless works of Pythagoras, Chuang Tzu, Sankara, Avicenna, Leonardo da Vinci, Beethoven and Edison, were created in inspired moments of Zen experience (even though they might not have heard of the word 'Zen'), when they were in a deep meditative state of mind distinctly different from their ordinary consciousness. Although ordinary followers may not realize it, all the greatest spiritual experiences of various religious teachers were achieved in moments of deep meditation – though they might have called it something else. For example, the great Christian saint Augustine explained that the way to attain union with God is through contemplation:

> Contemplation itself entails 'recollection' and 'introversion'. Recollection is concentrating the mind, banishing all images, thoughts, and sense perceptions. Having emptied the mind of all distractions, introversion can begin. Introversion concentrates the mind on its own deepest part in what is seen as the final step before the soul finds God.[1]

The importance of meditation in Islam is explicitly mentioned by Prophet Mohammed himself:

An hour of meditation is better than sixty years of acts of worship.
Prophetic tradition, Hadith[2]

Many readers may be surprised to know that Muslim meditation is very similar to Zen. For example, the Muslim teacher Mir Valiuddin explains that meditation, known as *muraqaba*, the essential discipline Muslims practise to return to God, operates at two levels: externally it keeps out all outside interference from the five senses; internally it fixes the heart unwaveringly on God.[3]

While superficially there may be many differences in terms of rites and practices between Christianity, Islam and Buddhism, at the highest level in their approaches to the Supreme Reality they are surprisingly similar.

Readers are reminded that the meditation techniques described in this chapter are very advanced; they are not for self-practice unless aspirants are initiated or supervised by a master.

YOGA, THE UNION WITH BRAHMAN

Meditation is explicitly the principal means to spiritual fulfilment in practices such as yoga and Taoism. The numerous but unorganized meditation principles and techniques of ancient India, many of which were mentioned in the *Vedas*, were first systematized in the 4th century BC by Patanjali, who became known as the father of yoga. Hence, the belief held by some people that Buddhist meditation was derived from yoga, is incorrect: Siddharta Gautama Buddha had already developed a comprehensive system of meditation 200 years before yoga emerged.

The aim of yoga is union with Brahman, the Supreme Reality, and the essential way is through dhyana or meditation. Other yoga practices – supple exercises in hatha yoga, breath control in pranayama, and religious devotion in bakti yoga – are preparatory, similar in principle to the cultivation of moral purity and devotional practices in Buddhism. Yoga meditation is very rich in its philosophy and techniques; the following brief description is from the yoga classic *Patanjali Yoga Sutras*.[4]

> Yoga meditation is the control of thought-waves in the mind, which is achieved through determined practice and detachment. One effective method is concentrating the mind on a single object, which will lead to four stages of examination, discrimination, joyful peace and simple awareness of individuality – similar to the four dhyana states in Buddhist meditation. In another method of mental concentration, no object is used, but the mind observes its own subconscious impressions. Other methods to achieve concentration include focusing on the breath, on an inner light, or on a divine form.

When the mind is concentrated, the aspirant attains the state of samadhi. If he applies this samadhi to a specific objective to the exclusion of everything else, he attains *samyama*, which may lead to various incredible powers. For example, by applying samyama to his ear, he develops supernatural hearing; by applying it to the back of his head, he is able to see celestial beings; by applying it to his changing thought-waves, he has knowledge of the past and the future; and by using samyama to obstruct the perceptibility of his body by beholders, he achieves invisibility!

But the acquisition of such powers is in fact petty when compared with the noble aim of yoga which is to attain union with Brahman. For this the aspirant needs to go beyond his mind to reach his *atman* or soul. Samyama is now employed for the greatest task of all – to attain the insight that brings awareness that mind and atman are different.

> From *samyama* on the distinction between perfected mind as pure consciousness and liberated soul as pure awareness comes insight into the genuine difference between such pure mind and such pure soul.[5]

With this accomplishment, the atman is liberated and unites with Brahman.

THE TAOIST QUEST FOR IMMORTALITY

The term 'Zen', or 'chan' in Chinese, is not found in Taoist literature, but when Taoists use *jing-zuo* ('silent sitting'), a term found in their sacred texts on spiritual fulfilment, they mean Zen. In Chinese Buddhist texts, jing-zuo is *zuo-chan*, or *zazen* in Japanese, which means 'sitting meditation'.

The aim of Taoism is to attain immortality. This quest for immortality may be interpreted in three ways: to achieve longevity in this earthly life; to become a celestial saint transcending the human realm; and, the highest goal of all, to be united with the eternal Cosmos, or the Supreme Reality. Some aspirants attempted to achieve their goal by taking an elixir of pills; others by means of ritualistic sexual union between men and women. These approaches – called the earth approach and the human approach respectively – are actually debased forms of Taoist practice, denounced by great Taoist masters. One reason why these debased practices came about was that Taoist arcane knowledge was deliberately written in symbolic language so as to hide its esoteric teachings from the uninitiated. As a result, some people mistook genuine Taoist practices for alchemy or sexual rituals. The genuine approach is through meditation, known as the heaven approach because the aspirant merges the vital energy in his body with the cosmic energy of the universe into one organic unity.

There are many different ways of Taoist meditation. The account which follows is a generalized description derived from numerous Taoist classics, such as *Golden Flower Doctrinal Instructions of Saint Lu, Confirmed Experiences of Golden Saints, Realization of Truth, Important Selections from Great Success* and *Simplified Records of Organic Awareness in True Taoism* (all written in Chinese).

The aspirant adopts a single or double lotus sitting position to circulate the vital energy around his body in what is known as a 'small universal energy flow'. He then accumulates his vital energy in the energy-field at his abdomen known as *guan-yuan* (gate of primordial energy). When he has built up a substantial pearl of energy, which may take months or years of cultivation, he transports it to the energy-field at his heart, known as *huang-ting* (yellow hall). At the third stage of cultivation, he transports the glowing pearl of energy to the energy-field at his third eye, known as *tian-mu* (heavenly-eye).

Meanwhile, throughout these three stages of spiritual cultivation, he visualizes his pearl of vital energy taking on the shape of his own human form, and he calls this pearl his 'heavenly baby'. The heavenly baby then manifests his consciousness in an astral body. When the heavenly baby is fully developed into his astral replica, he transfers his consciousness into this replica and floats out through the crown of his head. He can now, in his astral body, travel anywhere he likes at tremendous speed, without being obstructed by physical objects. He may return to his physical body if he likes, or discard it to become a celestial saint.

If the aspirant aims for the highest goal – uniting with the Cosmos – he does not transform his pearl of energy into a heavenly baby but lets it diffuse all over his body in what is called the 'big universal energy flow'. He uses his third eye to look inward into his body, and his psychic ear to listen to every internal sound. As he develops spiritually, he feels golden, vibrant energy penetrating into and shining through his every cell, and his soul attains harmonious and organic unity with the cosmos. Here the famous Taoist saint of the 7th century, Lu Dong Bin, describes his own comic experience of the highest Zen.

> In the stillness, there is infinity, freedom and freshness of consciousness, as if intoxicated in a blissful shower, perfect harmony of body and environment, golden shower blossoming, yet everything in perfect quiescence, full moon in the sky, the whole great earth is a realm of brightness and clarity, the mind and body clear and open, golden shower expanding ... in the perfect silence everything is fully revealed before the eyes, pure soft whiteness as if opening the eyes in clouds ... looking at the body finds that the body is not there, everywhere is pure soft whiteness, the internal and external being transparent.[6]

DEBASED FORMS OF ZEN

Due to shallow understanding, deviated traditions, evil intentions and other factors, some people, Buddhist and non-Buddhist, practise a debased form of Zen. Some examples include what are called 'oral Zen', 'language Zen', 'wild fox Zen', 'rotten wood Zen' and 'beat Zen'.

Oral and Language Zen

Oral and language Zen are quite similar except the former concerns spoken and the latter written application. The exponent does not practise any form of Zen cultivation (like meditation or pondering over gong-ans) or understand any Buddhist doctrines, especially those related to Zen Buddhism, but has learnt some Zen expressions in a parrot-like fashion, without understanding their Zen significance. He may, as is often the case with the Japanese poetic form *haiku*, appreciate its literary beauty. Let us take the following Chinese Zen poem as an example.

> When wind blows, the heart moves trees
> When clouds gather, arise dust and sand
> Being ignorant of daily affairs
> Have not understood the original man.

If we merely memorize the poem or appreciate only its literary but not its spiritual qualities, we debase the poem into a form of oral or language Zen. But if, from studying the poem, we can derive some understanding of Buddhist doctrines, or experience a flash of truth into cosmic reality, we have rewardingly employed the poem in Zen cultivation. For example, in Buddhist symbolism, the wind often symbolizes the arising of spiritual ignorance, and dust stands for the illusory phenomenal world. Thus, the first two lines suggest that because of our ignorance, we mistakenly think that the so-called external world is objectively real, whereas in fact it is illusory, created by our mind (which in Chinese is often written as heart).

The last two lines of the Zen poem suggest that due to ignorance we mistake the phenomenal world for ultimate reality. Hence, we do not understand the true significance of our existence, which is to 'see our original face', to actualize our cosmic reality. This spiritual realization is found in our daily life, and Zen practice, as we will learn in this book, can help us to understand and experience this cosmic reality.

Wild Fox Zen

The term 'wild fox Zen', which illustrates karmic retribution due to deviated Zen practice, is derived from a Zen story recorded in *The Meeting of the Five Lamps*.

An old man was always present to listen to the sermons of the Zen master Bai Zhang (Po Chang). One day, after all others had left, Bai Zhang asked the old man if he needed any help. With tears in his eyes, the old man explained, 'Long, long ago during the time of Kasyapa Buddha, I was a Mahayana teacher. A student asked me whether a Mahayana adept was subject to the law of karma. I answered, "Not subject to karma." For this grave mistake I was continuously reborn as a fox. But even as a fox, I continued to cultivate and this has been going on for 500 years. As a result of my cultivation, I can now transform myself into a human form, though I am basically in a fox body. But the question of karma still troubles me, and I beg you to enlighten me.'

'Why don't you ask me?' Bai Zhang said.

'Is a Mahayana adept subject to karma?'

'No taste of karma' came the answer clearly and forcefully.

At this instant the old man was awakened. He discarded his fox body and attained enlightenment.

But how did Bai Zhang's seemingly illogical answer bring about awakening in the old man? The old man remained in a fox body because he continuously felt guilty about his wrong answer. He was 'punished' not by any outside power, but as a result of his own thinking which created a mental force that had been carried on from rebirth to rebirth. Had Bai Zhang attempted a logical answer, the old man would have continued to think in the same way and this would have perpetuated the karmic effect. But his illogical answer literally jolted the old man out of his thinking, hence stopping further thought process. The master could have given other shocking answers related to karma, such as 'Kick the karma!' or 'Karma is for eating!' and still achieved the same result. But such an answer must be given in the correct shocking manner, and by someone with Bai Zhang's spiritual force, sincerity and compassion. A lesser person giving the same answer would not have the same effect.

A similar technique is used in the story mentioned in the previous chapter about a student asking his teacher how to find his true self. Instead of answering logically, Zhao Zhou enquired whether he had eaten his porridge. The real shock came when the teacher asked him to wash his bowl. Had Zhao Zhou given a logical explanation of the true self, the student would not have had a direct experience of awakening, because his mind would still have been bound by dualistic thinking; at best he would have received only an intellectual understanding. Because Zhao Zhou's illogical answer came out of the blue, the student was shocked beyond the mode of dualistic thought. He was thus awakened and able to see his own true self. Experiences of awakening and the nature of the true self will be explained in later chapters.

Rotten Wood Zen

The Meeting of the Five Lamps also supplies a story for illustrating rotten wood Zen.

A pious woman honoured and supported a Zen practitioner in his Zen training. After three years, she decided to test his progress. So, one night, her pretty young daughter suddenly embraced the monk from behind and said, 'You can do whatever you want! How about that?' The monk replied, 'A piece of rotten wood has been left leaning against a boulder. After three winters, it no longer has any warmth.' Hearing this, the mother was disappointed. 'I've supported a piece of rotten wood for three years!' she exclaimed.

Feeling ashamed of himself, the monk left them, but continued to practise Zen in a nearby cave. After another three years, he returned to the mother and pretty daughter, and asked to be given another chance. The woman agreed. Then, one night, the pretty daughter embraced the monk again, asking the same question, 'You can do whatever you want! How about that?' The monk replied, 'Heaven knows, earth knows, you know, I know, but don't let your mother know!'

The mother came out and congratulated the monk, 'Now at last you have been awakened!'

The monk's answer in his first test was a demonstration of his moral purity. His reaction was the perfectly proper thing to do, seen from the perspective of other Buddhist schools and other religious teachings. It represents the monk's gradual development. But Zen training stresses sudden awakening; that was why the woman was disappointed the monk had made no headway in three years.

In the second test, the monk's answer, if seen in ordinary circumstances, was flirtatious and irresponsible, unbecoming of a spiritual aspirant towards a young innocent girl. Yet the mother congratulated him. Why? Because, in the spirit of Zen, his answer showed he had been awakened – not sexually but spiritually. He had been awakened to the experience of cosmic reality, which is inexplicable. 'Heaven knows, earth knows' symbolizes the infinite consciousness of cosmic reality; 'don't let your mother know' suggests its inexplicability.

Beat Zen

The above example also shows that beyond its apparent playfulness and liberty, Zen is not only ethical and religious, but highly spiritual. This, of course, is vastly different from the attitude and philosophy of 'beat Zen', which sometimes camouflages a licence for capriciousness and irresponsibility. As you read on, you will meet some seemingly unrestricted demonstrations of wild actions and words – even hitting the teacher and scolding the Buddha! They are all serious means devised by the masters to help their pupils attain awakening. However, such extreme behaviour is confined to their school grounds or monastery surroundings; it is not to be, and never has been taken out of its legitimate environment for abuse in public.

Undoubtedly there is a lot of humour and good fun in Zen, but above all it is for mature people who are working determinedly towards their spiritual fulfilment. Not all people will be ready for spiritual training, yet they can still benefit very much from Zen, because there are many other worthy rewards besides the attainment of enlightenment. We shall examine these rewards in the next chapter.

3

THE BENEFITS OF ZEN

A Refreshed Mind, Humour, Healing and Longevity

*The most rewarding aspect of Zen, besides
spiritual fulfilment, is that it teaches us to find
joy and meaning in our daily lives.*

RELAXATION AND MIND CONTROL

In his last words before he entered *parinirvana*, or the final
nirvana, the Buddha gave this advice to humanity: 'Life is short.
You must work hard to liberate yourselves from samsara.' There
are many ways to liberate ourselves from *samsara*, or from the
suffering of the endless cycle of birth and rebirth, but Zen offers
the fastest and most direct way. If we are ready, or in Buddhist
terms if we have excellent spiritual roots, we can attain enlightenment instantly!

How to ascertain whether we have excellent spiritual roots,
and how to cultivate them if they are lacking, will be explained
in later chapters. Here, we discuss what benefits Zen can
provide for people who may not be ready for spiritual training.
Indeed, many people are already applying Zen in their daily
lives without realizing it, but if they were aware of the principles
and methods of Zen, they would obtain even better results,
irrespective of their religion, or lack of one. For example, when
a scientist plans a research programme, an executive presents
a business proposal, an artist creates a masterpiece, or a
sportsman focuses on a technique, they all involve in some way
or another certain aspects of Zen. If the scientist has clarity of
mind, the executive directness of purpose, the artist originality
of thought, and the sportsman concentration of effort, his or

her objective will be accomplished more successfully and effectively. All the qualities that contribute to the success of their endeavours are developed in Zen practice.

The first requirements are self-discipline, determination and perseverance, and two of the earliest skills a Zen practitioner needs to acquire are the ability to relax and to control the mind. If tense or anxious or constantly distracted by irrelevant thoughts, the student will be unable to make further progress. Many techniques are available to develop these skills, and a good Zen instructor can initiate his students into relaxation and mind control almost without their conscious knowledge. Some of these techniques will be explained in later chapters for those readers who wish to practise these skills.

Once we can relax, we are able to attain a state where mind and body can function at their optimum, with all our natural functions – defence, immune, regenerative and feed-back systems – enhanced. Not only can the Zen practitioner manage stress effectively and prevent illness, but any health or medical problems that he may have already, can be brought under control.

According to Chinese medical philosophy, the emotions are intimately connected with both internal energy flow and the mind (which the Chinese call the heart).[1] For example, the meridian system of the heart is connected with the feeling of joy, that of the liver with anger, and that of the stomach with anxiety. Zen cultivation promotes harmonious energy flow through the meridians. This explains why Zen practitioners are always cheerful, amiable and relaxed – not as the result of any extrinsic moral instruction they have received but because of qualities developed intrinsically as part of the training process. Zen practice is therefore an excellent method of stress management. Anyone – in whatever walk of life – who is exposed to stress will derive much benefit from practising Zen.

Constant practice in training the mind in meditation makes the mind sharp, serene and well focused. Such mental development enables the Zen practitioner to think clearly and deeply, to concentrate on work for long periods, and to make decisions quickly and confidently. Many artists and sportsmen and women will value these qualities. The Zen practitioner who advances and reaches deeper levels of consciousness may be able to tap into the universal mind which has provided inspiration and creative ideas to scientists, artists and philosophers throughout history.

With Zen cultivation, psychic powers like telepathy, clairvoyance and astral travel may be developed. After Dr Rhine, the father of parapsychology, had scientifically shown that one in every five persons readily demonstrates the power of extrasensory perception, numerous universities set up departments to investigate and develop psychic ability. The techniques they employed were similar to those used in Zen cultivation, except Zen practitioners have no need for elaborate laboratory equipment and are in general not interested in developing such powers.

> Huang Bo and a monk came to a river. While Huang Bo was looking for a boat to take them across, the monk employed his supernormal power to walk across the water without getting wet. Huang Bo followed suit, but when they reached the other side, he said, with characteristic Zen humour, 'I didn't know you could do that, or else I would have pushed you right down to the bottom of the river.'

HUMOUR AND MEANING IN DAILY LIFE

Having a good sense of humour is typical of Zen practitioners, whose training has enabled them to be detached so that their comic spirit can readily flourish. Christmas Humphreys observed that 'there is more honest belly laughter in a Zen monastery than surely in any other religious institution on earth. To laugh is a sign of sanity; and the comic is deliberately used to break up concepts, to release tensions and to teach what cannot be taught in words.'[2] Conrad Hyers, in *Zen and the Comic Spirit*, deals with this topic remarkably, as the following two examples illustrate.

> When the Zen master Teng Yin Feng was about to enter parinirvana, he asked his friends:
> 'I've seen monks die sitting and lying, but have any died standing?'
> 'Yes, some,' came the reply.
> 'How about upside down?'

'Never seen such a thing!'

Whereupon the comic Teng stood on his head and died. People who came to his funeral were astounded, and undertakers were not sure how to carry away his body. His younger sister, a nun, came grumbling at him:

'When you were alive you took no notice of rules and customs. Even now you are dead, you are making a nuisance of yourself.'

She poked him with a finger and he fell with a thud.

One day Zhao Zhou and his disciple Wen Yuan were having a leisurely stroll, and they decided to have a contest to see who could put himself into the lowest position. The winner was to pay the loser a piece of cake.

Zhao Zhou said, 'I am an ass.'

'I am the ass's buttocks,' answered Wen Yuan immediately.

'I am the ass's shit.'

'I am a worm in the shit!'

'What are you doing in the shit?' the master asked.

'I'm spending my summer vacation.'

Zhao Zhou, the loser, had to accept a piece of cake from Wen Yuan.

Zen is not only full of comic spirit, but it also teaches us to live and appreciate every moment of life, to be incredibly relaxed even in extremely demanding situations, and to find joy and beauty in otherwise simple deeds and day-to-day living.

The *vinaya* master You Yuan asked Zhao Zhou:

'Do you still practise spiritual cultivation?'

'I still practise.'

'How do you practise?'

'When rice comes, I eat; when tiredness comes, I sleep,' Zhao Zhou answered.

'Everyone does that; so everyone practises spiritual cultivation like you!'

'Not the same.'

'Why not the same?'

'When it's time to eat, they do not eat; they're tied down by hundreds of thoughts. When it's time to sleep, they do not sleep; they're troubled by thousands of calculating schemes.'

No wonder Zhao Zhou, a Zen master who found humour and meaning in daily life, was able to live to 120.

HEALTH AND HEALING

An exciting and rewarding area which Zen practitioners can both benefit from and contribute to is health and medicine. Illness can be, and has been, cured by means of meditation alone, without orthodox medication. Readers who are used to the Western paradigm of health and medicine, where the body is often treated like a machine and distinctly separated from the mind, will find this concept of meditation therapy difficult to comprehend. A paradigm shift in their way of thinking may be necessary in order to arrive at an understanding of how physical and mental illness can be overcome through meditation. They would need to examine the subject according to Buddhist philosophy.

Two basic Buddhist doctrines are relevant here: the belief that our body is an illusion created by the mind; and that every phenomenon, including our body, is a manifestation of *dharmas*, or subatomic forces and particles. A meditator who has great control over the mind can influence how and where dharmas are to be manifested. For example, if irritants in the lungs are causing asthma, or a hole in the stomach a peptic ulcer, a meditator can, through the power of the mind, direct the dharmas that are manifesting as irritants to be cleared, or create dharmas manifesting as healthy cells to patch up the stomach sores. I myself have successfully employed these principles, together with the relevant exercises, to help cure many patients of their so-called incurable diseases, including cancer. If you think this sounds like a fairy tale, perhaps these quotations from world renowned scientists concerning their celebrated discoveries will convince you.

Michael Talbot, an American professor of quantum physics, says:

Even the world we know may not be composed of objects. We may only be sensing mechanisms moving through a vibration dance of frequencies.[3]

In the words of well-known biologist, Professor Edmund Jack Ambrose:

> The matter in life has no permanence; only the pattern according to which it is arranged or organised has permanence. Life is basically a pattern of organised activity.[4]

Another modern scientist of world fame, Dr Andrew Scott, has this to say about our bodies:

> The particles from which our living bodies are constructed do not sit apart from one another in lonely isolation. In the first place they are all constantly on the move – rushing about, spinning, tumbling, bumping into and bouncing off one another.[5]

And the Cambridge physicist Alastair Rae echoes the view of modern scientists:

> Quantum theory tells us that nothing can be measured or observed without disturbing it, so that the role of the observer is crucial in understanding any physical process. So crucial in fact that some people have been led to believe that it is the observer's mind that is the only reality – that everything else including the whole physical universe is illusion.[6]

Scientists tell us that the external world is actually an illusion, that the matter which constitutes life has no permanence but is arranged in a pattern, that the subatomic particles that form this life-matter are constantly moving, and that the crucial factor that shapes 'reality' is mind.

It is also helpful to remind ourselves that the hundred trillion cells that constitute the pattern which we normally call our body, are constantly replaced. The rate of replacement varies, but scientists believe that in seven months, total renewal has occurred. In other words, the physical body you have now is completely different from the one you had seven months ago. Buddhist masters have known this fact since ancient times. Their knowledge is even more profound: they believe that not only body cells but all the ingredients that constitute a person – in Buddhist terminology the five *skandhas* of form, perception, thought, activity and consciousness – are transient.

Meditation Healing

If all our body cells are constantly replaced, why do cancer cells remain? The explanation for this is that although all cells, cancerous and otherwise, are replaced, the patterns upon which they are formed and behave, continue. In Buddhist terms, at the subatomic level, the karmic force of the individual dharmas that manifest as cancer cells, is transmitted from one cell-life to another. Just as the mind of an observer can affect the pattern of subatomic particles in a scientific experiment, the mind of a Zen practitioner during deep meditation can affect the pattern of dharma manifestation. By visualizing that the cancer cells are being eliminated and replaced by new healthy cells, the patient is literally translating his thoughts into physical reality at the cellular level.

The discovery of the famous Russian psychologist Dr Victor Krivorotov may one day serve as a bridge between ancient wisdom and modern science in the search for solutions to today's health problems, including cancer, aids and psychiatric disorders. He says:

> A disease is that state of the system in which full spiritual potential is unrealized ... Given this definition of disease, what does effective treatment consist of? Treatment consists in stimulating the patient's spirit, which affects all the systems, bringing them into a harmonious state ... For the most part, modern medicine effects somatic corrections. Consequently, treatment can be successful only in those cases where the initial source of the disease is in the body. But for modern man, the primary source of disintegration has become a negative system of conditioning (manifesting egotism, arrogance, vanity, envy, jealousy, etc), the system of values, and world-view.[7]

In modern society, therefore, conventional medicine is frequently unsatisfactory. In contrast, meditation therapy treats illness directly, and is therefore applicable to both psychiatric and somatic disorders.

In his masterpiece, *Six Marvellous Gateways*, a treatise on samadha and vispasyana meditation, the great Tian Tai master Zhi Yi (538–97) provided a fascinating explanation for the curing of illness by means of meditation. The five major therapeutic approaches he postulated involved:

1 Focusing the mind at the site of illness
2 Using six characteristic healing sounds
3 Using twelve major breathing methods
4 Applying visualization
5 Analysing the composition of the four 'elements' (earth, water, fire and air) in the body

It should be noted that meditation therapy is not necessarily always better than conventional medicine or other types of healing. There are a number of disadvantages with this method. The patient must have attained a reasonably high standard of meditation for such healing to be effective, and it requires a great deal of mental energy. Thirdly, it is mainly self-healing; it is not usually feasible – but not impossible – to use meditation therapy on another person.

There are, nevertheless, at least two areas where meditation therapy can contribute greatly to conventional medicine. Firstly, curing through meditation can be an excellent alternative healing system in diseases where conventional medicine is known to be inadequate, as in the whole range of degenerative and psychiatric disorders, such as cardiovascular dieases, diabetes, rheumatism, manic depression, schizophrenia and cancer. Secondly, if medical research scientists could only overcome their prejudice and start to investigate the claims of 'miraculous' cures by meditation masters, they may find that the principles and techniques they employ are valid and could be usefully incorporated into conventional medical practice without necessarily distorting its own basic traditions.

Therefore, while Zen cultivation is primarily for spiritual development, it can also bring more down-to-earth benefits to practitioners. For patients suffering from a range of diseases, from insomnia and diabetes to sclerosis of the liver and cancer, Zen provides not only hope but a good possibility of recovery. For others, it promotes physical, emotional and mental health and enhances longevity, as is amply substantiated by the lives of Zen masters such as Nan Quan (748–834), Bai Zhang (720–814), Shi Tou (700–90), Zhao Zhou (778–897) and Suzuki (1870–1966).

As a system of stress management, Zen is particularly useful in dealing with the problems inherent in modern, busy lives. It is direct yet elegant, simple yet effective; its training of the mind enables scientists and philosophers to think clearly and deeply, while poets and artists can find within it the source of their originality and creativity. Zen is indeed beneficial to everyone. The most rewarding aspect of Zen, besides spiritual fulfilment, is that it teaches us to find joy and meaning in our daily lives.

4

THE CHARACTERISTICS OF ZEN

From Awakening to Enlightenment

Enlightenment, of course, occurs in other religions too, although it may be known by other names.

THREE IMPORTANT QUESTIONS

If you decide to practise Zen you will be interested in the following three questions. What signs should you look for to check that your practice is correct? How do you know whether you have attained spiritual awakening? Are there further achievements beyond satori? The answers to these questions represent the three stages of Zen progress.

It should be noted that in this chapter, the term Zen is used generally to refer to all kinds of Zen; it may mean 'meditation', 'a glimpse of cosmic reality', and sometimes the 'Supreme Reality' or 'Ultimate Absolute' itself.

Since the way to both a cosmic glimpse and the Supreme Reality is through meditation, the practice of meditation constitutes the main part of Zen cultivation. A cosmic glimpse (satori) occurs from time to time to indicate that cultivation is progressing correctly; realization of the Supreme Reality, known as enlightenment, is the ultimate goal.

Meditation is best done under the guidance of a competent instructor. Those who practise on their own should be careful that they are proceeding correctly, for faulty practice may lead to harmful effects. While this warning is true, it should nevertheless not deter aspirants who wish to practise on their own. Harmful effects, just like good effects, take time to develop, and there are usually sufficient signals to warn that the practice is not being carried out correctly. If the student is so unwise as to ignore these warnings and persists in faulty meditation, then gradually over a period of time (a few years) the harmful effects can become very serious and lead to physical or mental illness.

SIGNS OF WRONG PRACTICE

The warning signs listed below are indications that Zen is being practised incorrectly. The actual techniques of meditation will be explained in a later chapter.

1 Pain in the body. This is probably caused by incorrect posture or breathing. The logical remedy is to correct the posture or breathing.
2 Becoming easily tired or drowsy during meditation practice. This is probably due to wrong or forced mental concentration during meditation. Choose a more congenial subject for mental concentration, which must be done gently.
3 Frequently feeling frightened or seeing unpleasant visions during meditation. This is probably due to a lack of confidence in your method or in yourself, having doubts, or feeling guilty about some past thought or action. You should stop your meditation practice for the time being, find out more about your own religion (if you profess one) and about meditation methods from qualified people or from good books, and practise tolerance, charity and kindness to enhance your moral purity. All religious teachers stress that moral purity is a basic requirement for spiritual development. There are practical reasons for saying this; they are not merely moralizing. Sometimes, however, changing your place of meditation can help you to overcome these feelings of fright or unpleasant visions.
4 Feeling giddy and uncomfortable during meditation practice and becoming easily irritated at other times. This can be caused by an energy blockage due to faulty technique. Practise some *chi kung* exercises (*see* Chapter 18) to harmonize energy flow before resuming your meditation practice.

On the other hand, the following beneficial effects indicate that you are making progress in your Zen cultivation.

1 Feeling fresh and relaxed
2 Experiencing a sense of inner peace
3 Developing a cheerful and caring attitude
4 Being able to focus on anything for longer and longer periods
5 Being surprised at the clarity and depth of your thinking
6 Finding that the world is suddenly more beautiful than before

THE SPIRITUAL AWAKENING

As you continue to practise Zen, you may one day experience a spiritual awakening, known as wu in Chinese, and satori or kensho in Japanese. Although this awakening is spiritual, it is not religious because its attainment does not depend on the acceptance of specific religious beliefs, nor will it affect unfavourably the present religious beliefs of the practitioner – on the contrary, it usually strengthens them.

The Japanese Zen master Daisetz Teitaro Suzuki describes satori as a change of view-point to an intuitive, non-intellectual kind of understanding: '. . . satori means the unfolding of a new world hitherto unperceived in the condition of a dualistic mind.'[1] There are two crucial points concerning satori. The change of view-point must transcend whatever is perceived by a dualistic mind; and this change must involve intuitive experience, not just intellectual and logical understanding. For example, in the past you might have regarded your wife or husband as someone who just happened to have married you; but now you regard her or him as someone really special, someone who has given the best of her or his life for your welfare and happiness. This change of view-point, which may have resulted from your Zen cultivation, is not satori, because, although it involves intuitive experience rather than intellectual understanding, it is still within the realm of dualistic thinking. It is dualistic because the change of view-point involves comparing the past with the present, and comparing an ordinary spouse with a special one.

In satori, breaking through this dualistic mode of thinking is essential. The organic oneness of cosmic reality will be explained in Chapter 6; here suffice it to say – though many readers may find this incomprehensible – that a change of view-point in satori will render your present spouse (who is now very special to you) timelessly linked to the past (when your spouse was just ordinary) and spatially linked to everything around you. If your Zen teacher were to ask you a question like 'Where is your spouse?', you would honestly and correctly say something like 'a bird is in the tree', because in your supposed satori you would see your spouse holistically linked to the bird and the tree! If you can appreciate this point, you will be able to comprehend that many of the seemingly illogical answers given in Zen stories are actually meaningful.

But if you were again asked that question, and you gave that apparently illogical answer, it would not be an indication of satori, because your change of view-point would be due to your intellectual understanding, not your intuitive experience. In other words, your change of view-point occurred because you intellectually understood what had just been explained, not because you experienced the phenomenon intuitively.

In his book *Zen and the Psychology of Transformation*, Dr Hubert Benoit describes an experience which he calls a 'little transitory satori':

> At this moment the calm in me is so pure that it amounts to a veritable suspense. Suddenly a sense-perception (an object which enters my field of vision, or a sound which reaches me) breaks this suspense; I see the object, or I hear the sound, as I never see or hear habitually; as if, habitually, forms and sounds only came to me through a screen which deformed them, whereas in this special moment, they come to me direct, in their pure reality. Still more interesting, my sense perception communicates to me simultaneously a knowledge of the outside world and of myself; in this moment I feel no longer any separation between the world and myself although they remain distinct; Not-Self and Self, while remaining two, are joined together to form a unity.[2]

The above quotation reveals a superficial understanding of satori based on reading Zen literature, not on personal experience. It is unlikely that the above author has practised Zen in the way it is traditionally practised. Benoit's experience may be an altered state of consciousness, but it is not satori. He first experiences a state of pure calmness, 'a veritable suspense'. Then a sense-object breaks the calmness and he perceives this object in a way he has never perceived it before. His experience is still phenomenal, not transcendental. He *feels* that he is not separated from the world – a feeling that is probably due to his intellectual, not intuitive, knowledge of Zen – yet he is aware of his separateness. A satori experience is usually, though not necessarily, the reverse. The pure calmness comes *after*, not before, the sense-object, which acts as a catalyst for the Zen awakening. The subject does not feel or think that he is organically linked to the world; he actually *experiences* this organic togetherness.

The disturbing point is that Dr Hubert Benoit's views on Zen are regarded in the West as authoritative. The London *Times* reports, 'He has understood their [the Zen masters'] secret', while Aldous Huxley comments, 'Dr Benoit has discussed the supreme doctrine of Zen Buddhism in the light of Western psychological theory and Western psychiatric practice.'

What is a satori or kensho experience like? The following is an example from an unnamed schoolteacher:

> My hand stretched to the watch on the desk, and I picked it up. At that moment, I encountered a very strange phenomenon. The watch seemed to be part of me. There was no differentiation between my hand and the watch. Truly, an extraordinary feeling! It was quite a different sensation from my ordinary routine one, and it impressed me strongly. I kept looking at the watch for some moments in amazement. The watch was its usual shape and gold color, and as far as these qualities were concerned, it was quite a different thing from my hand, which was holding it. Yet in another dimensional quality, it was not different from my hand.[3]

Satori, therefore, represents a touch of, or an encounter with, Zen. There are different degrees of satori. As the aspirant continues to cultivate, his satoris or awakenings will become more intense and transparent, until he attains nirvana or enlightenment. Thus, nirvana, which is experiencing cosmic reality beyond its phenomenal illusion, represents the realization of Zen. There are also different degrees of nirvana, the highest of which is known in Mahayana as Buddhahood.

There is much overlapping between the various degrees of satori and the various degrees of nirvana. The earlier stages of nirvana are the advanced stages of satori.

FOUR LEVELS OF ENLIGHTENMENT

The great 1st-century Indian Buddhist master, Asvaghosha, classified enlightenment into the following four progressive levels, which represent four stages of Zen achievement. The first three stages are known as non-perfect enlightenment, because the adept has not completely become one with the Supreme Reality; the highest stage is perfect enlightenment, where the adept has completely become one with the Supreme Reality and has become the Eternal Buddha. (Buddhahood will be discussed in Chapter 6.)

1 'Enlightenment of the Initiated' (nei fan jue), where the aspirant is initiated into the path towards perfect enlightenment
2 'Enlightenment of Resemblance' (xiang si jue), where the adept realizes that the phenomenal world is an illusion but still has attachment to self or dharmas
3 'Enlightenment of Convergence' (sui fen jue), where the adept realizes the transcendental aspect of cosmic reality, but for certain reasons – like wanting to save other sentient beings, as in the case of Bodhisattvas – still returns to the phenomenal realm
4 'Perfect Enlightenment' (jiu jing jue), where the adept completely and totally realizes the Supreme Reality and in other words, becomes one with the Supreme Reality or Tathagata[4]

Once we have understood, intellectually at least, that satori is an intuitive change of view beyond dualistic thinking, how do we know when we attain nirvana or enlightenment? What does the adept experience when he attains these various stages of enlightenment?

The question is actually irrelevant because if we attain satori or nirvana, we will inevitably know it, just as when we are happy or in love, we intuitively know although we may not be able to describe this feeling accurately. Nevertheless some descriptions may be helpful. But it must be emphasized that these descriptions at best are only an intimation and do not give a perfect picture of the real experience. In Buddhist terminology, nirvana is inexplicable. This does not mean that we cannot describe nirvana, only that whatever description we give will not accurately describe it, and the concept derived from the description may be totally wrong. For example, we may describe love as blind or as a many-splendoured thing, or as the production of so many types of hormones, but to a person who has not experienced love, the descriptions may give a totally misleading picture.

Asvaghosha describes four meditation states – figuratively referred to as mirrors – which are related to the four levels of enlightenment mentioned above. These four mirrors or meditation states are four reflections of Zen.

The Four Mirrors

1 External Developmental Mirror

The adept experiences inner peace, and the meditative state, figuratively described as a mirror, illuminates his mind according to his thoughts, and inspires him to continue his cultivation to free himself from defilement. Here, Zen is like a peaceful mirror.

2 Non-Phenomenal Mirror

The adept is free from emotional and intellectual hindrance and free from the illusion caused by a defiled mind. His mind is tranquil and transparent, and he understands that the phenomenal world is an illusion. Here, Zen is like a dust-free mirror.

3 Manifested Mirror of Reality

All the phenomena in the world, which are actually a creation of the mind, can be manifested in celestial light in this stage of enlightenment. The vision or feeling of the enlightened person is transcendental; he perceives not just his surroundings but also what is possibly hundreds of miles or years away. Here, Zen represents a magical, marvellous mirror.

4 *Empty Mirror of Reality*

This is the highest level attainable, where the Ultimate Absolute is totally and completely realized, where duality disappears, where the knower is the known and the subject is the object; it is incomprehensible to the unawakened. Here, Zen is the empty mirror of reality.

These four meditation states suggest what an adept experiences when he attains the various levels of nirvana or enlightenment. Of course there are countless individual types of enlightenment experiences, but these four states represent four typical descriptions, though overlapping may occur. Adepts at the 'enlightenment of the initiated' (Level 1) usually experience the 'external developmental mirror' and the 'non-phenomenal mirror', whereas those at the 'enlightenment of resemblance' and 'enlightenment of convergence' (Levels 2 and 3) usually experience the 'manifested mirror of reality'. The experience of those who have attained 'perfect enlightenment' (Level 4) is represented by the 'empty mirror of reality'.[5]

In the third Zen story mentioned (*see* pages 1–2), Fa Rong no longer saw wild animals protecting his house or birds bringing him flowers, because as he had attained perfect enlightenment, these phenomena, which were created by dualistic thought and therefore illusory, disappeared. In perfect enlightenment, the knower and the known merge into one holistic unity, so there were no such differentiated entities as Fa Rong and the animals or birds. Earlier, Fa Rong saw the animals and birds as separated from himself because of his dualistic thinking. When he overcame this way of thinking and attained enlightenment, the animals, birds and he himself became undifferentiated.

SOME EXAMPLES OF ENLIGHTENMENT

Enlightenment, of course, occurs in other religions too, although it may be known by other names. The spiritual ecstasy described by the Taoist saint Lu Dong Bin in Chapter 2 illustrates the experience of perfect enlightenment. The following is another example of perfect enlightenment from the Christian saint Marina de Escobar:

When in deep ecstasy, God unites the soul suddenly to His essence, and when He fills her with His light, He shows her in a moment of time the sublimest mysteries. And the soul sees a certain immensity and an infinite majesty – the soul is then plunged, as it were, into a vast ocean which is God and again God. It can neither find a foothold nor touch the bottom.[6]

The universality of the world's major religions is obvious when we compare the similar way in which great teachers describe their highest spiritual fulfilment. In the example below, the modern Zen master Tai Xu (1889–1947) describes his enlightenment experience, which is at the meditative level of the 'manifested mirror of reality'.

One day, while studying the [Great Prajna] sutra, suddenly I found myself dissolved into a realm without body and mind. In this tranquillity and spacelessness a spiritual light shines brightly, and countless worlds reveal themselves like mirage and illusion, illuminated without end. I sat there for a few hours, but it appeared like a flick of a finger. For many days afterwards, my body and mind appear to exist in light, purity, peace and happiness.[7]

This experience occurred to the master in 1909 while cultivating at the Xi Fang Temple in China, when he was just 19 years of age. Later when he studied the *Hua Yan Sutra* (Avatamsaka Sutra) he was surprised to find that it described an experience similar to his own.

Such great spiritual achievements are not exclusive to religion. The experience of the Confucian philosopher and chi kung master of the Song dynasty, Zhang Dai (1020–77) is awe-inspiring. In his meditation he discovered that:

The cosmos is a body of energy. Energy has the properties of yin and yang. When energy is spread out, it permeates all things; when it coalesces it becomes nebulous. When this settles into form it becomes matter. When it disintegrates it returns into its original state.[8]

Zhang Dai's experience was astounding on two points. Firstly, he was ahead of modern scientists by almost ten centuries in his knowledge that the cosmos is a body of energy, and that energy and matter are constantly changing into one another. Yet he did not use any elaborate instruments; he used only his mind in deep meditation. Secondly, Zhang Dai's achievement was highly spiritual, although the idea of religion was never in his mind. His meditation attainment surpassed the 'manifested mirror of reality' and bordered on the highest Zen, the level of the 'empty mirror of reality'. Although spiritual training was not his expressed objective, he had achieved 'the enlightenment of convergence', bordering on perfect enlightenment. Because the intention of his Zen or meditation was to investigate the cosmos and the nature of energy rather than to become a Buddha, Zhang Dai did not proceed further and become organically united with the Supreme Reality, though it would probably have been easy for him to do so had he wished.

The extract below from the famous *Heart Sutra* shows that Avalokistesvara Bodhisattva (Guan Yin Pu Sa in Chinese) attained the highest level of enlightenment.

> Form is not different from emptiness, and emptiness is not different from form. Form is emptiness, and emptiness is form. Feeling, thought, activity and consciousness are also thus.[9]

In perfect enlightenment, Avalokistesvara Bodhisattva realized that what we experience as the phenomenal world in our ordinary consciousness, is in fact empty. The ultimate reality, which is empty when experienced transcendentally, manifests as the phenomenal world because of the defilement of our minds. On realizing that the five groups of ingredients that constitute a person – form, feeling, thought, activity and consciousness – are empty, Avalokistesvara Bodhisattva achieved liberation from the attachment to self and became enlightened to the fact that the self, at the transcendental level, is unreal. He also realized that dharmas are unreal too (*see* quotation on page 60). Hence, with the liberation from both self and dharmas, Avalokistesvara attained Buddhahood and became one with Zen or the Supreme Reality. But because of his great compassion, he voluntarily came back to the phenomenal realm to save other sentient beings.

The *Heart Sutra* is one of the most important sutras in Mahayana Buddhism.[10] Although it is very short it incorporates all the significant doctrines of Mahayana philosophy, but because of its conciseness and profundity, many readers may not understand it. Why, for example, is form the same as emptiness? Answers to this and other questions necessary for a proper understanding of Zen will be explored in the next chapter.

THE BACKGROUND TO ZEN

The Fundamental Doctrines of Buddhism

*Generally speaking, a Theravadin is a moralist, a
Mahayanist a compassionate cosmologist, and
a Vajrayanist a spiritual magician.*

THE THREE MAIN TRADITIONS

Some readers may be surprised to find that when they study
Buddhism more deeply to gain a sound background to Zen,
many concepts that they may have accepted as valid, or even
as fact, may not be so! Many people, especially Westerners and
non-Buddhists, have accepted as historical fact that Gautama
Buddha was the founder of Buddhism. In all schools of Buddhism, this is not true! Some people think that Buddhism is
pessimistic and nihilistic because they mistakenly believe that
its basic doctrine is suffering and that its ultimate goal leads to
annihilation. Again, this is totally untrue. Many people,
including some Buddhists, say that Buddhism does not believe
in God, or in the existence of souls. This varies between different
Buddhist schools of thought – though all schools accept the
existence of gods and most accept the existence of souls. It also
depends on whether the doctrine is interpreted in the phenomenal or the transcendental dimension. These and other
interesting concepts will be discussed in this and the following
chapters.

Is Buddhism confusing if there are different answers to fundamental questions? Certainly not. Buddhist teaching is very clear
on these answers; misunderstandings arise because of the profundity of Buddhism, not its indecisiveness. There are three
main reasons for such misunderstandings.

There are three main traditions in Buddhism today: Theravada, Mahayana and Vajrayana. Hence, if your information about Buddhism comes from only one source, it is likely to be unbalanced, and your answers to many questions may conflict with those of people who derive their information from other sources. For various reasons, most Western readers derive their understanding of Buddhism mainly from a Theravada source, which is, according to Mahayanists and Vajrayanists, only a preparatory stage for higher Buddhist wisdom. Theravadins, of course, vehemently oppose this view, and claim that Mahayanist and Vajrayanist sources are a later adulteration of the original teaching, despite the fact that Mahayana literature is generally much older. Mahayana Buddhism has enjoyed a continuous tradition up until now, whereas the Theravadin Sri Lankan monastic order, for example, died out in the 17th, 18th and 19th centuries (when monks had to be repeatedly imported from Burma and Siam) and was revived only in about 1880.[1]

The Buddha's teaching was transmitted mainly in Sanskrit and Pali, but was not recorded until about the 1st century BC (about 400 years after the Buddha's parinirvana). Then, for socio-political reasons, Pali almost disappeared in India, while Sanskrit continued to flourish. It was not until about 400 AD that some old Pali suttas were found in Sri Lanka, and great translators like Buddhaghosa and Buddhadatta translated the Pali texts into Sinhalese, the main language of Sri Lanka. On the other hand, Mahayana literature had been translated from Sanskrit into Chinese as early as the 2nd century AD, often under the patronage of Chinese emperors. For example, the Amitabha Sutra was translated by the famous Parthian prince-turned-monk An Shi Kao in AD 148, the Dhammapada Scripture Texts by the Indian Buddhist monks Wei Zhi Nan and Zhu Lu Yen in 224, and the Abhidharma-vibhasha by Sanghabhuti, Dharmanandi and Buddharaksha in 383. By about 410, the celebrated translator Kumarajiva – an eminent Hinayana master before his conversion to Mahayana, and who led the imperial translation bureau of Emperor Yao Hsing – had alone translated more than 300 Buddhist works!

The second cause for misunderstanding is that language is used provisionally in Buddhism. Buddhist masters have often found that words and expressions, in whatever language Buddhist concepts are described, do not always convey the intended meaning precisely. For example, no amount of description can accurately convey the concept of awakening or enlightenment to someone who has not experienced it. Thus, Buddhist masters have always insisted that spiritual fulfilment is an experiential rather than an intellectual process; they have always advised their followers to seek direct experience of the teaching and not rely entirely on book learning. This is particularly so in Zen Buddhism, where numerous ingenious methods – meditation, koan solving, shouting and even hitting – are used to help students experience spiritual awakening. Nevertheless, since words and expressions, despite their imperfection, need to be used, their use is usually provisional to the situation.

To illustrate this point, when the Buddha said that life is suffering, he was comparing the suffering in samsara to eternal bliss in nirvana. To regard this statement as unchangeable dogma or to misinterpret it to mean that there is no joy in living, is to miss its significance by failing to appreciate the provisional use of language in Buddhism. Similarly, when the Buddha said that nirvana is extinction, he referred to the extinction of pain and suffering. To interpret this as total extinction is to miss its deeper meaning.

The third cause of misunderstanding is the failure to differentiate between ordinary knowledge and higher wisdom in Buddhism. The great 2nd-century Buddhist master, Nagarjuna, said that if a person does not understand the higher wisdom of Buddhism, he will miss the essence of the Mahayana teaching. The same can be said of Vajrayana Buddhism too. Higher wisdom refers to the ability to comprehend from many dimensions at the same time, whereas ordinary knowledge comprehends from only one dimension at one time. In some contexts, higher wisdom refers to awareness of the transcendental as well as the phenomenal aspects of cosmic reality (to be explained in the next chapter).

Ordinary people, understandably, use ordinary knowledge. For example, when we look at water, we normally regard it as a liquid that can be used for drinking, washing and so on. Under special circumstances, when performing an experiment in electro-analysis, say, we regard water as a compound of hydrogen and oxygen, and when we look at water under an electron microscope, we see it as patterns of subatomic particles. This way of perceiving water, seeing its different dimensions at different times, is the result of ordinary knowledge. When an awakened person with higher wisdom views water, he comprehends all these different aspects of water at the same time; he may, for example, be aware that while water as a liquid can quench fire, as a compound of hydrogen and oxygen it provides the ingredients for the fire it is supposed to quench.[2]

It should be stressed that Theravada, Mahayana and Vajrayana are not three Buddhisms, but three traditions of the same Buddhism. The core of Buddhist doctrines common to all three traditions constitute Theravada Buddhism. Beyond this core we find the majestic and splendid philosophy of Mahayana Buddhism concerning cosmic reality, and the mystical and arcane practices of Vajrayana Buddhism dealing with supernormal powers, which are for the most part unacceptable to Theravadins. Generally speaking, a Theravadin is a moralist, a Mahayanist a compassionate cosmologist, and a Vajrayanist a spiritual magician.

The basic teaching of Theravada Buddhism, which both Mahayana and Vajrayana Buddhism accept but regard as only the preliminary teaching, may be summarized in the Four Noble Truths, the Eightfold Path, and the Doctrine of Dependent Origination.

THE FOUR NOBLE TRUTHS

As the *Cattari Ariyasaccani* states: 'The heart of the Buddha's teaching lies in the Four Noble Truths.'[3]

1 The First Noble Truth is the doctrine of *dukkha*, which states that living is suffering.
2 The Second Noble Truth is the doctrine of *samudaya*, which explains that the cause of suffering is craving.
3 The Third Noble Truth is the doctrine of *nirodha*, which teaches the emancipation of suffering to attain nibbana, the Pali term for the Sanskrit nirvana.
4 The Fourth Noble Truth is the doctrine of *magga*, showing the path to nibbana, known as the Eightfold Path.

As mentioned earlier, the First Noble Truth concerning suffering is meant to compare suffering in samsara to eternal bliss in nibbana. The Buddha taught that if a person chooses to remain in samsara (caught up in the cycle of birth and rebirth), he will miss the eternal bliss of nibbana. Interpreting this truth to mean that life is nothing but suffering and pain is 'highly unsatisfactory and misleading'.[4]

The cause of samsara is craving. When a person craves for sensual pleasures and continued existence, he sets into operation the doctrine of dependent origination that perpetuates the endless cycle of birth and rebirth. But by following the Eightfold Path, he can liberate himself from this cycle and attain the eternal bliss of nibbana.

THE EIGHTFOLD PATH

The Eightfold Path (*Ariya-Attbangika-Magga*) is sometimes called the 'Middle Way' (*Majjhima Patipada*), because it avoids the two extremes of sensual pleasure and self-mortification. It consists of eight tenets, namely:

1 Right Understanding (*samma ditthi*), which is essential for starting spiritual cultivation, because perverse views will lead the follower astray
2 Right Thought (*samma sankappa*), which is of particular importance in Buddhism since thought initiates the karmic process
3 Right Speech (*samma vaca*), which means to abstain from telling lies, backbiting, slandering, using abusive language, and indulging in foolish gossip
4 Right Action (*samma kammanta*), which promotes moral conduct, and forbids killing, stealing, adultery, covetousness and anger
5 Right Livelihood (*samma ajiva*), which discourages engaging in occupations that bring harm to other beings
6 Right Effort (*samma vayama*), which means not doing evil but doing good and persevering in spiritual cultivation
7 Right Mindfulness (*samma sati*), which is stilling the mind in tranquillity meditation by means of various methods
8 Right Concentration (*samma samadhi*), which is concentrating the mind in insight meditation to acquire *panna*, or wisdom, for attaining enlightenment

These eight tenets are meant to develop the three fundamental

Buddhist disciplines of *sila* (moral purity), *samadhi* (meditation), and *panna* (wisdom). The eight tenets are to be practised simultaneously, not one after another.

The Eightfold Path represents the practical approach of Theravadins in their spiritual cultivation. Its successful cultivation produces the Arahant, or the Worthy One, who is the Theravadin ideal. As we can see from the tenets above, the cultivation of Theravadins is centred on themselves, and they are seldom concerned with the cultivation of other people. This is not to imply that they are selfish, but they believe everyone has to work for their own enlightenment.

Perhaps because of their deep respect for Gautama Buddha, Theravadins believe that he is the only Buddha in our era, though they also believe there have been many Buddhas before, and will be many after, Gautama. As Gautama Buddha is not the first Buddha, a doctrine accepted in all schools of Buddhism, he cannot be the founder of Buddhism, the teaching of Buddhas. The Arahants are not Buddhas, but they still can enjoy the benefit of enlightenment like a Buddha.

THE DOCTRINE OF DEPENDENT ORIGINATION

Buddhists, like many other peoples in ancient civilizations, believe that our phenomenal world is an illusion – a concept accepted by quantum physicists today. If that is so, why do we see a table as a table, or an elephant as an elephant? Does another sentient being, like a fairy or a bacterium, see an elephant as an elephant? And how does craving for sensual pleasures or existence lead to the perpetuation of the cycle of birth and rebirth? These and other related questions can be explained by the doctrine of dependent origination, which lists 'twelve causes of dependent origination' (*paticcasamuppada* in Pali, *shi er yuan qi* in Chinese) in the following cyclical developmental stages:

1 Ignorance (*avijja, wu ming*)
2 Activities (*sankhara, xing*)
3 Consciousness (*vinnana, shi*)
4 Modality (*namarupa, ming se*)
5 Six entries (*salayatana, liu ru*)

  6 Contact (*phassa, chu*)
  7 Perception (*vedana, shou*)
  8 Desire (*tanha, ai*)
  9 Attachment (*upadana, qu*)
10 Becoming (*bhava, you*)
11 Life (*jati, sheng*)
12 Death (*marana, si*)

The cause of our illusion is ignorance. If we eliminate ignorance, we will achieve nibbana or enlightenment. Because of ignorance, we endlessly carry on our cycle of activities in the phenomenal realm. These activities bring about karmic effects which are imprinted in our consciousness.

Our consciousness acts as a link between our past, present and future lives, human or otherwise. This consciousness, together with the karmic effects of our previous lives and our thoughts at the time of death, will determine our future parents and time of conception, as well as other aspects of our next life as a foetus. The resulting modality, the totality of our mind and body, will influence our development – from a foetus through childhood to an adult – in the human or other planes of existence. It will also determine the six entries (five senses plus mind) with which we perceive the phenomenal world. Our six entries determine the types of contact we make with the world. For example, because the hearing-entry of a bat is different from that of a human, a bat will be able to hear sounds which are outside the hearing range of humans. Similarly, because an awakened person has enhanced his six entries, he will be able to have visual, audio, and other kinds of contact with beings not perceptible to ordinary people.

Different types of contact, which in turn are due to myriad other factors, give rise to different perceptions. Thus, a mass of dharmas (subatomic particles and forces) that appear to us as an elephant, will appear as something else to a different being. For example, that same mass may be invisible to a fairy, but a bacterium may perceive it as a universe.

Different kinds of perception lead to different kinds of desire. Many people desire material wealth and power because they perceive them as things which will satisfy their sensual pleasures, but spiritual aspirants may perceive material wealth and power as a hindrance to their spiritual development.

Because of its different perception, the desire of a bacterium would again be vastly different. But it would be presumptuous of us to imagine that the desire of a bacterium must be simple and primitive; we are not in a position to speak for bacteria or other sentient beings because we do not have their perception.

Desire causes attachment; the more a person desires something, the more he is attached to it. Attachment causes the arising or 'becoming' of phenomena. Becoming leads to life, and then death. If a being is still not enlightened at death, his ignorance will continue the cycle of dependent origination. Because a person is attached to phenomena, he experiences them. Dharmas are everywhere around us; they manifest as objects or processes perceptible to us only when we are attached to them. This Buddhist concept may seem outlandish, but its validity has now been confirmed by modern physics. As Cambridge Professor of quantum physics, Alastair Rae, says:

> Because our knowledge of the outside world (if it does exist!) comes only through our sense impression, it is only the sensual data of whose existence we can be sure. When we say, for example, that there is a table near us, all we actually know is that our mind has acquired information by way of our brain and our senses that is consistent with the postulate of a table . . . A quantum theory based on consciousness, however, goes further than this: the very existence of an external universe, or at least the particular state it is in, is strongly determined by the fact that conscious minds are observing it.[5]

This explains that realms of different sentient beings can exist simultaneously in place and time without being aware of one another's presence. In other words, heavenly beings may be sharing the same room with you, but you are unaware of each other.

Thus, the Buddhist concept of karma does not merely explain that if you sit under an apple tree and an apple falls, it will fall on your head. It goes further to explain why, for example, you are you and not an apple, or why the apple chooses to fall on your head. All these explanations are made possible by the doctrine of dependent origination, using factors like consciousness, modality, contact and perception. It is too complicated to scrutinize the complex matrix of karmic effect to explain why you become you, and not an apple, but a much simplified explanation could be as follows.

Long, long ago, because of your spiritual ignorance, you were manifested as a phenomenon. Favourable reincarnations over the centuries led to you being born as a human, not an apple. Countless factors went into shaping you as you are, with your present type of consciousness, mode of six entries, nature of contact, and so on. Had you been less meritorious in your previous reincarnations and been born as an insect, the falling apple would not have dropped on your head. If you had been an insect beneath the apple at the time of its falling, it would either have missed you altogether or squashed you into your next life.

DOES THE SOUL EXIST?

The question that has probably caused the most controversy in Buddhism is whether the soul exists. The Theravada master, Walpola Rahula, says:

> Buddhism stands unique in the history of human thought in denying the existence of such a Soul, Self, or *Atman*. According to the teaching of the Buddha, the idea of self is an imaginary, false belief which has no corresponding reality, and it produces harmful thoughts of 'me' and 'mine', selfish desires, craving, attachment, hatred, ill-will, conceit, pride, egoism, and other defilements, impurities and problems.[6]

This however refers only to Theravada Buddhism, because there is no doubt in Mahayanist and Vajrayanist teaching that the soul does exist.

Professor Kenneth Ch'en reports that 'During the Han period the main tenets of Buddhism were the indestructibility of the soul and the cycle of rebirth and karma.'[7] In fact the soul was one of the main topics on which Confucian and Taoist opponents attacked Buddhism when it first spread to China. For example, Fan Chen attacked the Buddhist concept of the indestructibility of the soul, stressing the Confucian view that because one did not even know life, how could one know death? Hui Lin, in his *Pai Hei Lun* (Treatise on White and Black), accused the Buddhists of tempting or frightening people by creating the concept of heaven and hell for their souls. In defence against the attack, the 3rd-century lay Buddhist Mou Tzu, in *Li Huo Lun* (Treatise on the Settling of Doubts, the first treatise on Buddhism written by a Chinese), said that belief in the soul was already present in native Chinese practice. The famous 4th-century Chinese Buddhist master, Hui Yuan, in his *Shen Pu Mieh Lun* (Treatise on the Indestructibility of the Soul), quoted from Chuang Tzu and Wen Tzu to support the Buddhist concept of the soul. Another famous Chinese master, Tao Sheng, asked: 'If there is no permanent self in samsara, is there a permanent self in nirvana? If there is no self, what is it that enters into nirvana?'[8]

Belief in the soul is also unquestionable in Vajrayana Buddhism. For example, in the great liberation through hearing in the *bardo*, a service performed by the Tibetans for their dead (popularly described in *The Tibetan Book of the Dead*), the soul is guided through the bardo, or the interval between death and birth, in the hope that it may be liberated and not have to be reborn. The following is one of the prayers for deliverance that the officiating monk teaches the soul in the bardo to recite:

> When through intense desire I wander in samsara,
> on the luminous light-path of discrimination wisdom,
> may Blessed Amitabha go before me,
> his consort Pandaravasini behind me;
> help me to cross the bardo's dangerous pathway
> and bring me to the perfect buddha state.[9]

The Buddha did not categorically say there was no soul. On occasion he mentioned the *pudgala*, or the self; at other times he spoke about the non-self, but there were also occasions when he mentioned neither self nor non-self. All schools of Buddhism, including the Theravada, accept the 500 past lives of Gautama Buddha. Passing through those 500 reincarnations was the same self. The Buddha clearly stated that in one of these reincarnations, the self called Sunetra was himself.

The concept of the soul or self is also mentioned in important Theravada scriptures. Dr Rune E A Johansson reports that 'the Digha Nikaya mentions a great number of speculative views. The subjects discussed were especially the nature of the soul and the world, the nature of virtue and its results, the existence of another world, and whether the soul and the world are caused or not.'[10] The Abhidharma describes the eight types of enlightened beings as the eight pudgalas, or selves. The Western Buddhist scholar, Professor Edward Conze, concludes that 'the orthodox teachers had to admit these passages, but maintained that they do not mean what they say'![11]

In the quotation below, the Theravadin scholar, Professor Jayatilleke, has avoided using the term 'soul' or 'self' by substituting the words 'discarnate spirit'.

> The law of continuity, popularly known as rebirth, ensures the persistence of the dynamic consciousness of the individual with the death of the physical body. If this unconsciousness is not attuned to higher worlds by moral and spiritual development of the individual it is said generally to persist in the spirit-sphere (pettivisaya) as a discarnate spirit, and subsequently get reborn as a human being.[12]

Even among Hinayanists, from whom the Theravada school originated, there were many who explicitly believed in the existence of the soul. These schools were collectively known as the *Pudgalavadins*, because of their unequivocal belief in the pudgala or self. The Pudgalavadins formed a very substantial portion of the Hinayanists: the famous Chinese pilgrim Yuan Zang in the 7th century counted 66,000 Pudgalavadin monks out of a total of 250,000.[13]

Why, then, did the Buddha teach the doctrine of non-soul? Without an understanding of Buddhist higher wisdom, this very important doctrine – which is crucial for the attainment of the highest enlightenment – can easily be taken to mean that Buddhists do not believe in souls. The answer will become clear in the next chapter when we study the majestic splendour of Mahayana philosophy.

6

ZEN AS COSMIC REALITY

The Higher Wisdom of Buddhism

*What, then, is the higher wisdom which
Mahayanists claim Theravadins lack – the
difference that contrasts the grandeur of
Mahayana philosophy with the comparatively
simple, down-to-earth practice of common
Theravada Buddhism?*

THE MORAL, THE COSMOLOGICAL AND THE METAPHYSICAL

Some people think that Buddhism is just a philosophy for a moral way of living, with no mention of cosmology or metaphysics. This mistaken view is probably due to their understanding of Buddhism only from a Theravada source, which emphasizes the moral aspect of Buddhism. Were they also to study Mahayana and Vajrayana Buddhism in some detail, an exceedingly rich cosmological and metaphysical knowledge would be revealed.

The Mahayanists, for example, describe macro and micro worlds in terms and accuracy that would astound modern astronomers and physicists. They refer to not just one but countless universes, each with galaxies and stars as numerous as the sands of the River Ganges, separated by millions and millions of light years. At the micro level, they discover complete worlds in a mote of dust, each one reflecting and containing the macro worlds in a mutual interpenetration of simultaneously arising dharmas – a concept that modern quantum physicists are only now beginning to appreciate. Such a cosmic view is an expression of Zen.

The magic and mysticism of the Vajrayanists has always awed or fascinated the general public. How does a siddha, or spiritual magician, use his supernatural powers to perform miracles like creating rain or looking into the future? 'When we draw down the power and depth of vastness into a single perception, then we are discovering and invoking magic,' explains the Tibetan master, Chogyam Trungpa.[1] Yet, these powers are not ends in themselves, but an incidental bonus of the spiritual quest. 'By magic we do not mean unnatural power over the phenomenal world but rather the discovery of innate or primordial wisdom in the world as it is,' the master continues. This discovery of primordial wisdom is similar to awareness in Zen.

But it is a mistaken view that the cosmic splendour in Mahayana and the magic of wisdom in Vajrayana are not to be found in Theravada. Professor Jayatilleke says:

> The Early Buddhist conception of the cosmos is in essence similar to the modern conception of the universe. In the Pali texts that have come down to us we are literally told that hundreds and thousands of suns and moons, earths, and higher worlds, constitute the minor world system, and a hundred thousand times this is the middling world system, and a hundred thousand times the middling world system is the major world system. In modern terminology it would seem as if a minor world system (culanika-loka-dhatu) is a galaxy of which we observe a hundred millions through our best telescopes. The Buddhist conception of time is equally immense.[2]

Theravada masters are well versed in performing miracles too. But such cosmic and metaphysical knowledge is not emphasized in Theravada Buddhism. Theravadins are more concerned with moral purity, which is the prerequisite of Zen.

THE HIGHER WISDOM OF COSMIC REALITY

What, then, is the higher wisdom which Mahayanists claim Theravadins lack – the difference that contrasts the grandeur of Mahayana philosophy with the comparatively simple, down-to-earth practice of common Theravada Buddhism – even though Theravada masters are not unfamiliar with the splendours of Buddhist cosmology and metaphysics? The higher wisdom they refer to concerns the transcendental and phenomenal aspects of cosmic reality.

Cosmic reality – known by various names, including Supreme Reality, Ultimate Absolute, Universal Mind, Original Face, Buddha Nature, the Tathagata, the Eternal Buddha, the Cosmos, Brahman, and God – is infinite, eternal, immanent, omnipresent and omniscient. In its transcendental aspect, cosmic reality is impartial and undifferentiated. This means that everything there is, is a holistic unity; there is no difference or separateness whatsoever between you and me, between this book and the eyes you are using to read it, between subject and object, between the knower and the known. Buddhists call this the void, or the emptiness, meaning that the Ultimate Truth is devoid of phenomena, emptied of all objects and processes.

This universal wholeness is known in all religions, as revealed to their greatest teachers. Of her deepest religious fulfilment, Saint Teresa experienced that

> God establishes himself in the interior of this soul in such a way that when she returns to herself, it is wholly impossible for her to doubt that she has been in God, and God in her.[3]

In his religious realization, the great Muslim master, Mansur al-Hallaj, expressed the same thing in a way that lesser minds would regard as blasphemy: 'I am He whom I love and He whom I love is I.'[4]

In Taoism and Hinduism, the holistic oneness of the Supreme Reality, called respectively the Cosmos and Brahman, is well known. The famous Taoist master, Chuang Tzu, said: 'The cosmos and I live together, Everything and I are one.'[5]

This universal oneness that transcends any form of duality is expressed by Arjuna to the Godhead, manifested as Sri Krishna, in the *Bhagavad-Gita*:

> You are the original Personality of Godhead, the oldest, the ultimate sanctuary of this manifested cosmic world. You are the knower of everything, and You are all that is knowable. You are the supreme refuge, above the material mode. O limitless form! This whole cosmic manifestation is pervaded by You![6]

What is significant is that if we replace terms such as 'God', 'cosmos' and 'Brahman' in the above quotations with the Buddhist term 'Tathagata', we may think they are descriptions of spiritual fulfilment in Buddhism. Even more significant is that if we use a neutral term like 'Ultimate Truth' or 'Supreme Reality' instead of the religiously connotative words, any one of the descriptions can be applied to any religion. Thus, the world's great religions are in effect similar, their apparent differences due only to historical, cultural, linguistic and other factors.

Descriptions of transcendental cosmic reality are readily found in Chinese Buddhist literature, but because the classical Chinese in which much of the Mahayana texts are written is very concise, and the ideas profound, many people do not understand their real significance, or interpret them merely at a superficial level. If you do not understand the significance of the quotations or examples given here, do not despair. The great masters have acknowledged that the concept of cosmic reality is difficult even for highly intelligent or religious people.

Cosmic reality can be expressed in two dimensions: transcendental and phenomenal. Transcendental cosmic reality is unconditioned and absolute. Phenomenal cosmic reality is conditioned and relative. When cosmic reality is experienced transcendentally, it is undifferentiated and tranquil. In other words, when cosmic reality is not conditioned by any factors, that is, when we have reached the ultimate, primordial truth of cosmic reality, beyond which we cannot go further, 'everything' and 'everywhere' is the same, there are no separate objects or processes, but a universal spread of cosmic consciousness. A useful, though imperfect, analogy would be looking at the universe through a gigantic electron microscope: things like people and houses, the sky and the earth (differentiated objects when seen with the naked eye) disappear and you see only the undifferentiated spread of cosmic energy!

The earth on which we live is actually a minute speck in the universe. Suppose you were deep in outer space, what would you see? Andrew Scott reports:

> Hydrogen is believed to account for about 92.7 per cent of all the atoms in the entire universe, and helium for around 7.2 per cent. This leaves a tiny 0.1 per cent for all the other types of atoms, of which there are 90 known to occur naturally.[7]

Because, with your naked eyes, you cannot see hydrogen, helium and other atoms, transcendentally you will see 'emptiness'. In the same way, a being from outer space arriving at our

earth, will also see 'emptiness' – if his experience is transcendental. In fact, transcendentally, there is no separateness or
differentiation between you and that being, between outer space
and this earth. Transcendentally the whole cosmos is void; it is
infinite, holistic and undifferentiated.

Yet you will not see emptiness or the void unless you have
attained enlightenment. You will experience the universe
phenomenally, not transcendentally, and your experience will
be conditioned and relative. In other words, whether you are
on earth or in outer space, the ultimate cosmic reality, which
is originally undifferentiated, will be experienced by you as
differentiated phenomena. The kinds of phenomena that will
be manifested will be conditioned by the doctrine of dependent
origination explained in the previous chapter. The phenomena
are relative, not absolute. For example, the collection of undifferentiated energy that appears to you as a differentiated apple
falling on your head, may appear to bacteria like a collapsing
universe; and what may appear to scientists on earth as barren
rocks on the moon, may appear to celestial beings as a garden
of Eden.

MISINTERPRETED MAHAYANIST EXPRESSIONS

When Buddhist masters say that our phenomenal world is an
illusion, they do not mean that we imagine things that are not
there; they mean that what many people regard as the 'objective
external world' is really a function of their defiled mind due to
ignorance. The mind is originally pure but, because of ignorance, it is shrouded in layers of defilement. One way to regain
purity is to tear down the layers of defilement, though this may
take many years or even lifetimes. This approach to enlightenment is gradual, and is used in Theravada and many Mahayana
schools. In Zen Buddhism the approach is sudden, reaching the
mind directly to disperse ignorance. As soon as ignorance is
overcome, the many layers of defilement fall off in an instant.
How this is done will be explained in subsequent chapters.

With some understanding of the transcendental and phenomenal aspects of cosmic reality, let us examine some common
Mahayana expressions and compare what ordinary people think

they mean with their actual meaning in relation to higher wisdom.

Many people think the expression 'everything is empty' refers to the Buddhist tenet of detachment from worldly pleasures and material possessions. Actually, except for monks who have renounced worldly lives for specific reasons, there is nothing in Buddhist teaching against lay followers having legitimate pleasures and possessions, though they are advised not to over indulge. 'Empty' in this instance does not mean total nothingness; rather, emptied of phenomena. In other words, when we are enlightened, we experience cosmic reality not as differentiated and illusory, but as undifferentiated and absolute.

Similarly, 'nirvana is tranquil' does not merely mean that when you attain nirvana, you become very still in your bodily form and joyously peaceful in your heart. The expression refers to the state where an enlightened being realizes the ultimate truth that cosmic reality is infinitely quiescent, where absolutely no thoughts arise in the mind. If thoughts arise, they start the transformation into the phenomenal realm.

'Realizing the nature of dharma to become a Buddha' does not merely mean understanding the teaching of the Buddha and becoming morally pure and free from suffering, like Gautama. This condition is a prerequisite; the expression goes beyond this preparatory stage. It means realizing that the nature of dharma is actually empty (that the phenomenal world is illusory) and thus attaining perfect enlightenment. Here dharma refers to the subatomic forces and particles that are manifested as phenomena; it does not refer to the teaching of the Buddha. 'Buddha' in this expression refers to the Eternal Buddha or Supreme Reality, not the physical manifestation in Gautama Buddha.

Indeed, according to Mahayana teaching, it is precisely the failure to understand this concept of dharma and the Buddha that prevents Theravadins from proceeding to higher wisdom. Liberation is of two kinds: from self and from dharma. In other words, an enlightened person realizes that both his own self and the phenomenal world are illusion, that in Supreme Reality the self and the dharmas that manifest as phenomena do not exist.

To help Buddhists to understand the illusion of the self at the transcendental dimension, the Buddha taught the doctrine of non-self. At the transcendental level, the self as well as other separate entities do not exist, because the Ultimate Absolute is undifferentiated. But the self, like other separate entities, exists at the phenomenal level. According to the Mahayanists, because the Theravadins do not understand this higher wisdom concerning transcendental reality, they interpret the doctrine of non-self only at the phenomenal level. Hence, they miss the significant fact that this doctrine of non-self is provisional, specially taught to help Buddhists overcome the attachment to self, just as the doctrine of suffering is provisional, specially taught to help Buddhists liberate themselves from samsara. If we fail to understand the provisional use of language in these two doctrines, it is easy to mistake them for unchangeable dogma which dictates that the self or soul does not exist and that life is suffering.

Mahayanists say that although Theravadins succeed in liberating themselves from the attachment to self, they fail to liberate themselves from the attachment to dharma Theravadins realize that self is illusory, but they postulate that dharmas are real entities, though existing only momentarily. Indeed, the Sarvastivada, which was a leading Hinayana school but is now comparatively unknown, derived its name from its doctrine that dharmas were real. On the other hand, Mahayanists postulate that both self and dharma are illusory. At the transcendental dimension, they believe that cosmic reality is empty, that the illusory existence of self and phenomena is due to the defilement of the mind. This constitutes one of the basic philosophical differences between Mahayana and Theravada. Ontologically, Vajrayana is similar to Mahayana, but its practice has strong elements of mysticism.

DIFFERENCES BETWEEN MAHAYANA AND THERAVADA

As set out above, Theravadins believe that dharmas are real, though momentary, and Mahayanists believe that dharmas are empty. The *Abhidhammattha Sangaha*, a standard Theravadin text on Buddhist philosophy, says:

With His supernormal knowledge the Buddha analysed this so-

called paramanu and declared that it consists of paramatthas –
ultimate entities which cannot further be subdivided.[8]

Paramanu is the Buddhist term for atom. There are four types
of *paramatthas*, described figuratively as air, earth, water and fire.
It should be noted that they are not literally these substances, as
is sometimes thought, but because their characteristics are
similar these four 'elements' are used as symbols for the four
different types of subatomic forces or particles.

Mahayana philosophy accepts that in the realm of human
thought, phenomena are fundamentally composed of these subatomic forces and particles, but teaches that they are not
ultimate or absolute; their existence is conditioned by mind,
and is relative. For example, because the condition of the
mind of a cat or a *deva* (heavenly being) is different, a cat or a
deva may not perceive these fundamental entities as the four
paramatthas. If paramatthas were ultimate reality, then the cat,
the deva or any other sentient being would perceive them as the
same. Even among similar human minds, the perception is
relative. Western scientists, for example, would perceive the
different fundamental entities not as air, earth, water and fire,
but as possessing top-, bottom-, up- or down-spins.

More significantly, Mahayana philosophy teaches that these
entities exist only in the phenomenal dimension. At the transcendental dimension, they are non-existent. This Mahayana
concept is expressed by the popularly known, but not popularly
understood, Chinese phrase *si da jie kong*, which means 'the four
universals (of air, earth, water and fire) are empty'.

The philosophical difference between Mahayana and Theravada concerning the 'stuff' that makes up reality, leads to a
fundamentally different concept of nirvana. Generally, Theravadins are quite reluctant to define nirvana, saying that nirvana
is inexplicable, and that one has to experience it to know what
it is. This is of course true: no matter how accurately nirvana is
described, an inexperienced listener or reader may not derive a
correct concept. Nevertheless, some form of description, despite
its imperfection, is usually helpful and often necessary. Since
achieving nirvana is the supreme aim of Buddhism, it is very
important for Buddhists to know what nirvana is, for the definition of the aim, whether in religion, science or any other field

of endeavour, not only influences the methods to be used, but also affects the ultimate goal.

Let us see how authoritative Theravada scriptures define nirvana. The *Samyutta-nikaya* says:

> Calming of all conditioned things, giving up of all defilements, extinction of 'thirst', detachment, cessation, Nibbana.[9]

And since nirvana is the realization of the Absolute, let us see what the same text says about the Absolute:

> O bhikkhus, what is the Absolute (*Asamkhata*, Unconditioned)? It is, O bhikkhus, the extinction of desire (*ragakkhayo*), the extinction of hatred (*dosakkhayo*), the extinction of illusion (*mohakkhayo*). This, O bhikkhus, is called the Absolute.[10]

The modern Theravada master, Paravahera Vajiranana Mahathera, while quoting Sariputra (the Buddha's disciple and greatly honoured by Theravadins) who said that 'Nibbana is the extinction of lust, hatred and delusion', advises that

> it must not be thought that Nibbana is nothing but the mere extinction of these mental states. From the doctrinal aspect the statement implies that these lower tendencies of the mind must be destroyed by cultivating the opposite qualities; that is, by moral and intellectual development with Nibbana, freedom, as the result.[11]

In Mahayana philosophy, nirvana is never conceptualized as extinction; it is usually described as the direct experience of cosmic reality. There is nothing to be destroyed: it is not destroying negative qualities like lust, hatred and delusion, then substituting positive qualities like equanimity, compassion and insight. This process of moral development is a prerequisite, to be cultivated before nirvana. During nirvana, there is no difference between lust and equanimity, or between hatred and compassion, because such dualistic thought has been transcended.

Perhaps wishing to emphasize this difference of interpretation, besides 'nirvana', Mahayana masters often use terms like *bodhi*, *jue* (awareness), *Zhen Ru* (True Suchness) and Buddhahood to mean enlightenment. The description in Zen Buddhism is even more direct, with terms like Buddha's Nature and Original Face.

The experience of the Buddha's enlightenment is graphically

described in sutras such as the *Garland Sutra* (*Hua Yen Jing* or *Avatamsaka Sutra*) and the *Lotus Sutra* (*Lian Hua Jing* or *Saddharma-Pundarika Sutra*). For example, the *Garland Sutra* says:

> When the Buddha first attained enlightenment, the whole earth became purified, adorned with all types of jewels and flowers, and sweet-smelling perfume filled its every corner. Flowering vines entwined themselves around the Buddha, and on them were strewn strange jewels: gold, silver, lapis lazuli, agate, cornelian, coral and amber. From the leaves and the branches of the trees there was emitted a bright shining light. The change was brought about by the mysterious supernatural power of the Buddha.[12]

This majestic splendour of cosmic reality which is not perceptible to ordinary beings is experienced in the enlightenment state known as 'ocean-mirror samadhi' in the Hua Yen school of Mahayana Buddhism, and is similar to the 'manifested mirror of reality' described in Chapter 4.

In the *Vimalakirti Sutra*, enlightenment as experienced in another samadhi state known as 'empty mirror of reality', is described as 'the Spiritual Gate of Nonduality, the portal to the Dharma where all opposites are resolved'.[13] Here, enlightenment is the direct experience of cosmic reality as the Absolute, where there is no duality, and where all forms of differentiation have disappeared.

This undifferentiated, impartial aspect of transcendental cosmic reality that is experienced in nirvana, is well described in the famous *Heart Sutra* (*Ban Ruo Xin Jing* or *Prajnaparamita Hridaya Sutra*), though many who have read it may not realize its meaning because of the conciseness of the language:

> All phenomena are emptied of characteristics: non-arising, non-ceasing; non-defiled, non-pure; non-adding, non-subtracting. Thus, in emptiness there is no form, no feeling, no thought, no activity, and no consciousness.[14]

Briefly, the above extract says that in nirvana, the enlightened person is aware that all dharmas, in their ultimate reality, are empty, that is, not real. Therefore, in the transcendental aspect of cosmic reality, there are no dharmas arising or ceasing, no phenomena that are defiled or pure, and no Buddhas added to or ordinary persons subtracted from the total when ordinary persons become Buddhas. This is because transcendental cosmic reality is impartial and undifferentiated, emptied of all separate form, perception, thought, activity and consciousness.

Related to their different concepts of nirvana is the Theravadin and Mahayanist attitude towards salvation. Theravadins who postulate that nirvana is ontologically separate from samsara and achieved when negative factors like craving, attachment and suffering are eliminated, believe that salvation is a personal affair, that everyone has to work out their own enlightenment. On the other hand, Mahayanists postulate that nirvana and samsara are actually the same. The apparent difference is one of spiritual perspective. When reality is perceived from the transcendental perspective, we experience nirvana; when reality is experienced from the phenomenal perspective, we experience samsara. Because cosmic reality is ultimately a holistic unity beyond all duality, Mahayanists believe that salvation is a cosmic responsibility.

The Theravada ideal is the Arahant, the Worthy One; whereas that of the Mahayana is the Bodhisattva, the Enlightened Sentient Being. Because the Arahant is mainly concerned with his personal enlightenment, he is often described as being cold and emotionless, whereas the Bodhisattva who has vowed to work for universal salvation is seen as helpful and compassionate.

Theravadins regard Gautama Buddha as *the* Buddha, meaning the one and only Buddha in our aeon; though they also accept other Buddhas in other aeons before and after Gautama. Mahayanists also regard Gautama Buddha (whom they more often call Sakyamuni Buddha), as the Buddha, meaning the first and most important Buddha in our aeon, and also recognize other Buddhas in other aeons, but in addition they believe that there have been countless other Buddhas throughout the ages and there are countless others here and now. Both Theravadins and Mahayanists define a Buddha as one who is enlightened. The difference, therefore, lies not in the definition but in their interpretation of what constitutes enlightenment. Theravadins believe that Gautama Buddha is the only one who has attained perfect enlightenment, whereas Mahayanists believe that anyone, including non-humans, can attain perfect enlightenment – a view which is perhaps more in line with Gautama's teaching, otherwise he would not have dedicated his entire human life to this very purpose. Vajrayanists, on the other hand, place more emphasis on Vairocana Buddha (the

Personification of Cosmic Reality) than Gautama Buddha, although the latter is still regarded as the Buddha of this aeon.

Considering that the Theravadins reserve the attainment of nirvana exclusively for Gautama Buddha, it is surprising that their concept of nirvana is less 'majestic' than that of the Mahayanist. Thus, it is often said that Theravada Buddhism aims for nirvana, whereas Mahayana Buddhism aims for Buddhahood. This suggests that in Theravada, when a person achieves enlightenment he has extinguished all his desires, suffering and illusions, and attains a mental state of supreme bliss. In Mahayana, achieving enlightenment means that a person has liberated himself from the imaginary confinement of his physical body and is aware that he is in actuality the whole cosmos!

Because Mahayana masters realize that people are spiritually at different developmental stages, they have devised many and varied means to help them attain enlightenment. For those who lack intellectual understanding or spiritual insight, devotional practice (like praying to the Buddha and Bodhisattvas) will increase their spiritual merits so that they may continue their spiritual development in future lives. Others may recite the name of Ambitabha Buddha so as to be reborn in the Buddha land for future cultivation. The spiritually more advanced may use tranquillity and insight meditation to acquire enlightenment in this life. The fastest and most direct, but not necessarily the easiest, method is Zen, and the next chapter will explain the development of Zen Buddhism with classical examples of instant enlightenment.

7

THE SPREAD OF ZEN FROM INDIA

The Coming of Bodhidharma from the West

Although many people, including the Japanese Zen master Suzuki, believe that Zen (Chan in Chinese) is actually the product of the Chinese mind, most Chinese Zen masters gratefully acknowledge its Indian origin and trace its source back to Gautama Buddha.

THE CONTROVERSY OVER BODHIDHARMA

Within the study of the history of Zen Buddhism certain scholars have persistently insisted on information which conflicts with what generations of Zen practitioners have believed and cherished. While such insistence is also found in other disciplines and fields of study, it is particularly illuminating in Zen Buddhism because it happens despite the existence of so much evidence to the contrary which these scholars are obviously unaware of.

It must be emphasized that any claims to facts or differences of opinion with the traditional practitioners are not made out of malice or selfish intentions – the scholars are generally sincere in their endeavour. It must also be acknowledged that, although the possibility is very slight, the scholars may be right after all. Their work in providing basic and extensive information, especially from their standpoint of expert observers rather than involved practitioners, is invaluable and much appreciated.

The main topic of controversy is whether Bodhidharma started Zen Buddhism in China. Some scholars, who may not have practised Zen Buddhism at all, claim that Zen Buddhism was developed not from Bodhidharma but from Chinese monks such as Dao An (Tao An, 312–85) Dao Sheng (Tao Sheng, 360–434) and Hui Yuan (334–416), who emphasized meditation in their spiritual cultivation and were much influenced by Taoist thought. What the scholars probably do not realize is that the Chinese term *chan shi* which was often applied to these masters, was taken to mean 'meditation masters', not 'Zen Buddhism masters'. (As you may recall from Chapter 1, 'chan' can mean 'meditation' or 'Zen Buddhism'.) Even Alan Watts, who has contributed much to the knowledge of Zen Buddhism in the West, says 'The origins of Zen are as much Taoist as Buddhist.'[1] Some scholars even suggest that Zen Buddhism is Taoism in Buddhist attire. Other critics have questioned whether Bodhidharma existed at all.

Some scholars, who are not Chinese, argue that the Chinese invented Bodhidharma in order to claim a link between Zen and India, the home of Buddhism. This seems to go against the grain of the Chinese people, who are known to be fiercely proud of their civilization, often boasting that it is the greatest in the world. Throughout history, especially at the height of Zen development during the glorious Tang dynasty, the Chinese claimed that they were the centre of the universe and needed nothing from external 'barbarians'. It is thus untenable to suggest that a proud, often chauvinistic, people would invent a non-Chinese for their Patriarch. The reverse is more likely; even today some Chinese erroneously believe that Lao Tzu went west to convert Siddharta Gautama! Unless the facts were convincing, no Chinese persons, from pauper to emperor, would have accepted Bodhidharma as the First Patriarch.

Indeed it is hard to find any other topic of controversy where the evidence is so overwhelming. Imperial documents clearly recorded that Bodhidharma arrived in China and had an audience with Emperor Liang Wu Di, and official monastery history shows that since 527 Bodhidharma taught Zen at the famous Shaolin Monastery, the imperial temple where emperors of various dynasties prayed to heaven on behalf of the empire. There are no records whatsoever to show Zen Buddhism existed in China before Bodhidharma's arrival. It is pertinent to note that throughout Chinese imperial history, anyone wilfully providing false information to the emperor would have had his head chopped off.

In the Shaolin Monastery, which was the source of Zen Buddhism (from Bodhidharma) as well as Shaolin Kungfu and Shaolin Chi Kung, huge Chinese characters for 'Shaolin Zen Monastery' were prominently written on one of its long walls. The building where Bodhidharma taught Zen was named Bodhidharma Chamber; it was also called 'Standing-in-the-Snow' Pavilion, because his successor Hui Ke stood in the snow while waiting for Bodhidharma's teaching.

Not far from the monastery proper, but within the huge area under its control, was the Bodhidharma Cave where Bodhidharma meditated for nine years. Nearby were the Temple of the First Patriarch, the Temple of the Second Patriarch, and the Temple of the Third Patriarch, all in memory of the first three Zen patriarchs in China who taught at the Shaolin Monastery. There was no temple for the Fourth Patriarch, Dao Xin (whom we read about in Chapter 1 helping Fa Rong to gain enlightenment), because he taught Zen at the Dongshan Temple at Huangmei (Yellow Plum) Mountain. All this hard evidence, including the Chinese characters on the monastery wall, still stands today.

Imperial records clearly show, directly or indirectly, that Bodhidharma was the First Patriarch of Zen Buddhism in China. For instance, around 790, Shen Hui was decreed the Seventh Patriarch by imperial order and his teacher, Hui Neng, the Sixth, thus continuing their genealogical line that led back to Bodhidharma, the First Patriarch. Genealogies were remarkably well maintained by Zen masters and students, and all genealogical lines without exception started from Bodhidharma.

All Zen masters, again without a single exception, accepted and honoured Bodhidharma as the First Patriarch. Bodhidharma's picture or statue was, and is, often revered in Zen temples. The koan 'What is the intention of the First Patriarch coming from the west?' was frequently used to test students' development in Zen cultivation. The First Patriarch was never mentioned by name because everyone accepted that this title referred to Bodhidharma. Indeed the acceptance of Bodhidharma as the First Patriarch of Zen Buddhism in China is so established that telling Zen practitioners Bodhidharma was a myth is like telling scientists that Newton did not exist but had to be invented for naming the laws of motion.

ZEN AND TAOISM

How valid is the argument that, even if Bodhidharma existed, Zen Buddhism, despite its name, was derived from Taoism? The Zen concept of wu-xin, or 'no-mind', is similar to the Taoist concept of *wu-ji*, or 'extreme void'. The Zen concept of *ben-xing*, or 'original nature', is similar to the Taoist concept of *wu-wei*, or 'spontaneity'. The carefree attitude of Zen Buddhists is similar to the romanticism of Taoists. Hence, some scholars argue that Zen Buddhism was derived from Taoist philosophy. But deeper analysis shows that this argument is superficial.

Similarity between the Taoist wu-ji and the Zen wu-xin (both of which refer to transcendental cosmic reality) arises because they are both expressions for the Ultimate Absolute. As explained in the previous chapter, this concept of cosmic reality is found not only in Taoism and Zen, but in all the world's great religions.

The concepts of wu-wei and ben-xing represent the principle behind the practice of returning to the ultimate reality. Although in both the principle is similar, the practice is clearly different. The characteristic Zen practice of using gong-ans (koans) is not found in Taoism. On the other hand, Zen Buddhists never talk about the elixir of life, and ritualistic sex is strictly forbidden, although these two practices are debased forms of Taoism. Even the approach to meditation, the essential way to spiritual fulfilment in both Taoism and Zen, is different: Taoist meditation uses visualization extensively, Zen meditation focuses on emptiness. Moreover, the similarity in principle between ben-xing and wu-wei is not exclusive; the same principle is also found in other systems under different names, like the Confucian *zi-ran*, or 'naturalness'.

If we examine the romanticism of Taoism and the carefree attitude of Zen more deeply, we will find that the similarity is only superficial. At a deeper level, they are quite different.[2] Taoist romanticism is a result of retreating from society, like declining high office to lead a solitary life, whereas the carefree attitude of Zen is a result of finding joy and meaning in daily living, being in society but not contaminated by it.

In dialectics, the romantic attitude is employed in Taoism to speculate and philosophize, whereas in Zen it is used ingenuously as a practical tool to help students achieve awakening. While both Taoist and Zen literature are imbued with humour, wit and the spirit of freedom, each has a beauty of its own and is distinctly different from the other. Compare, for example, the following famous piece from the great Taoist master Chuang Tzu (Zhuang Zi in romanized Chinese) about his dream, with any of the Zen stories in this book. Here, like Zen masters elsewhere, Chuang Tzu suggests that life is an illusion, but his treatment of the subject and its effect, is very different:

> One day I dreamt that I was a butterfly, fluttering here and there, enjoying myself to the fullest. I had no doubt I was a butterfly, not realizing that I was really Chuang Chou. Then I woke up from my dream, and had no doubt that I was Chuang Chou. Now I am not sure whether I *was* a man dreaming myself to be a butterfly, or I *am* a butterfly dreaming myself to be a man.

More significantly, all these Zen features, which critics argue were developed from Taoism, existed in Buddhism before Zen developed in China. The philosophy of wu-xin or no-mind is based on the Mahayana concept of transcendental cosmic reality. The principle and practice of ben-xing or original nature are derived from the Mahayana concept of original enlightenment. The carefree attitude owes much to the Buddhist doctrine of detachment.

Anyone who doubts that Zen Buddhism is Buddhism should study the similarities between Zen Buddhism and Theravada Buddhism described by the modern Theravada master, Walpola Rahula:

> Some important axioms, considered particula
> keeping with the original Theravada teaching
> puts much emphasis on the sudden attainmer
> ticular distinction, and relates stories to illustr
> Examples of this kind of 'sudden' awakenir
> ment of arahantship are not lacking also in Pa
> acrobat named Uggasena attained arahantship
> balanced on the top of a bamboo pole in the

risky acrobatics, when he heard from the Buddha an utterance almost like a Zen *koan*:

> Let go in front;
> Let go behind;
> Let go in the middle,
> Gone beyond existence,
> With a mind free everywhere.
> Thou comes not again to birth and decay.[3]

It is also unlikely that the early formative Zen masters were much influenced by the works of Taoist masters like Lao Tzu and Chuang Tzu. It is a strong Zen tradition to discard book learning and seek awakening and enlightenment through direct experience. Much of Zen philosophy is shaped by the teachings of their two greatest masters, Bodhidharma and Hui Neng. Bodhidharma is well known for his distrust of book learning; he asked his students to burn all their books and concentrate on practising meditation, though he valued and preached the *Lankavatara Sutra*. Besides, his understanding of the Chinese language would not have been adequate for him to study Taoist literature even if he had wanted to.

Hui Neng, on the other hand, was illiterate, and thus would not have read Lao Tzu's and Chuang Tzu's works. Indeed throughout his teaching, his thoughts, which often revealed great insight, were mainly derived from the *Diamond Sutra*, which he learned from his teacher, Hong Jen. Hui Neng's thoughts were summarized in the *Platform Sutra*, from which many subsequent Zen masters drew their teaching and inspiration. These three sutras form the foundation of Zen philosophy. In fact all the concepts which bear some semblance to Taoist teaching can be found in these three sutras.[4]

Nevertheless, while Zen Buddhism is not a Taoist reaction to Indian Buddhism by the Chinese mind, after its formative years it was influenced by Taoism and Confucianism, and vice versa. Taoist romanticism, though not the source of Zen humour and freedom, must have influenced Zen thinking and attitude. Of all the various Buddhist schools, in China and elsewhere, Zen Buddhism is the most boisterous. On the other hand, Zen philosophy had a strong influence on the neo-Confucianism of the ng and Ming dynasties. Much of the neo-Confucian literature and tastes of Zen. For example, the following ecstatic exclamation from Hu Zhi, a Confucian philosopher of the Ming dynasty, could easily be mistaken for the words of a Zen master:

> One day, suddenly my mind was enlightened; there were no irrelevant thoughts. I saw all the myriad things in the world inside me, making me exclaim that the whole cosmos is me.[5]

FROM INDIA TO CHINA

Although many people, including the Japanese Zen master Suzuki, believe that Zen (Chan in Chinese) is actually the product of the Chinese mind, most Chinese Zen masters gratefully acknowledge its Indian origin and trace its source back to Gautama Buddha. The genealogical line is very clear, and Chinese Zen masters accept it without doubt. There are also many records of the typical Zen tradition of transmitting Zen from heart to heart while Zen Buddhism was still in India, and two examples are described below.

> One day on Vulture Peak (*Mount Grdhrakuta, Ling Shan*), God Brahma offered a golden kumbhala flower to the Buddha, and requested the World-Honoured One to deliver a sermon. The Buddha ascended his dharma throne, showed the flower to the gathering of 80,000 disciples, including heavenly beings, but remained silent for a long time. No one understood him except Mahakasyapa, who smiled serenely. The Buddha then said to Mahakasyapa:

> > Here's the eye of true teaching,
> > The marvellous mind of enlightenment,
> > Reality with no characteristics,
> > Techniques of subtle amazement.
> > Not recorded in language and words,
> > Transmission beyond the tradition,
> > Directly pointing at the mind.
> > Enter Buddhahood in an instant.

This is the first typical heart-to-heart transmission, and constitutes the first gong-an. Hence, transmission of Zen is also called transmission of the Buddha-heart, or Buddha-mind. The above verse spoken by the Buddha has become the essence of Zen teaching. Mahakasyapa is therefore the First Patriarch in Zen Buddhism.

Ananda, the Buddha's favourite attending-disciple, asked Mahakasyapa what the Buddha had transmitted to him. Mahakasyapa told him to go out of the temple into the bamboo grove and find the answer there. Ananda went, but returned without finding the answer. Mahakasyapa then told him, 'Take down the banner!' Ananda instantly understood and was enlightened. Ananda became the Second Patriarch.

In the deeper meaning of Mahakasyapa's words, the temple symbolized a body of spiritual teaching, and the banner outside the temple indicated that preaching, which necessarily used words, was going on. An intimation of this meaning can be found in the above verse.

Hui Neng in his *Platform Sutra* says that, at first, sudden enlightenment was transmitted to seven Buddhas:

1 Vipasyin Buddha
2 Sikhin Buddha
3 Vestabhu Buddha
4 Krakuchanda Buddha
5 Kanakamuni Buddha
6 Kasyapa Buddha
7 Sakyamuni Buddha[6]

Since Sakyamuni (the name Mahayanists usually used for Gautama Buddha), Zen Buddhism was transmitted from patriarch to patriarch for 28 generations in India. The genealogical line, as given in the *Platform Sutra*, is as follows:'[7]

1 Mahakasyapa
2 Ananda
3 Madyhanitka
4 Sanavasa
5 Upagupta
6 Dhritaka
7 Buddhananti
8 Buddhamitra
9 Parsva

10 Punyayasas
11 Asvaghosha
12 Kapimala
13 Nagarjuna
14 Kanadeva
15 Rahulata
16 Sanghanandi
17 Gayasata
18 Kumarata
19 Jayata
20 Vasubandhu
21 Manorhita
22 Haklennayasas
23 Aryasimha
24 Basiasita
25 Upaguta
26 Sangharaksha
27 Vasumitra
28 Bodhidharma

Because the same master was known by more than one name, and because of different traditions within Zen Buddhism itself and variations in translation techniques, some lists of patriarchs are slightly different. For example, the modern Zen teacher Hui Guang lists Nagarjuna, regarded by many as the second Buddha, as the Fourteenth Patriarch, instead of the Thirteenth as listed above,[8] and some writers refer to Bodhidharma's teacher as Prajnatara, not Vasumitra.[9]

THE TEACHING OF BODHIDHARMA

Bodhidharma (Da Mo in Chinese, Daruma in Japanese) third prince of Kancipura in South India and Twenty-eighth Patriarch in India, became the First Patriarch in China. He arrived in China in 520 to spread Buddhism. The emperor Liang Wu Di, who was sometimes known as the Asoka of China because of his great work in promoting Buddhism, asked the Indian master:

'Since becoming the emperor, I have built temples,

translated sutras, and ordained monks beyond what can be remembered. What merit have I gained?'

'No merit at all!' replied Bodhidharma.

'Why have I no merit?'

'These good deeds bring only small rewards, resulting in being born in heaven. Their causes are conditioned, like shadow following the body, but have no ultimate reality,' explained the master.

'What then brings real merit?'

'Purity and wisdom in perfect enlightenment; body and self being empty and tranquil. This kind of merit is not obtained in the mundane world.'

'What is the first principle of holiness?' asked the Emperor.

'There is only emptiness, no holiness.'

'Who is now before me?'

'Don't know.'[10]

Bodhidharma is clearly explaining a very important cosmic truth to help Liang Wu Di to be awakened. All the good deeds the emperor had done were meritorious only for moral purity, a preparatory stage, and he would be rewarded with rebirth in some heavenly realms – a small reward when compared with enlightenment. But such deeds, however many a person might perform, were in themselves not enough to attain enlightenment.

This, of course, does not mean that one should not perform good deeds. As mentioned earlier, doing good deeds promotes moral purity, a prerequisite for enlightenment. Purity and higher wisdom, which is obtained from meditation, lead to enlightenment, where all the illusion of phenomena and self disappears, and where ultimate reality is empty and tranquil. The merit required for cosmic realization comes not from mundane activities but from persistent spiritual cultivation.

At this highest level of enlightenment, there is no dualistic thinking. Hence, there is no difference between profanity and holiness, between defilement and purity, between the knower and the known, because transcendental reality is undifferentiated; there is only emptiness.

There is no differentiation in ultimate reality: the differentiation into separate entities, into Liang Wu Di and

Bodhidharma, is an illusion. Hence, when the emperor asked Bodhidharma who he was, the ultimate answer was he did not know.

As the emperor was not ready, he missed this opportunity to experience an awakening. Bodhidharma then went north. According to legend, as he came to Yangtze Kiang, Bodhidharma stepped on a floating reed and used his supernormal powers to cross this river that separates south and north China. The expression 'Crossing the river on a reed' is now a popular phrase in the Chinese language.

Bodhidharma settled in Shaolin Monastery in 527 to teach Zen. His teaching can be divided into two approaches: 'entry through understanding' and 'entry through practice'. Understanding refers to wisdom achieved through meditation, with the aspirant attaining insight into cosmic reality. Practice refers to practising the following four tenets in daily living:

1 Tolerance – if suffering the painful effect of previous bad karma
2 Equanimity – when rewarded by good karma
3 Determination – to overcome the suffering of samsara and work hard for nirvana
4 Realization – that all phenomena and the mind are of the same nature

These two approaches have greatly influenced the cultivation methods as well as the way of life of subsequent Zen practitioners.

Bodhidharma discovered that the monks at Shaolin Monastery were too weak for the vigorous meditation that was necessary for attaining enlightenment. Unlike some masters who postulated that the mind was most important in spiritual cultivation and thus neglected the body (sometimes referred to as a 'smelly skin receptacle') Bodhidharma expounded that the body too is important, because physical, emotional and mental health are all necessary for spiritual development. To this end he taught the Shaolin monks two sets of exercises: the *Eighteen Lohan Hands* and *Sinew Metamorphosis*.

The Eighteen Lohan Hands is a set of 18 meditative/respiratory exercises to promote agility, flexibility, physical strength, circulation of the blood and vital energy, and general health. Some examples are provided in Chapter 18. These exercises later developed into the famous Shaolin Kungfu, considered by many as 'the best martial art under heaven'.

The Sinew Metamorphosis is a set of internal exercises to develop amazing internal force, increase energy levels and improve mental freshness. The exercises look bafflingly simple, but the results have to be seen or, better still, experienced to be believed. Sinew Metamorphosis has since developed into Shaolin Chi Kung, the Shaolin art of training vital energy. Because of the tremendous power that chi kung could generate, in the past this art of energy training was kept secret, taught only to special disciples. But conditions have changed, and chi kung is now available to the general public, though often in adulterated forms. Shaolin Chi Kung exercises are explained in Chapter 18.

The early history of Zen Buddhism in China, and how it came to acquire Chinese characteristics, is described in the next chapter.

8

EARLY HISTORY OF ZEN IN CHINA

From Hui Ke's No-Mind to Hui Neng's
Buddha-Nature

*Transcendentally, nirvana is samsara and samsara
is nirvana; the illusory difference is one of
spiritual perspective.*

HUI KE SEEKING THE DHARMA

Ji Guang (487–583), a weakly Confucian scholar, went to Shaolin
Monastery to seek teaching from Bodhidharma. When Bodhidharma first saw him, the master said, 'I don't accept disciples
who are physically weak.' So the master taught Ji Guang the
Eighteen Lohan Hands to strengthen him.

After a year of training, Ji Guang asked the master for further
instruction. Bodhidharma was then sitting on his meditation
seat in the cave, now called Bodhidharma Cave, not far from
Shaolin Monastery. 'If you can pull me down from my seat, I'll
teach you.' Ji Guang tried hard but to his surprise could not
move the master. So Bodhidharma taught him Sinew Metamorphosis to develop his internal strength.

After another year, Ji Guang, now a symbol of health and
vitality, sought Bodhidharma in his favourite cave for further
training. Bodhidharma said, 'The birds outside the cave are
making too much noise for you to learn effectively.' Ji Guang
chased away the birds, but they flew back as soon as he walked
away. He even used his internal strength to break a huge branch
upon which the birds sat, but they flew into the top of the tree.
As Ji Guang was wondering what to do, Bodhidharma went

into meditation and, using his supernormal power, created a strong wind that rustled the leaves so much, the birds flew away. Then Bodhidharma taught Ji Guang meditation.

After three years of meditation practice, Ji Guang sought his master again, but each time Bodhidharma avoided him. One wintry day in Shaolin Monastery, Ji Guang found his master meditating inside a chamber, now named Bodhidharma Chamber. It was snowing heavily but Ji Guang stood waiting in the snow. He waited and waited until the snow reached up to his knees. He was able to stand the cold because of his Sinew Metamorphosis training. Hence, this building is now called Standing-in-the-Snow Pavilion. At last Bodhidharma emerged.

'Please teach me the way, master,' Ji Guang pleaded.

'No!'

'Please, master, when can you teach me?'

'When the snow turns red.'

Calmly, using his internal strength, Ji Guang severed his left arm; blood gushed out, making the snow red.

Equally calmly, Bodhidharma asked. 'What is troubling you?'

'My mind is troubling me. Please calm my mind, master.'

'Bring out your mind and I shall calm it,' the master said.

Suddenly a smile spread over Ji Guang's face. 'I searched for my mind, but I cannot find it. I have no mind!'

'You are awakened!' Bodhidharma said. 'From now on you shall be called Hui Ke, meaning Able to Transmit Wisdom.'

Bodhidharma transmitted the *Lankavatara Sutra* to Hui Ke (Eka in Japanese). When Bodhidharma entered parinirvana, he handed the cotton *kasaya* (monk's robe), the insignia of Zen patriarchate, to Hui Ke who therefore succeeded him as the Second Patriarch.[1]

Two points are worth remembering in this story. Firstly, the procedure taught by Bodhidharma is the Shaolin tradition of Zen cultivation, involving teaching students first to be healthy through kungfu, then to develop their internal force through chi kung, and finally to enhance their minds through meditation. When a student is well prepared, he may achieve awakening or even enlightenment in an instant when the right time comes.

The second point concerns Hui Ke severing his arm. Many readers will be aghast at this, but one has attained a very high spiritual level, losing an arm for a spiritual awakening is nothing. After all, the arm and everything else in the phenomenal world are illusory; in transcendental reality, the whole cosmos is undifferentiated. Like many other Zen practitioners we shall read about later, Hui Ke had reached the extreme of dualistic thinking and was ready to sacrifice anything for enlightenment. Most ordinary people, of course, would value their arm more.

THE MIND IS THE BUDDHA

The situation in which Hui Ke transmitted Zen to his successor was similar to the one in which he had received it from Bodhidharma.

At the Shaolin Monastery, an aspirant, whose name was not known, asked Hui Ke:
'My body is full of sins. I request Your Venerable to help me repent.'
'Bring out your sins and I'll help you repent.'
'But when I search for my sins, I cannot find them!' the aspirant said.
'I've helped you repent. The monastic order is with the Buddha's teaching.'
'When I see Your Venerable, I understand the monastic order. But what is the Buddha's teaching?'
'The mind is the Buddha. The mind is the teaching. The Buddha and the teaching are not different. The monastic order is the same too.'
'Hearing this, now I understand. Right at the beginning the nature of sin is not inside, outside or in the middle. So it is with the mind. Thus the Buddha and the teaching are not different.'
'You are a treasure to the monastic order, I name you Seng Can,' the master said.

Seng Can ('glory of the monks') later succeeded Hui Ke as the Third Patriarch.

The Buddha, the teaching (known as Dharma, or *fa* in Chinese) and the monastic order (*sangha*, or *sengjia* in Chinese) are the Three Treasures or the Triple Gem of Buddhism. The Triple Gem of Shaolin, which leads to Zen realization, comprises kungfu, chi kung and meditation.[2] The crucial line in the above Zen encounter was when Hui Ke told Seng Can that the Buddha, the Dharma and the sangha are not different from the mind. (This will be dealt with in subsequent chapters.) Immediately Seng Can was awakened; he realized that the mind (that is cosmic reality) is universal and undifferentiated.

THE ULTIMATE TRUTH IS WITHIN US

When Dao Xin (Tao Hsin, 580–651) met his teacher at the Shaolin Monastery, Dao Xin was only 14 years old. He asked Seng Can:
    'Master, may you have compassion on me. Teach me the way to be liberated.'
    'Who ties you?' Seng Can asked.
    'Nobody ties me.'
    'Since nobody ties you, why do you seek liberation?'
    Dao Xin was instantaneously awakened.

Dao Xin continued studying Zen under Seng Can for another nine years, and succeeded him as the Fourth Patriarch. Later he moved to Dongshan Temple in Huangmei District in Hubei Province. Since the time of Bodhidharma, the main scripture for preaching had been the *Lankavatara Sutra*. But when Dao Xin moved from Shaolin Monastery to Dongshan Temple, he changed the main scripture to the *Diamond Sutra*, because this scripture was already popular in Huangmei District.

    Zen, as mentioned earlier, is directly pointing at the mind. Instead of philosophizing on liberation, Seng Can asked Dao Xin who had tied him. He pointed out that as Dao Xin was not tied, he did not have to seek liberation. What he needed was this realization.

    All of us have the Buddha nature, or divine spark, in us. We do not have to search for Buddhahood outside because we are all originally Buddhas. In Christian terms, we do not have to search for God's kingdom outside because the Kingdom of God is within us. Similarly, in Islam the essence of human life is *roh*, which is the spirit of God; and in Hinduism the atman inside is an expression of Brahman, the Universal Spirit. In Zen, when a person realizes this cosmic truth, when he realizes that the transcendental reality of which he is an integral part is undifferentiated, he attains awakening.

REINCARNATED TO BE AWAKENED

Dao Xin was very young when he attained his awakening, but his successor was even younger.

> Dao Xin said to his student, Zai Song, who was an old man, 'I would like to transmit the Zen teaching to you, but you are too old now. How about coming to me again in your next life?'
>
> Zai Song then met a young woman washing clothes by a river, and asked her, 'May I stay with you?'
>
> 'You may, but I have my parents at home.'
>
> When she returned home she became pregnant though she was unmarried. Her parents chased her from the house. When she delivered the baby she was surprised to see that he glowed in celestial light. The mother and child begged food together. As the boy had no father, villagers used to call him 'Wu Xing Er' (child without surname). One day, when he was seven years old, he was seen by Dao Xin on his way back to Dongshan Temple.
>
> Dao Xin asked, 'Boy, what is your *xing*' (By 'xing', Dao Xin meant the boy's surname.)
>
> 'I have a xing, but it is not an ordinary xing,' the boy answered.
>
> In the Chinese language, xing can also mean 'nature', so the boy's answer was either 'I have a surname, but it is not an ordinary surname' or 'I have a nature, but it is not an ordinary nature.'
>
> 'What type of xing?' the master asked.
>
> 'Fu xing,' the boy replied.

The Chinese word for 'Buddha' is now pronounced 'fo', but in ancient time it was pronounced 'fu', which was also the sound for 'no'. Hence, the boy's second answer could mean 'I have no surname' or 'I have Buddha-nature.'

'So, you don't have xing,' Dao Xin said.

'Xing is empty; that's why there isn't any.'

Dao Xing recognized that the boy was the reincarnation of Zai Song. He took the boy back to Dongshan Temple and named him Hong Jen ('Great Tolerance', Gunin in Japanese). Hong Jen (602–75) later succeeded Dao Xin as the Fifth Patriarch.

The significance of this Zen encounter lies in the pun on 'xing' and 'fu' When the master asked the boy his surname, he answered that his nature was extraordinary. The master asked what was so extraordinary about his surname. He said he had Buddha-nature. The master concluded that the boy had no surname. The boy said that because Buddha-nature is empty, there is no Buddha-nature, which is the same as saying the Universal Mind is no mind. It is no-mind because ultimate reality is beyond any separate entities.

This Zen story also illustrates that there is no limitation on age or position in Zen awakening. The awakened may be an old man or a child, a prince or a pauper.

ULTIMATE REALITY IS UNDIFFERENTIATED

Hong Jen became a very successful Zen teacher with more than a thousand pupils. His most outstanding disciple was the head monk, Shen Xiu (605–706, Junshu in Japanese), a well-educated Buddhist scholar whom everybody expected to succeed Hong Jen. However, a very important development occurred that was to change the course of Zen history when Hui Neng (638–713, Yeno in Japanese) joined the Dongshan Temple.

Hui Neng was a poor illiterate who peddled firewood to support his mother. While selling firewood he heard a customer reciting the Diamond Sutra (Vajrachchedika Sutra). Hui Neng understood the teaching and was awakened. Learning that the Diamond Sutra was taught by Hong Jen, Hui Neng travelled to Dongshan Temple and begged to be accepted as a pupil. Hong Jen said, 'You are a barbarian from the south; how could a barbarian become a Buddha?' Hui Neng's answer – that although people might be differentiated into northerners and southerners, there is no differentiation in Buddha-nature – surprised the master. Hui Neng was then asked to pound rice in the temple kitchen.

Hong Jen announced that whoever could compose the best *gatha* (poem) to illustrate his understanding of Zen would be chosen as his successor. As everyone expected Shen Xiu to succeed, no one else offered a gatha. Perhaps out of modesty or caution, Shen Xiu did not present his gatha openly, but wrote the following poem on a wall at night:

> The body is the bodhi tree,
> The mind like the mirror bright.
> Clean it diligently every time,
> Do not ever let dust alight.

When Hong Jen saw the poem the next morning, he knew it was written by Shen Xiu. He praised the head monk, but said that his understanding was still not perfect.

Later Hui Neng heard a boy reciting this poem, but as soon as he heard it, he realized it was not complete. He recited another poem and asked someone to write it on an adjacent wall, as follows:

> Bodhi is actually not a tree,
> The mind not a mirror bright.
> Buddha-nature is always tranquil,
> Wherefore can dust alight?

When Hong Jen saw the poem he was surprised at the depth of Hui Neng's understanding. In order to grasp the poem's deeper meaning, it is necessary to be aware that the crucial line, 'Buddha-nature is always tranquil' does not mean that the nature of a person who follows the Buddha's teaching is always calm and peaceful. It means that ultimate reality is always undifferentiated and impartial, that, transcendentally, there are no separate objects and processes. 'Buddha' here refers to ultimate reality, not to Gautama Buddha. 'Tranquillity' refers to undifferentiation and impartiality, not to calmness or the peacefulness of a person's disposition.

Hence, Hui Neng's poem showed his understanding of transcendentalism; he knew that the Ultimate Absolute is 'beyond

all duality' (meaning that there are no separate entities). Therefore, there is no dust to be wiped off, nor tree nor mirror to
represent the body and the mind.

Shen Xiu had not understood this cosmic truth. His thinking
was still dualistic. He still perceived body, tree, mind and mirror
as separate entities. His concept, like that of the great majority
of people, including Buddhists, was polaristic, separating purity
and nirvana on one side from defilement and samsara on the
other. His idea, therefore, was to constantly keep away defilement, symbolized by dust in the poem, so that nirvana, which
was separated from samsara, could be achieved.

Shen Xiu's attainment, therefore, was still Hinayanist; his
spiritual aspiration was to attain moral purity. This aspiration
would result in his rebirth in some heavenly realms, or at a
higher spiritual level in his future human life, but by itself was
insufficient to lead him to enlightenment. He had not reached
the Mahayanist stage, as emphasized by the great Indian Zen
patriarch Nagarjuna, where, transcendentally, nirvana is
samsara and samsara is nirvana.

Realizing Hui Neng's cosmic wisdom, Hong Jen called him
to his room at night and transmitted the *Diamond Sutra* to
him. Although Hui Neng was illiterate, he comprehended the
sutra after hearing it only once. The master passed the cotton
kasaya and the patriarchal bowl to Hui Neng, thus choosing
him as his successor, but asked him to leave the temple that
night so as to avoid a possible uproar the next morning when
the others learned that an unknown rice pounder was the next
patriarch.

IT IS YOUR MIND THAT MOVES

Hui Neng, the Sixth Patriarch, went south and maintained a
low profile for 16 years. In 676 he arrived at Guangzhow
(Canton) and heard a dispute between two monks in front of
Fa Xing Temple (Temple of Dharma Nature) over a banner
fluttering in the wind. One monk said it was the banner that
was moving; but the other said it was the wind. Hui Neng told
them, 'Neither the banner nor the wind moves; it is your mind
that moves.' When their teacher, Yin Zong, an expert on the
Nirvana Sutra, heard about this, he was so impressed with Hui

Neng's wisdom that he wanted to become his disciple. But Hui Neng was not even an ordained monk, because when he was at Hong Jen's Dongshan Temple he was only a lay rice pounder. Yin Zong shaved Hui Neng's head so he could become a monk, and about three weeks later another vinaya teacher, Zhi Guang, ordained him. A pagoda was built to preserve his hair. Later, in 1151, Fa Xing Temple was renamed Guang Xiao Temple (Temple of Glorifying Filial Piety) by imperial decree. If you visit the temple today, you will find not only the pagoda, but also the Sixth Patriarch Hall, the Wind and Banner Hall, and the huge bodhi tree under which Hui Neng preached.

For 37 years Hui Neng taught Zen in numerous famous temples in the south – Da Fan Temple (Temple of Great Brahma), Guo En Temple (Temple of National Beneficence), and Nan Hua Temple (South China Temple) – but his most important base was the Bao Lin Temple (Temple of Precious Grove) in Cao Xi (Tsao Hsi) District. There he had thousands of students, among whom were 43 famous disciples who later spread Zen far and wide.

NORTHERN AND SOUTHERN SCHOOLS

Shen Xiu succeeded Hong Jen at the Dongshan Temple, and taught Zen for more than 25 years. He was very successful in north China, and in 700 was appointed Imperial Teacher; even the powerful Empress Wu prostrated before him. The empress declared Shen Xiu as the Sixth Patriarch, and retrieved the cotton kasaya from Hui Neng, but compensated him generously, including an imperial kasaya which Hui Neng accepted and used.

An intriguing aspect of this appointment was that Empress Wu did not give the cotton kasaya to Shen Xiu, but to Zhi Xi, one of his junior classmates. This was because when the empress had asked Shen Xiu, Zhi Xi and some of the other senior disciples of Hong Jen whether they still had desire, all except Zhi Xi answered 'no'. He said, 'As long as a person lives, he has desire; he has no desire only when he is dead.' Like most people, the empress perceived the world at the level of ordinary knowledge. She said Zhi Xi was honest, so presented the cotton kasaya to him, but Shen Xiu continued to be the most respected.

He lived for 100 years, and two of his disciples, Pu Ji and Yi Fu, also became imperial teachers to succeeding emperors. Pu Ji succeeded Shen Xiu as the Seventh Patriarch.

Rivalry among some followers led to accounts depicting Shen Xiu as a malicious person attempting to usurp Hui Neng's position and influence. These writings are unfair to Shen Xiu. Had he been malicious, with his influence and power it would not have been difficult for Shen Xiu or his successors to eliminate Hui Neng's school, especially when it first developed. Hui Neng was free to teach and practise whatever and wherever he wanted. There is no record at all to suggest that Hui Neng or his successors were oppressed. On the contrary, Shen Xiu advised Empress Wu to invite Hui Neng to the capital, although Hui Neng, realizing that their doctrinal differences would make it difficult for them to work together, declined the imperial offer.

To place these events in their proper historical perspective, it should be remembered that this period was the golden age of Buddhism in China, when other Buddhist schools besides Zen Buddhism also flourished. Most of the important schools of Chinese Buddhism which later spread to Japan and other places, were founded around this time, including the Tian Tai (Lotus) School founded by Zhi Yi (Chih I, 531–97), the Hua Yen (Garland) School by Du Shun (Tu Shun, 557–640), and the Fa Xiang (Ideation) School founded by Xuan Zang (Yuan Tsang, 596–664). To be chosen from the large number of great masters from all schools for the position of Imperial Teacher (who also doubled as the nominal head of the Buddhist faith in the entire empire), is indicative of the respect Shen Xiu commanded.

What, then, was the difference between Shen Xiu's teaching, now called the northern school, and Hui Neng's teaching, the southern school? The most notable difference was that in the northern school enlightenment was attained gradually, whereas in the southern school it was sudden. However, it must be pointed out that Shen Xiu did not rule out sudden enlightenment, nor did Hui Neng rule out gradual enlightenment, but their approaches were such that the northern school was sometimes called the school of gradual enlightenment, and the southern school the school of sudden enlightenment.

Each man's approach was necessarily affected by his training methods. Both schools used meditation: the northern school stressed doctrinal studies and moral purity; the southern school pointed at the mind, sometimes with ingenious methods like seemingly illogical questioning, shouting and even hitting to assail the mind so as to reveal in an instant its true nature. It is sometimes said that the southern school disregarded meditation; this is not true. As will be shown later, meditation is an essential aspect of Zen Buddhism, whose name actually means the Meditation School of Buddhism.

The northern school, despite its initial glory, eventually faded away. All the important Zen schools that subsequently flourished in China belonged to the southern school. This was mainly due to the efforts of Hui Neng's outstanding disciple Shen Hui. His first decisive effort was to organize a large assembly at Da Yun Temple (Temple of Great Clouds) in Huatai in 735, 22 years after Hui Neng's parinirvana, to declare publicly that it was Hui Neng's teaching, not that of the northern school, which was the genuine Zen teaching from Bodhidharma. He repeated the declaration at another important assembly in Loyang.

The northern school took no counter action against Shen Hui, but 18 years later, in 753, at the advanced age of 85, he was banished to Jiangxi for inciting large crowds. Rebellion broke out two years later, and when the government was re-established in 757 the emperor recalled Shen Hui to raise funds for the government. His reputation soared and consequently the southern school became popular. Around 790 Shen Hui was declared the Seventh Patriarch by imperial order and Hui Neng the Sixth.[3]

Today in China there is no clear-cut distinction between the northern and southern schools of Zen. In fact the differences between various Mahayanist schools have faded away, and most Chinese Buddhists regard themselves as Mahayana Buddhists rather than Buddhists of specific schools, though Zen and the Pure Land sect remain most popular.

Nevertheless, almost all the puzzling Zen stories that readers are likely to come across nowadays are related to masters from Hui Neng's succession line. Hence, in order to make sense of these stories, it is necessary to have a basic idea of Hui Neng's teaching, which forms the foundation of Zen Buddhism and is summarized in his *Platform Sutra*. One good indication of whether a person is ready for satori or awakening in Zen – or in Buddhist terms, whether he has good spiritual roots – is whether he has awareness of higher wisdom. Thus, an understanding of Hui Neng's fundamental teaching on Zen, which touches on higher wisdom, is an effective preparation for awakening. The main doctrines taught in the *Platform Sutra* are explained in the next three chapters.

9

ZEN OF THE SIXTH PATRIARCH

The Teaching of Hui Neng on Meditation and
Wisdom

*Readers, including Buddhists, familiar with
traditional ways of mind training, will find Hui
Neng's method very different (and effective) as
evident from the great number of Zen
practitioners who achieved awakening by
following his teaching.*

THE IMPORTANCE OF THE *PLATFORM SUTRA*

Some people, rightly or wrongly, consider that Hui Neng is the
founder of Zen Buddhism, not Bodhidharma, because much of
Zen Buddhism, they argue, is derived from his teaching. Moreover, Hui Neng gave Zen Buddhism in particular, and
Mahayana Buddhism in general, a Chinese perspective which
made it distinctly different from Indian Buddhism. According
to this trend of thought, masters from Bodhidharma to Hong
Jen, Hui Neng's teacher, are regarded as forerunners of Zen
Buddhism.

To evaluate this opinion, or for that matter to arrive at an
adequate understanding of Zen Buddhism, it is necessary to
examine Hui Neng's teaching in some detail. Fortunately this
is not difficult, because the essence of Hui Neng's teaching is
recorded in his *Tan Jing*, or *Platform Sutra*. The great importance
Chinese Buddhists place on this work is evident from the fact
that the term 'sutra' is usually reserved for records of teachings
by the Buddha himself, but the *Platform Sutra* is one of the very
few exceptions in the very extensive Buddhist literature. Indeed,
many people consider Hui Neng the Chinese Buddha. Like

Gautama, he achieved enlightenment by his own effort; when his teacher passed on the patriarchate to him, he was already enlightened.

Hui Neng himself said that the *Platform Sutra* represented his fundamental teaching, and those who have not received this teaching have received nothing. He also told his ten special disciples, 'If you do not transmit the teaching of the *Platform Sutra*, you have not transmitted my teaching.'

It is called the *Platform Sutra* because the core of its content was preached by Hui Neng on a specially erected platform to a large gathering of over 10,000 – lay people as well as monks – at the Da Fan Temple (Temple of Great Brahma) in Shaozhou District in south China. The magistrate who had invited Hui Neng to preach, instructed Hui Neng's senior disciple and head monk, Fa Hai, to record the master's teaching. There are some minor differences in the different versions of the scripture that have come down to us. For example, in the English translation by Wing-Tsit Chan,[1] which also provides the Chinese original, the general who intercepted Hui Neng to seek his teaching was named Hui-shun, whereas in Wong Mou-Lam's translation, where the sutra is presented under main topics, he was called Hui Ming.[2] But the main points taught are the same. A commendable feature of the sutra is its clarity and directness of language, especially when compared with the poetic and often illustrative style of other sutras. Its profound ideas, though described in simple words, may need some explanation and reflection before they can be readily comprehended. The *Platform Sutra* also contains Hui Neng's comments on the difference between his and Shen Xiu's teaching, on the recitation of Amitabha and on the *Lotus Sutra*.

Readers who expect a scripture to sing the glory of God, expound rewards in heaven, or implore people to do good, will be very surprised at the content of the *Platform Sutra*. Although God, in the rather prosaic term of 'true nature' is immanent in the sutra, there are hardly any glories sung to Him. To be reborn in heaven is not the aim of Zen practice, and because moral purity is an understood prerequisite for spiritual development, doing good is mentioned only in passing. The gist of the scripture concerns mind. For those who wish to train their mind for Zen awakening, an understanding of Hui Neng's teaching is certainly helpful. But readers, including Buddhists, familiar with traditional ways of mind training, will find Hui Neng's method very different – and effective, as evident from the great number of Zen practitioners who achieved awakening by following his teaching. Those who wish to find deeper meaning in tantalizing Zen stories can also derive guidance from the *Platform Sutra*.

The sutra starts with Hui Neng providing some autobiographical material. Then the Sixth Patriarch expounds his main doctrine with special reference to meditation and wisdom, and follows this with an explanation of the Three Bodies of the Buddha, the Four Great Vows, the Triple Gem, and the perfection of great wisdom and cosmic reality. Next the master explains sudden enlightenment and answers important questions concerning Bodhidharma, Amitabha, Shen Xiu's teaching, and the *Lotus Sutra*. Finally, he offers useful advice on attaining enlightenment.

THE WISDOM OF ENLIGHTENMENT

After the preliminary autobiography, including the transmission of the patriarchate from Hong Jen, Hui Neng begins the preaching proper by declaring that his teaching has been transmitted from past patriarchs, and that it is not his own knowledge:

> Learned audience, the wisdom of enlightenment (bodhi-prajna) is inherent in all people; it is due to the delusion of their minds that people are not awakened to their own original enlightenment. Hence they have to seek the compassionate and wise to help them to see their own nature. Learned audience, once awakened, you will attain the wisdom of enlightenment.

Those who are not sure about the role of meditation in Hui Neng's teaching will find a definite answer in the master's own words:

> Learned audience, meditation (*ding*) and wisdom (*hui*) are the fundamentals of my teaching. First of all, do not be deluded that meditation and wisdom are different. Meditation and wisdom are of the same body, that is, meditation is the body of wisdom, and wisdom is the application of meditation. Hence, when wisdom is

present, meditation is in wisdom; when meditation is present, wisdom is in meditation.

One possible cause of misunderstanding or inadequate understanding is that the Chinese word 'ding' is translated to mean something else besides meditation, probably because many people believe that the only Chinese terms for meditation are *chan* (dhyana) and *jing-zuo* (silent sitting). For example, in his remarkable work, Professor Wing-Tsit Chan has translated this word as 'calmness',[3] which, in my opinion, although literally correct, has missed its figurative significance. *Ding* here is the short form for *chan ding*, which is the established Chinese term for the Sanskrit *dhyana-samadhi*, though this term may not be widely known outside initiated circles. The standard Chinese terms for the three Buddhist disciplines of moral purity (sila), meditation (dhyana) and wisdom (prajna) are *jie*, *ding* and *hui*.

Wong Mou-Lam, being a practising Buddhist, clearly understands the significance of *ding*. He translates the above quotation as follows:

> Learned Audience, in my system (Dhyana) Samadhi and Prajna are fundamental. But do not be under the wrong impression that these two are independent of each other, for they are inseparably united and are not two entities. Samadhi is the quintessence of Prajna, while Prajna is the activity of Samadhi. At the very moment that we attain Prajna, Samadhi is therewith; and vice versa.[4]

Why is meditation not different from wisdom? By wisdom here is meant the realization that cosmic reality is transcendental – the attainment of the Ultimate Absolute or Buddhahood. This realization of the ultimate reality can be attained only in a state of deep meditation, which transports ordinary consciousness not only to a greatly heightened level of reality, but to the very ultimate, where duality is transcended. At our ordinary level of consciousness, we experience reality as a delusion because of our gross sense of perception; it is only in deep meditation that we can transcend the phenomenal realm conditioned by our senses and attain transcendental cosmic reality, known in Buddhism as nirvana or Buddhahood. Thus, meditation is essential in all schools of Buddhism. Indeed, meditation, known by different names, is essential in all the world's great religions as a way of attaining the highest spiritual fulfilment.

The master compares the correlation between meditation and wisdom with that between words and thoughts. If a person speaks of good deeds but his thoughts are full of wickedness, there is no correlation between words and deeds. Similarly, a person in which there is no correlation between meditation and wisdom will not attain enlightenment. Hence, the master advises that having a straight mind – being sincere without wickedness and malice – is necessary. He quotes from the *Vimalakirti Sutra* saying that 'The straight mind is the place for spiritual training; the straight mind is the Pure Land.'

HUI NENG'S BASIC DOCTRINE

Explaining his basic doctrine, the master says:

> Right from the start, irrespective of whether enlightenment is attained suddenly or gradually, non-thought constitutes the basic doctrine, non-characteristics the basic body, and non-abiding the basic foundation. What is non-characteristics? Non-characteristics is to be in the midst of characteristics yet free from characteristics. Non-thought is to be in the midst of thoughts yet free from thoughts. Non-abiding is the original nature of man. Thoughts after thoughts arise, yet they do not abide. Past thoughts, present thoughts, future thoughts – thoughts after thoughts are connected, without breaking off, without end. If a thought is broken off, the spiritual body is free from the physical body. During the continuous process of these thoughts, do not let any thought abide at any dharma. Once a thought abides, all thoughts abide. This is called bondage. When all thoughts do not abide at dharmas, then there is no bondage. This is the meaning of saying non-thought is the foundation.

This is a crucial passage explaining the method of Hui Neng's teaching in particular and Zen cultivation in general. If you understand this passage, you will understand why, in the Zen stories in Chapter 1, Huang Bo said that Lin Ji was practising Zen, why the student attained awakening when Zhao Zhou asked him to wash his bowl, and why after enlightenment Fa Rong no longer found birds bringing him flowers. You will also appreciate the deeper meaning in many other Zen stories.

Non-characteristics constitutes the basic body of Hui Neng's teaching. Although Zen practitioners exist in the phenomenal world, where the phenomena express countless characteristics, the awakened realize that these characteristics are illusory, conditioned by their gross sense perception. When a person is awakened to this realization he is free from characteristics, which is the nature of ultimate reality, although he may still exist in the midst of characteristics in the phenomenal realm.

Non-abiding is man's original nature, which is the Zen jargon for transcendental reality. In other words, in transcendental reality, even if there are thoughts, they do not abide at dharmas, that is, they do not manifest as separate objects and processes as in the phenomenal world. An enlightened person will experience transcendental reality as a holistic, organic unity. But ordinary people experience reality as the phenomenal world. This is because since millennia thoughts after thoughts arise continuously without end and, being conditioned by our sense perception, these thoughts manifest as what we ignorantly regard as 'external reality'. Other beings, whether in our own realm of existence – like insects and plants (which certainly possess consciousness) – or in other realms – like ghosts or angels (whose existence many people out of ignorance are not aware of) – will experience the same cosmic reality very differently. In other words, so-called 'external reality' is actually a creation of the mind. Before modern physicists discovered this fact, many people thought that Buddhist masters were talking non-sense.

If a person can break off a thought from its abiding, then his spiritual body is liberated from his physical body. This again is Zen jargon, meaning that if a person can attain the state of non-thought, he will realize that what he previously considered to be his physical body is actually an illusion, and that in his timeless moment of enlightenment, there is no differentiation between 'himself' and his surroundings. For example, he will experience, without the help of scientific instruments, that what he normally calls his skin is in reality not a line separating his so-called interior from his so-called exterior, and that there is a constant flow of subatomic particles across this illusory line.

For unenlightened people, once a thought abides, all thoughts abide, because thoughts are continuously linked. In this way we are bound – endlessly tied to arising thoughts which perpetuate the cycle of birth and rebirth. The objective of Buddhism is to liberate oneself from this bondage; in Zen this liberation often comes suddenly.

SITTING MEDITATION

Next, the master explains meditation. If this teaching is inadequately understood, it can be construed that he advocates doing away with meditation:

> In this method, the fundamental purpose of sitting meditation is neither looking at the mind nor at the void; nor do we say there is no activity. If we say we look at the mind, the mind is originally deluded; delusion is like illusion, so there is nothing worthwhile to see. If we say we look at the void, man's nature is basically the void; it is because of delusion that the void of the Supreme Reality is obstructed. Liberated from deluded thought, basic nature is the void. If we do not see the void of our basic nature, but allow thoughts to arise so as to see the void, what we see is a deluded void. Delusion has no real existence, thus we know that what we see is illusory. The void has no physical forms or characteristics. But ordinary people create physical forms and characteristics and say this is the purpose of meditation.

The Chinese word *jing* in the original passage is usually translated as 'pure', for example *jing tu* is 'Pure Land'. In a Buddhist context, 'pure' usually means 'the void', that is, devoid of impurities or illusory phenomena. Hence, in order that readers grasp the intended meaning of the master more easily, in the above translation 'the void' is used instead of 'pure' or 'purity' which are often found in other translations.

It is very clear that the master teaches what not to do during meditation, and not that meditation can be done away with. Hui Neng's method of meditation, nevertheless, is vastly different from what most people are familiar with.

In Mahayana meditation the meditator usually focuses on the void, whereas in Theravada meditation the meditator usually focuses on an actual or imaginary object so as to achieve a one-pointed mind, and in Vajrayana meditation the meditator usually employs visualization. Sometimes, especially at advanced levels in all the schools, the meditator observes his own mind. In Zen meditation as taught by Hui Neng, the meditator does none of these things. As indicated elsewhere, the aim of Hui Neng's meditation is to let the mind be natural, spontaneous – to be in the midst of characteristics yet not affected by them, to be in the midst of thoughts yet not bound to them. In this way, Hui Neng teaches, we can more easily see our own nature and attain transcendental cosmic reality. Once we use our mind to focus on the void or an object, to visualize or to observe itself, thoughts abide. Hui Neng advises that this spontaneity of mind be adopted not only during sitting meditation, but while standing and walking – in fact at all times.

This emphasis by Zen practitioners on spontaneity in meditation and in all spheres of activities has led some scholars to postulate that Zen is developed from Taoism, because Zen spontaneity is similar to Toist spontaneity or wu-wei. As explained in Chapter 7, although there may be some superficial similarities, and Taoism and Zen Buddhism may have influenced each other, their philosophies are different. This will become obvious as we examine some basic Zen concepts in the next chapter. Meanwhile, notice the directness and simplicity of Hui Neng's language, as shown in the quotations from the *Platform Sutra*, which is so untypical of Taoist writing. In Taoist texts, the above information would be presented in a more arcane manner, such as: 'In our way of preparing the elixir of life, do not look at the mercury or add distilled water; nor do we advocate that there is no interaction of ingredients . . .'

The Patriarch continues to explain sitting meditation:

> Hence, in our teaching, what is meant by zuo-chan or sitting meditation? In our teaching, when there is no obstruction whatsoever – externally to all entities and space, internally no thoughts arise in the mind – that is *zuo* (sitting). Perceiving the original nature without any perturbation is chan (meditation). What is chan ding (dhyana-samadhi, or cosmic stillness)? Externally being free from all characteristics is chan (dhyana), and internally being unperturbed is ding (samadhi).

This important passage, which is very clear in the original Chinese version, can be easily misunderstood, especially if read from translation without adequate commentary. Some scholars mistakenly believe that by sitting meditation, Hui Neng meant free from interference from outside and calm inside, without having to be in any formal meditation posture. It should be noted that this passage, coming immediately after Hui Neng has explained what not to do during sitting meditation, is about what one should do during sitting meditation. The master teaches that when we sit, externally we should be free from the interference of myriad phenomena, and internally we should be free from thoughts. Only then, we have achieved the objective of zuo, or sitting.

When we meditate, we should perceive that our original nature is unperturbed, that cosmic reality is tranquil and undifferentiated. Only then have we achieved the objective of chan, or meditation. Having achieved the objective of sitting meditation, we arrive at the state of chan ding (cosmic stillness), which is the gateway to enlightenment. What is chan ding? Externally, to be free from the illusion of phenomena (although in the midst of phenomena) is chan, or attaining the cosmic mind. Internally, to be blissfully tranquil without thoughts arising is ding, or stillness.

Thus, meditation in Zen Buddhism as taught by Hui Neng is distinctively different from the kind of meditation traditionally taught in Indian Buddhism which aims to achieve a one-pointed mind. The way Zen Buddhists live and practise and their interpretation of certain Buddhist concepts are also quite different. In the next chapter we shall find out Hui Neng's teaching on these concepts.

10

FUNDAMENTAL CONCEPTS IN ZEN BUDDHISM

The Transformation of Indian Buddhism to Chinese Buddhism

*Some critics say that saving all humans on this
earth is daunting enough. How practical, they
ask, is the vow to save all sentient beings in all
universes? Hui Neng provides a profound
answer.*

UNDERSTANDING AND EXPERIENCE

Have you ever thought of yourself as the whole universe? Do
you believe that you can create your own heaven or hell? How
would you save others when you save yourself? These and
other Zen concepts taught by Hui Neng in the *Platform Sutra* are
what make Chinese Buddhism distinct from Indian Buddhism.

Although Zen practitioners have always focused on direct
experience rather than book learning, some concepts need to be
known in order to facilitate awakening. Zen Buddhism is not
against book learning – in fact there are probably more books
written on Zen than on any other single school of Buddhism –
but what it emphasizes is that we should not become so
immersed in book learning that we forget about direct experience, for spiritual fulfilment in any religion is basically an
experiential, not an intellectual, process.

A special and very important principle in Buddhism is that
a follower should base his religion on his personal understanding and experience, and not on faith or on the authority of
scriptures alone. Although a significant source of understanding

comes from book learning, the supreme attainment is not the mere understanding of what enlightenment is, but its direct experience. Understanding is necessary because it leads to experience; hence, if you wish to prepare yourself for the experience of sudden enlightenment that often occurs in Zen, you will find it helpful to understand the following concepts taught by Hui Neng:

1 The Three Bodies of the Buddha
2 The Four Great Vows
3 The Triple Gem
4 The Mahaprajna-paramita, or the perfection of higher wisdom to realize the Supreme Reality

Except for the Four Great Vows, these concepts are present in all schools of Buddhism, but Theravada Buddhism does not place as much emphasis on the vows of helping other sentient beings to attain enlightenment. Although their basic philosophy is the same, some schools may interpret some or all of these concepts differently. The Zen Buddhist interpretation is outlined below.

THE THREE BODIES OF THE BUDDHA

All Buddhist schools believe in the Three Bodies of the Buddha: the transformation body (*nirmanakaya*), the reward body (*sambhogakaya*) and the spiritual body (*dharmakaya*). The transformation body, sometimes referred to as the physical body (*rupakaya*), though there are fine differences, is the one that the Buddha employs to appear to us. The human form of Siddharta Gautama is the physical body of the Buddha. In Mahayana and Vajrayana Buddhism, the myriad phenomena that we see are regarded as the transformational bodies of the Buddha.

The reward body is normally not perceptible to ordinary people, only to awakened beings like Arahants, Bodhisattvas and Siddhas as a 'reward' for their spiritual development. These awakened beings are able to experience what some people may regard as fakery or hallucinations, what scientists may regard as shadow matter or anti-worlds, and what Buddhists regard as the reward bodies of the Buddha, such as heavenly scenes and celestial beings.

While the concepts of the transformation body and the reward body are generally similar among all Buddhist schools, the Theravada concept of the spiritual body is quite different from that of the Mahayana and Vajrayana schools. To Theravadins the spiritual body of the Buddha represents the summation of all the teachings, values, qualities and features of all Buddhas who have appeared and will appear. To Mahayanists and Vajrayanists the spiritual body is everything there is, not only in our universe but in all universes. The spiritual body of the Buddha is the Supreme Reality, the Ultimate Absolute, or what many people would refer to as the Almighty God.

As Zen Buddhism is a school of Mahayana Buddhism, its concept concerning the three bodies of the Buddha is naturally Mahayanist. Nevertheless, Hui Neng provides a profound interpretation that has greatly influenced Zen thought and practice. The Sixth Patriarch says:

> What is the pure, tranquil spiritual body of the Buddha? Learned audience, man's original nature is inherently pure. All dharmas are in self-nature . . .
>
> What are the thousands, millions, billions of transformation bodies of the Buddha? When there is no thought, self-nature is void and tranquil. Once there are thoughts, self-transformation operates. Evil thoughts transform a person into hells; good thoughts transform him into heavens. Malicious, wicked thoughts transform a being into a beast; kind, compassionate thoughts transform him into a Bodhisattva. Wisdom and merits transform a person into higher realms; ignorance and doubt transform him into lower planes. Self-nature can be transformed in countless ways; but deluded people are ignorant of their self-nature. Once we think of goodness, knowledge arises; this is called the transformation body of self-nature.
>
> What is the perfect reward body? A single light can eliminate the darkness of millennia; a single piece of wisdom can dispel the ignorance of a million years. Do not worry about your past, always think of your future, and for your future always think of good thoughts. This is the reward body . . .
>
> From the spiritual body, when thoughts arise, that is the transformation body. Always think of good thoughts, that is the reward body. If you are awakened yourselves, and cultivate yourselves, that is *guai-yi* (taking refuge). Our bones and flesh constitute our

physical bodies; they are only dwelling places, and cannot be spoken of as guai-yi (refuge). If you understand the three bodies, you comprehend my main idea.

Here the Sixth Patriarch exhorts people to think good and do good. However, his exhortation is not mere moralizing but the result of a cosmic truth. Our own self-nature is the cosmic reality, called the spiritual body of the Buddha, but due to our deluded thoughts we are ignorant of this cosmic fact and regard ourselves as confined to physical bodies. Deluded thoughts cause transformation of the spiritual body, in numerous stages, into myriad illusory phenomena, called transformation bodies. The kinds of phenomena that will be manifested depend on the kinds of thoughts. If a person harbours malicious, wicked thoughts, the phenomena manifested will be hellish; if he has good, compassionate thoughts, the phenomena manifested will be heavenly. These outcomes are not platitudes or trite axioms; they can be readily explained by the doctrine of dependent origination described in Chapter 5. What we experience is a creation of our mind, conditioned by our senses, and is called the reward body. As a rough analogy, in science reality can manifest as a particle or a wave, depending on the experimenter's intention and the instruments used to measure the manifestation.

The ultimate reality is called the spiritual body, which is infinite, eternal and undifferentiated. Thoughts transform the originally undifferentiated reality into differentiated phenomena, called the transformation body. Different thoughts will result in different manifestations, experienced by that person as the reward body.

Awakening to this fact, and thus cultivating for realization of the original transcendental reality, is called guai-yi, commonly translated as 'taking refuge', which may have a negative connotation of running away from responsibility. If anything, guai-yi calls for great responsibility and sacrifice; it means giving up everything for the sole and noble aim of spiritual realization. The Sixth Patriarch says that our physical body is only a temporary dwelling place and thus cannot be spoken of as a refuge. The proper place for guai-yi is the Three Bodies of the Buddha.

This philosophical interpretation of the Three Bodies of the Buddha and its relationship with doing good is a distinctive contribution of Hui Neng, and is different from the practice of moral purity as part of the Eightfold Path, or of the six paramitas traditionally taught in Indian Buddhism. Hui Neng's interpretation, however, does bear some semblance to, but is not the same as, that of Asvaghosha in his great work, *Awakening of Faith in Mahayana*, where he teaches that since the Supreme Reality is by nature morally pure, an aspirant has to be morally pure too; otherwise he would not be able to realize transcendental cosmic reality as he would be inconsistent with it.[1]

THE FOUR GREAT VOWS

Bodhisattvas, which Mahayanists strive to be before attaining Buddhahood, vow to save all sentient beings. Some critics say that saving all humans on this earth is daunting enough. How practical, they ask, is the vow to save all sentient beings in all universes? Hui Neng provides a profound answer. The master says:

> Now we have taken guai-yi (refuge) in the three bodies of the Buddha, let us make four great vows. Learned audience, please follow me and say together three times:
>
> > Infinite sentient beings I vow to save
> > Infinite defilements I vow to abolish
> > The infinite dharma I vow to practise
> > The supreme Buddhahood I vow to accomplish
>
> Learned audience, regarding the vow to save infinite sentient beings, it does not mean the accomplishment is by me. In our mind, every sentient being in his own body and nature saves himself. What is meant by saving himself through his own nature? In his physical body there are perverse views, defilements, doubts and delusion. Everybody has the nature of original enlightenment; use this right understanding for deliverance. Once a person is awakened to right understanding, and is awakened to higher wisdom, he can save himself from doubts and delusion. All sentient beings save themselves. When there are perverse views, save with right understanding; when there is delusion, save with awakening; when there is ignorance, save with knowledge; when there is wickedness, save with goodness; when there is defilement, save with enlightenment.

Deliverance in such a manner is genuine deliverance. Regarding the vow to eliminate infinite defilements, deliver illusion with your own mind. Regarding the vow to learn the infinite dharma, learn the supreme correct teaching. Regarding the vow to attain the supreme Buddhahood, always implement with the mind, respect everything, be free from delusion and attachment, generate wisdom, eliminate illusion, thus attain Buddhahood through self awakening, diligently implement the vow.

Thus, the Sixth Patriarch explains that since our mind when awakened is the undifferentiated cosmic reality which includes all sentient beings, we can save all of them by purifying our own mind. This is the Hua Yen doctrine of mutual interpenetration of simultaneously arising dharmas, where the whole universe can be contained in a mote of dust. This concept may seem outlandish, but modern physicists are even now seriously investigating it. The world renowned physicist David Bohm, for example, who proposes the explicate order where reality is separated as we normally experience it, and the implicate order where separateness vanishes and reality becomes an unbroken whole, says that 'everything interpenetrates everything'.[2]

THE TRIPLE GEM

In all schools of Buddhism, followers place their guai-yi at, or take guidance from, the Triple Gem. As mentioned earlier, although guai-yi (*namo* in Sanskrit) is often translated into English as 'take refuge in', it is a poor translation because it may imply that the 'refugee' is running away from responsibility or from society. Actually guai-yi means 'giving up everything for the sole and noble aim of spiritual development'. It takes great courage to make this important decision; a Chinese saying states that having the courage for guai-yi is something that even generals and prime ministers may not measure up to. Hence, for want of a better expression, I would use 'take guidance from' instead of 'take refuge in' for the term guai-yi.

The Triple Gem comprises the Buddha, the Dharma and the Sangha. The Buddha of our aeon is Gautama Buddha, the Dharma is the Buddhist teaching, and the Sangha is the monastic order. Notice that the word 'dharma' (*fa* in Chinese) has numerous meanings; it can mean both 'phenomena' and 'teaching'. Sometimes it can mean 'spiritual', as in dharmakaya (*fa shen*) which is 'spiritual body'. Because fa in Chinese in an ordinary context may also mean 'law', the 'spiritual body' of the Buddha is sometimes mistakenly translated as the 'law-body'.

While accepting this concept of the Triple Gem common to all Buddhist schools, Hui Neng gives a novel interpretation that was not found in Indian Buddhism. The Sixth Patriarch says:

> Learned audience, let us take guidance from the Triple Gem. The Buddha is enlightenment. The Dharma is the right teaching. The Sangha is purity.
>
> When our own mind takes guidance from enlightenment, deviation and delusion will not arise, craving diminishes and we become contented, free from greed and lust. This is called the most honoured of all who walk on two legs.
>
> When our own mind takes guidance from the right teaching, every thought will not be perverse, and there will be no desire. When there is no desire, it is called the most honoured without attachment.
>
> When our own mind takes guidance from purity, although all conditioned activities and deluded thoughts may be in self-nature [ie phenomenal aspect of cosmic reality, or the phenomenal world], self-nature is not polluted [ie we can experience the transcendental aspect of cosmic reality, or the ultimate reality]. This is called the most honoured among sentient beings.
>
> Ordinary people would not understand this. Day and night, they may say they take guidance from the Triple Gem. If they say they take guidance from the Buddha, where is the Buddha? If they cannot see the Buddha, then they have no guidance. If there is no Buddha from whom to take guidance to say taking guidance from him is a delusion.
>
> Learned audience, you yourselves must observe and examine; do not misunderstand the meaning. The scriptures say take guidance from the Buddha in yourselves, not take guidance from the Buddha outside. If you do not take guidance in your self-nature, there is nowhere to take guidance from.

The crucial difference between Indian Buddhism and Chinese Buddhism is that while Indians regard the Buddha, the Dharma and the Sangha literally, the Chinese regard them figuratively.

For example, regarding taking guidance from the Buddha, Buddhists of the Indian tradition refer to Gautama Buddha, whereas Buddhists of the Chinese tradition refer to the Supreme Reality which can be reached through one's mind. Referring to taking guidance from the Sangha, Indian Buddhists mean becoming monks or learning from monks, whereas Chinese Buddhists mean practising moral purity as symbolized by the monastic order. Theravadins, who claim to represent the original Buddhism as taught by Gautama Buddha, place great importance on monkhood; they believe that only by becoming a monk can one hope to attain Arahantship. Mahayanists believe that while becoming a monk is a great help, it is not an essential condition for attaining enlightenment. Hui Neng categorically says that a person practising at home has the same opportunity as one practising in a monastery to become a Buddha. To become a Buddha is to be enlightened, to become the cosmic reality!

GREAT WISDOM

To become the cosmic reality must appear outlandish or ridiculous to many people. How can we become the universe! This, in fact, is the aim of Buddhism; this is what is meant by becoming a Buddha. Mahayanists and Vajrayanists are very clear and definite on this point; Theravadins, as revealed in their statements on nirvana, seem to be uncertain. From the teachings of Theravada scriptures and masters, the conclusion one gets is that their understanding of nirvana or nibbana is the total extinction of lust, suffering and desire. Nirvana, to Mahayanists and Vajrayanists, is a direct experience of cosmic reality.

Buddhism teaches that the phenomenal world we see in our ordinary consciousness is an illusion and that reality at its ultimate is impartial and undifferentiated (not divided into parts or differentiated into separate entities). Why, then, do we see hills and streams, elephants and houses? This is because they are the creation of our mind!

It is indeed significant that confirmation of this ancient wisdom comes from modern-day science. Listen to what some of the world's famous scientists have to say:

The stuff of the world is mind stuff.

Sir Arthur Eddington[3]

We cannot put down a particle and say that it is such-and-such an entity. Instead we must regard every particle as somehow made up of every other particle in an endless Strange Loop.

Paul Davies[4]

For what quantum mechanics says is that nothing is real and we cannot say anything about what things are doing when we are not looking at them.

John Gribbin[5]

John Gribbin reminds us that 'quantum theory represents the greatest achievements of science', without which 'physicists would be unable to design working nuclear power stations (or bombs), build lasers, or explain how the sun stays hot. Without quantum mechanics, chemistry would still be in the Dark Ages, and there would be no science of molecular biology – no understanding of DNA, no genetic engineering – at all.'

Great wisdom, or *mahaprajna-paramita*, is needed to understand cosmic reality. The Sixth Patriarch explains:

Mahaprajna-paramita is a Sanskrit term. In Chinese it means 'great wisdom to reach the opposite shore'. This doctrine must be cultivated, not just recited by mouth. If it is not cultivated, it is like an illusion or phantom. If a person cultivates mahaprajna-paramita, his spiritual body becomes the same as the Buddha.

What is maha? Maha means 'great'. The mind is great, like the infinite void. If you sit in meditation in emptiness, you can attain the infinite void. The void can contain the sun, the moon and stars, the great earth, mountains and rivers, all trees and plants, wicked people and good people, wicked teaching and good teaching, heavens and hells, everything is contained in it. People's nature is also empty; it is also the same as the void . . .

What is prajna? Prajna is wisdom. At all times and in all places, let every thought be not foolish, always act wisely; this is the cultivation of prajna. One foolish thought, prajna will be cut out; one wise thought, prajna will be brought forth again . . .

What is paramita? This is in Sanskrit. In Chinese it is 'reach the opposite shore'. It means liberated from life and death. If you attach yourselves to any phenomenal spheres, the cycle of life and death arises. This is like waves in the water, and is called this shore. Once you are detached from phenomenal spheres, there is no life and death; it is like ever flowing water. Hence it is called the opposite shore, or paramita.

Learned audience. Hence, defilement is bodhi (enlightenment). Deluded thoughts make one an ordinary person; once enlightened he becomes a Buddha. Learned audience, mahaprajna-paramita is the most supreme, the highest and the foremost. It is non-abiding, non-going, and non-coming. All Buddhas of the past, present and future emerge from it. Apply this great wisdom to reach the other shore, to destroy the five skandhas (aggregates), defilement and delusion. The most supreme, the highest and the foremost! Let us praise this highest, supreme teaching. If you cultivate it you will definitely become a Buddha. Non-going, non-abiding, non-coming. It is the same as ding-hui (dhyana-prajna or meditation and wisdom), without attachment to any phenomena. All Buddhas of the past, present and future emerge from it, transforming the three 'poisons' (greed, hatred and delusion) into jie-ding-hui (sila, dhyana, prajna, or morality, meditation and wisdom).

The imagery of waves and water is often used in Buddhism to represent the arising of thoughts (waves) in transcendental reality (water), thus transforming reality which is ultimately undifferentiated into countless phenomena. This imagery can be traced to a very important incident long, long ago when a man and his mother were drowned while crossing a sea, despite his desperate attempt to save her. His dying thought was to save all other sentient beings crossing the sea of suffering. This noble thought became stronger and stronger with each of his reincarnations, until after cultivation for 500 lives he was eventually reborn Siddharta Gautama, the historical Buddha.

Prajna is not just ordinary knowledge; it is also not just being wise in everyday affairs. It particularly refers to the understanding that what ordinary people regard as 'external reality' is actually an illusion, and that cosmic reality is ultimately impartial and undifferentiated. The objective of Zen, or of any other schools of Buddhism, is to experience this transcendental reality directly.

What does Hui Neng mean when he says mahaprajna-paramita is non-abiding, non-going and non-coming? He means that when a person has cultivated this higher wisdom in order to arrive at the opposite shore of enlightenment, he will realize that cosmic reality is actually tranquil and undifferentiated, and that there are no phenomena because there are no thoughts abiding. 'Thus,' Hui Neng explains, 'self-nature is Zhen Ru (Tathagata, or the Supreme Reality).'

An enlightened person will realize that enlightenment does not entail going to another place called nirvana, that transform-ation from the phenomenal realm to transcendental reality is neither spatial nor temporal. What it actually involves is a change of spiritual perspective – like changing from seeing the world with your naked eyes where reality is manifested as countless objects and processes to seeing it through a cosmic microscope where reality is manifested as a unified spread of cosmic energy.

While the non-going doctrine explains why defilement is the same as purity and samsara the same as nirvana, the non-coming doctrine explains why an ordinary person is the same as a Buddha. When deluded, he is an ordinary person; when enlightened he becomes a Buddha. It does not mean that a new Buddha has come in to the world – he is the same person; the transformation is a change of spiritual perspective.

In Zen Buddhism this concept of becoming a Buddha instantly is distinctly different from the concept of the Buddha in Theravada Buddhism. Theravadins believe that there is only one Buddha in our aeon – Gautama Buddha. The highest a Theravadin can aspire to is an Arahant, the Worthy One, the Conqueror who has destroyed all lust, suffering and desires, and who, like the Buddha, attains nirvana.

In the next chapter, the Sixth Patriarch's teaching on sudden enlightenment will reveal how a Zen practitioner may become a Buddha in an instant, in contrast to gradual enlightenment which may take many years or lifetimes in other schools. He also gives his views on the teaching of the 'northern Zen school' of Shen Xiu, the four vehicles mentioned in the *Lotus Sutra*, and the recitation of Amitabha for rebirth in the Pure Land.

11

THE ZEN OF SUDDEN ENLIGHTENMENT

Seeing Your Original Face in an Instant

To be reborn in paradise is not the highest aim of
Buddhism, because the paradise, even though it
is a place of bliss, is still in the phenomenal realm.

THE PHILOSOPHY OF SUDDENT ENLIGHTENMENT

Zen Buddhism is known for sudden enlightenment, where the practitioner attains realization of cosmic reality in an instant. Hui Neng is famous for saying that: 'When unenlightened, Buddhas are sentient beings. When enlightened, in an instant sentient beings are Buddhas.'

Sudden enlightenment is another important feature that differentiates Chinese Buddhism from traditional Indian Buddhism. In the Indian tradition, a Theravadin has to cultivate for many reincarnations before he can be reborn as a monk to dedicate his life to achieving nirvana. In other schools of Mahayana Buddhism an aspirant spends many lifetimes as a Bodhisattva before attaining enlightenment. Zen Buddhists, on the other hand, aspire to attain enlightenment in their own lifetime.

However, sudden enlightenment is not necessarily easier, or even quicker, than gradual enlightenment for some people. Those who have 'poor roots' (who are not spiritually ready) may never attain sudden enlightenment even if they cultivate for many lifetimes. For them gradual enlightenment would be more appropriate. This would involve practising good precepts like charity and kindness, reciting scriptures, and praying to

Bodhisattvas or Buddhas so that they could be reborn at higher spiritual levels in future to cultivate for enlightenment. In this way enlightenment is gradual, and takes numerous, sometimes countless, reincarnations.

In a way, Zen Buddhism is a reaction against this slow process. Zen Buddhists believe that enlightenment can be achieved in this very life. But what should a Zen student do if he has poor roots to start with? Improve his spiritual roots in this very life! First, we must know the difference between having good roots and having poor roots. The Sixth Patriarch says:

> Prajna (or higher wisdom) does not vary among sentient beings. It is because their minds are deluded that they seek Buddhahood by external cultivation. They do not realize their own nature; hence they are regarded as having poor spiritual roots.
>
> Those who know the doctrine of sudden enlightenment do not depend on external cultivation, but train their own mind so that their own nature perceives the right view concerning defilement, delusion and sentient beings, resulting in instant enlightenment.

Therefore, the crucial different between those with good roots and those with poor roots is that the former possess prajna and cultivate internally, whereas the latter do not possess prajna and cultivate externally. Prajna is the higher wisdom to realize that the one and only cosmic reality can be manifested in its absolute, transcendental dimension or in its relative, phenomenal dimension.

In the absolute, cosmic reality is impartial and undifferentiated, and its experience is nirvana. It is absolute because it is unconditioned; there is nothing beyond it, and all enlightened beings, irrespective of whether they are humans or gods, ultimately experience the same reality.

But in its relative aspect, cosmic reality is manifested as countless entities and processes, and its experience is samsara. It is relative because its manifestation is conditioned by numerous factors, and different beings experience its manifestation differently. The same reality, for example, will appear different to humans and to gods.

Because ordinary people, with their deluded minds, do not understand this great cosmic truth, they practise external cultivation like observing rituals, praying to gods and seeking help from priests. They do not realize that their own nature, perceived in the transcendental dimension, is actually cosmic reality.

Those who realize this great truth do not depend on external cultivation, because whatever attainment is made in this way does not enable them to go beyond the phenomenal to the transcendental. For example, gods may answer their prayers, priests may guide them to a better life in heaven, but all these are still in the phenomenal dimension.

Those who have higher wisdom realize that samsara is the same as nirvana – they are the same cosmic reality – but the former is perceived phenomenally and the latter transcendentally. Hence, the transformation lies in internal cultivation (cultivating the mind) and not in external practices. When the mind is trained to have the right perception concerning defilement, delusion, and the illusory confinement of universal consciousness into different individuals, enlightenment is attained instantly. Understanding this higher wisdom, therefore, enables a person to change his roots from poor to good.

THE WAY TO SUDDEN ENLIGHTENMENT

Hui Neng does not merely talk about sudden enlightenment but provides a method which aspirants can practise to achieve it. The master teaches:

> Learned audience, once you are awakened, you realize Buddhahood. In your own nature and mind, use prajna to introspect and reflect. You will be illuminated inside and outside, and you will know your original mind. Once you have known your original mind, you are liberated. Liberation means to attain samadhi of prajna. To realize the samadhi of prajna is non-thought.

It is easy for those not familiar with Zen cultivation to miss the crucial point that in the above passage Hui Neng is explaining meditation. Although the word 'meditation' is not mentioned, it is what this passage is about, for the following reasons. Firstly, it follows closely the passage quoted earlier about prajna and internal cultivation. These two passages are on the same topic; the earlier passage explains the philosophy, the latter passage describes the method. Internal cultivation is meditation.

Secondly, because Hui Neng was speaking to an informed audience who knew about meditation and that it is the way of Zen cultivation, he did not need to start by saying something like 'when you are in sitting meditation . . .' because the audience already understood that – just as when a modern coach lectures to his trainees on football or swimming, he does not have to preface his instructions with 'when you are on the field' or 'when you are in the pool'.

The third reason is that key words like 'introspect', 'reflect', 'illuminated inside and outside' and 'samadhi' clearly indicate that the passage is about the meditation process. Indeed, the passage does not make much sense if read in any other context.

The master explains that when sitting in meditation, you should let the mind introspect and reflect upon the higher wisdom that cosmic reality is tranquil and undifferentiated. When you have successfully done this, you will feel that you do not have a physical body, that what you previously thought was your body is now illuminating light, radiating continuously to what you previously thought were your external surroundings, although now there is no boundary. In this way you will know your original mind, which is the same as cosmic reality. You are now liberated, no longer confined by your physical body. This is samadhi of prajna (stillness of higher wisdom), which is non-thought. The master continues:

> What is non-thought? Non-thought of phenomena means to see all phenomena but not be attached to any phenomena; to be everywhere but not be attached anywhere. Our self-nature is always void; let the six kinds of consciousness emerge from the six gates, but they are neither separated from nor attached to the six forms of defilement. Let the coming and going be free. This is the samadhi of prajna. It is spontaneity; it is liberation. It is called the cultivation of non-thought. If you suppress thinking so as to stop thought, that is bondage of phenomena, and it is a perverse view. Those who realize the method of non-thought can understand all phenomena. Those who realize the method of non-thought can see the realms of all Buddhas. Those who understand the method of sudden enlightenment through non-thought will attain Buddhahood.

It is necessary to understand this concept of non-thought. Non-thought is neither thought nor no-thought. Thus, non-thought transcends dualistic thinking. Let us say you think of a lotus – this is having the thought of a lotus. Now you suppress this thought of the lotus, ie the thought of the lotus is no longer in your mind – this is no-thought. Neither of these two processes – having thought or not having thought – is non-thought. In a way, non-thought is before thought and no-thought arise. Yet, from another perspective, non-thought can be both thought and no-thought! Thus, non-thought can also occur after thought and no-thought arise. Incidentally, concepts in quantum physics – like the case of Schrodinger's cat which is either dead or alive, or neither dead nor alive – resemble this kind of Buddhist philosophy.

When we are in the state of non-thought in our enlightenment, we can perceive all phenomena, yet at the same time we are aware that all these phenomena mutually interpenetrate into an organic whole. We can be everywhere, yet at the same time we are not at any particular place. This is because we are actually the void.

In this meditative state, we let our six kinds of consciousness (of sight, sound, taste, smell, touch and thought) emerge from our six sense organs (eyes, ears, tongue, nose, body, mind), but the consciousness is not contaminated by the distortion of reality caused by our six senses. When the flow of consciousness coming from our perception or going out from our sense organs is free from delusion, we have attained the samadhi of prajna, the meditative state of enlightenment derived from the application of higher wisdom. In other words, when other people look at an enlightened person sitting in meditation, they see him and the physical objects around him in the usual way, but the enlightened person experiences himself and the surrounding objects as pure consciousness, without any differentiation.

This is spontaneity – cosmic reality in its unconditioned state, or detachment from phenomena. This is liberation – consciousness not limited to a physical body, or detachment from self. This meditation is called the cultivation of non-thought, and an aspirant who practises this method will attain sudden enlightenment and achieve Buddhahood.

Meditation through the cultivation of non-thought is different from meditation through the suppression of thinking to stop thought. Many people may be mistaken that they are the same because superficially they appear similar. The suppression of thought in meditation is a perverse method, because it involves thought and no-thought, which are different from non-thought. Thought and no-thought are dualistic and therefore fall in the realm of phenomena. Thus a person who uses this dualistic method is in the bondage of the phenomenal realm, unable to break through to the transcendental dimension.

Although Hui Neng articulated some very profound concepts and made meditation techniques clear and simple for us to understand, some readers may still find them difficult. This teaching, as mentioned earlier, was preached to inform an audience with some knowledge of Zen philosophy and some practice of Zen meditation. Less experienced people may not be able to practise the advanced meditation described above, even if they have understood it intellectually. For them more suitable preliminary exercises are explained in later chapters of this book.

BODHIDHARMA AND AMITABHA

It is significant to note that without a single exception all important scriptures and all great Zen masters, including Hui Neng himself, refer to Bodhidharma as the First Patriarch, and Hui Neng as the Sixth. It is mainly scholars who suggest that it was Hui Neng rather than Bodhidharma who founded Zen Buddhism.

Although Hui Neng is famous for teaching sudden enlightenment, this teaching was not his invention. Since Gautama Buddha first transmitted Zen to Mahakasyapa, sudden enlightenment was transmitted from patriarch to patriarch. The Sixth Patriarch Hui Neng emphasized that his teaching had been transmitted in China by Bodhidharma, the First Patriarch. One day the magistrate asked Hui Neng why Bodhidharma had said that Emperor Liang had accumulated no merit despite building monasteries, translating sutras and ordaining monks. The Sixth Patriarch's answer provides a very important explanation:

> Building monasteries, doing charity and honouring monks are only cultivation of blessings. We must not mistake blessings for merit. Merit is in the spiritual body, not in the field of blessings.

The master explains that blessings and merit are different.

Blessings generate karma to enable a person to be reborn at a higher station in future lives in this world or in some heavenly existence. These rewards are still in the phenomenal realm. Merit enables a person to 'jump' beyond the phenomenal realm to transcendental cosmic reality – to Buddhahood. Merit is not cultivated in the 'field of blessings', a term referring to performing good deeds and generating good karma in the phenomenal world. Merit is cultivated through prajna and dhyana (wisdom and meditation).

Another practice that some people mistakenly think may have merit for enlightenment is reciting the name of Amitabha Buddha so as to be reborn in Western Paradise. The Sixth Patriarch explains:

> There are two classes of people, but the teaching is the same – the deluded and the awakened; hence, attaining enlightenment can be slow or fast. Deluded people recite the name of Amitabha Buddha to be reborn there [in the Western Paradise]; the awakened purify their own minds. Therefore, the Buddha says, 'as his mind is purified, he attains the Buddha's Pure Land'.

Because deluded people do not understand prajna, internal cultivation that purifies their minds is not suitable for them. Hence they recite the name of Amitabha Buddha so as to be reborn in the Western Paradise. Yet, to be reborn in paradise is not the highest aim of Buddhism, because the paradise, even though it is a place of bliss, is still in the phenomenal realm. In the Western Paradise, these blissful souls continue to cultivate under the guidance of Amitabha so that eventually they will attain Buddhahood by actualizing transcendental cosmic reality.

This is not to say that reciting the name of Amitabha Buddha is an inferior method of spiritual cultivation. Indeed, for many people who may not have attained the intellectual or spiritual level for sudden enlightenment, this may be the best method.[1] In Buddhism, reciting the name of Amitabha, Zen and other cultivation methods are expedient means to help people of different abilities and needs in their spiritual development.

Those who are awakened naturally attain enlightenment faster. In Zen they can achieve enlightenment in this very life, without having first to go to a paradise. Because they understand that the apparent difference between the phenomenal realm and transcendental reality lies in whether their minds are defiled or pure, they seek enlightenment directly by purifying their minds. Once their minds are purified, they attain the Pure Land or Buddhahood instantly.

SUDDEN AND GRADUAL ENLIGHTENMENT

Sudden enlightenment is a convenient term for the attainment of enlightenment instantly or quickly, as compared to gradual enlightenment which takes a much longer time, sometimes extending over aeons. Some Zen masters say that enlightenment cannot be attained in parts; it must be total, in the sense that one is either enlightened or unenlightened, never partially enlightened, because ultimate reality is impartial and undifferentiated. In this interpretation, therefore, enlightenment cannot be gradual.

Nevertheless, when comparisons are made between sudden and gradual enlightenment, what is usually being compared is not the instant of enlightenment but the training that brings about this enlightenment. Even Zen masters need time for their training, possibly many years in a Zen monastery, but when compared to an ignorant being's countless lifetimes spent reincarnating in the endless cycle of the six planes of existence (hell's denizens, hungry ghosts, titans, animals, humans, heavenly beings), the master's training time is 'sudden'.

Moreover, the enlightenment itself can be regarded as sudden or gradual. Notwithstanding what has been said about total enlightenment earlier, enlightenment can occur at different levels. As detailed in Chapter 4, Asvaghosha classifies four levels: initiated, resemblance, convergence and perfect. In this interpretation, sudden enlightenment would refer to an experience of convergence enlightenment or perfect enlightenment directly; glimpses of initiated and resemblance enlightenment would be instances of satori. Gradual enlightenment, on the other hand, would refer to experiencing these various levels of enlightenment progressively, with different levels spaced out in between, usually between lifetimes.

Do these two different interpretations – one saying that enlightenment must be total, the other that it comes in stages – imply any contradiction? No. The difference is another example of the limitations of language. When the masters say that enlightenment must be total, they refer to perfect enlightenment. On the other hand, when we say that enlightenment in Zen is sudden, we relate this to the present life of the Zen practitioner. But if we take into consideration all his previous reincarnations, his attainment of enlightenment is gradual; he has prepared himself in countless past lives to be born in his present life to practise Zen. Similarly, a deluded person now practising external cultivation will, in a future life when he is ready, attain enlightenment in an instant.

THE DIFFERENCE BETWEEN HUI NENG'S AND SHEN XIU'S TEACHING

While attaining enlightenment in Zen is considered sudden, when the northern Zen school of Shen Xiu is compared with the southern Zen school of Hui Neng, the former is regarded as gradual, the latter as instantaneous. Yet this comparison is relative and arbitrary. Referring to the northern and southern schools, the *Platform Sutra* says:

> There is only one teaching, although people may be differentiated as southerners and northerners. For this reason there is the southern school and the northern school. Why then is there gradual enlightenment and sudden enlightenment? The teaching is the same, but its understanding may be slow or fast. Those who understand slowly will be enlightened gradually, those who understand fast will be enlightened suddenly. The teaching itself is neither gradual or sudden. Because people's intelligence can be sharp or dull, enlightenment can be gradual or sudden.

When Hui Neng discovered that Zhi Cheng had been sent by his teacher Shen Xiu, the patriarch of the northern Zen school, to learn from him, he said, 'I heard that in his transmission your teacher taught only the disciplines of morality, meditation and wisdom. Can you tell me about his teaching?' Zhi Cheng responded:

> According to the Venerable Shen Xiu, abstinence from doing all evils is morality; performing all good deeds is wisdom; purifying the mind is meditation. These disciplines are called *jie-ding-hui* (morality, meditation and wisdom). This is what he says. I wonder what are your views, Your Venerable?

Hui Neng replied, 'His teaching is wonderful, but my views are different. How are they different? Understanding can be slow or fast.' The master continued:

> When the mind has no evil, that is morality of self-nature. When the mind has no disturbance, that is meditation of self-nature. When the mind has no delusion, that is wisdom of self-nature. The disciplines of morality, meditation and wisdom taught by your teacher are meant for people of low intelligence. My disciplines of morality, meditation and wisdom are meant for people of high intelligence. But for those who realize their self-nature, it is not necessary to set up the doctrines of morality, meditation and wisdom.

Zhi Cheng requested the master to elaborate. Hui Neng explained:

> When self-nature has no evil, no disturbance, no delusion, prajna illuminates every thought, and he is constantly free from the characteristics of the phenomenal world. What is there, that can be set up. Cultivating self-nature is sudden, whereas setting up doctrines is gradual. Thus, it is not necessary to set them up.

THE *LOTUS SUTRA* TEACHING

The *Lotus Sutra* (*Saddharma-Pundarida Sutra* in Sanskrit, *Miao Fa Lian Hua Jing* in Chinese, meaning 'Scripture of the Lotus of the Wonderful Teaching') is one of the most important scriptures in Mahayana Buddhism. A monk, Fa Da, sought Hui Neng's explanation on the *Lotus Sutra*. As Hui Neng was illiterate, he asked Fa Da to read the sutra to him. After hearing it only once, the master understood. He told Fa Da that there is only one teaching, but the Buddha used three vehicles to convey his teaching because people's intelligence varied.

The three vehicles are the vehicle of Sravadas, for those who attain enlightenment on hearing or reading the Buddha's teaching; the vehicle of Pratyakabuddhas, for those who attain enlightenment by their own effort; and the vehicle of Bodhisattvas, for those who seek enlightenment for all sentient beings. Hui Neng says all the Buddhas appeared in the world for one great cause – world salvation. Hence, the three vehicles are expressions of just one vehicle, the Buddha vehicle. The master explains the one vehicle, which is the essence of the sutra:

When the human mind is free from thought, it is originally void and tranquil, and is free from all perverse views. This is the same as the effect of the one great cause. When a person is free from delusion internally and externally, he is free from two extremes. Externally, people are deluded about the characteristics of phenomena. Internally, people are deluded about the emptiness of self. When a person is free from the attachment to phenomena while in the phenomenal realm, and free from the attachment to the emptiness of self while existing in emptiness, he is not deluded internally and externally. Awakening to this teaching, the mind is instantly open, and this attainment occurs in this very world. What is the mind open to? Open to Buddha-knowledge. Buddha means enlightenment, and is classified into four gates, namely to open us to enlightenment-knowledge, to show us enlightenment-knowledge, to awaken us to enlightenment-knowledge, and to enter us into the way of enlightenment-knowledge. We can go through any of these gates – open, show, awaken, enter – to enlightenment, to see our own original nature, to go beyond the phenomenal realm.

The phenomenal world is the result of thought. Therefore, when the mind is free from thought, it returns to its original nature, which is the ultimate reality. This is the same as the effect of the great cause for which all Buddhas appear in the world. Buddhas appear to help people attain enlightenment, which in Zen terms is to see their original face. Ordinary people cannot see their original face because of two extremes: they are attached to phenomena, and they are attached to self, both of which they mistakenly think of as real. If they are awakened to the cosmic truth that both phenomena and self are illusory, they will realize prajna, the Buddha-knowledge that will lead them to enlightenment. They will be able to go beyond the phenomenal realm to arrive at ultimate reality.

REALIZING THE BUDDHA OF SELF-NATURE

In the *Platform Sutra* the Sixth Patriarch provides a few verses to help us attain enlightenment, or see our original face. It is fitting to conclude these three chapters on the *Platform Sutra* with the final verse of this great Zen teacher before he entered parinirvana. Its concepts and expressions may appear exotic to some readers, but if they have understood Hui Neng's teaching as explained in this and the previous two chapters, they should find the verse comprehensible.

The great significance of this verse is best illustrated by the master's own comment on it. He says, 'I leave behind a verse called "Liberation Through the Buddha of Self-Nature". If deluded people of future generations understand the meaning of this verse, they will realize the real Buddha of self-nature in their own mind. I will leave you this verse and depart.'

> The pure nature of Supreme Reality is the real Buddha,
> Perverse views and the three poisons of greed, hatred
>   and delusion are the real evil.
> Evil resides in people with perverse views,
> The Buddha will meet those with right views.
> When perverse views and the three poisons are found in our
>   nature,
> This means the Devil has come to stay.
> When right view eliminates the three poisons from the mind,
> The Devil will be transformed into the real Buddha.
> Transformation body, reward body and spiritual body,
> The three bodies are originally one body.
> If in our body we seek our own realization,
> This is the cause of wisdom for attaining Buddhahood.
> From the transformation body pure nature is born,
> Pure nature is constantly in the transformation body.
> Our nature enables the transformation body to seek the right
>   way,
> It will achieve perfection, real and boundless.
> The nature of lust is originally form purity,
> Eliminate lust then the body of pure nature reveals.
> If our nature is free from the five sensual desires,
> In that instant we see our ultimate reality.
> If in this life we are awakened in the doctrine of sudden
>   enlightenment,
> In our enlightenment we will see the World-Honoured One
>   in front of our eyes.
> If we wish to cultivate to seek the Buddha,
> And do not know where to seek the real,

If we can perceive reality in our mind,
Perceiving reality is the cause of Buddhahood.
If we do not seek reality but seek the Buddha outside,
Seeking thus is certainly a deluded person.
The doctrine of sudden enlightenment I bequeath,
For salvation everyone himself must cultivate.
Now I tell the world's seekers of the Way,
Do not waste your time by not cultivating this teaching.

12

THE FLOWERING OF ZEN IN CHINA

Ingenious Ways to Help Disciples Attain Awakening

Zen masters after Hui Neng used fantastic means to help their students attain awakening – means that are not found in any other Buddhist schools, or any other spiritual cultivation. To the uninitiated, these methods are simply illogical, if not crazy.

ZEN FLOWER OF FIVE PETALS

Buddhism reached its golden age in China during the Tang (618–906) and Song (960–1279) dynasties. During the Yuan dynasty (1260–1368), Zen Buddhism and Vajrayana Buddhism were the two prominent religious practices in the Mongol Empire. The founder of the succeeding Ming dynasty, Zhu Yuan Zhang, was previously a Zen monk, hence Zen Buddhism was the chief religion during this time. However, in the following Jing dynasty (1644–1911), the Manchus, like the Mongols earlier, were Vajrayanist Buddhists, drawing their spiritual inspiration mainly from Tibet. During this time the gradual evolution of various Chinese Buddhist schools into a synthesized Mahayana form – a process which had began in the Song dynasty – became more definite as sectarian characteristics were discarded. From that time right up to the present day, the two most influential features in Chinese Buddhism have remained Zen and reciting Amitabha.

Although Hui Neng was the Sixth, and not the First, Patriarch of Zen Buddhism, the flowering of Zen was mainly due to him. When the First Patriarch, Bodhidharma, brought Zen Buddhism from India to China, the patriarchate was transmitted from one master to his successor, with the cotton kasaya (monk's ceremonial robe) as the insignia. When the kasaya reached Hui Neng, it was taken away from him by Empress Wu, who recognized his senior classmate, Shen Xiu, as the Sixth Patriarch. When Hui Neng's most senior disciple, Fa Hai, asked the master who his successor would be, Hui Neng said he would not limit the successorship to one person but would asked his various disciples to spread the Zen teaching.

Earlier, Bodhidharma predicted that the flower of Zen would blossom into five petals. True enough, about 250 years after Hui Neng, Zen Buddhism developed into five sects, all of which stemmed from Hui Neng's southern school. Although initially Shen Xiu had had a large following, his northern school faded away about 100 years later.

Hui Neng had thousands of students, 47 of whom were masters themselves. The two outstanding ones whose genealogies led to the five Zen schools were Nan Yue Huai Rang (Nangaku Ejo in Japanese, 677–744) and Qing Yuan Xing Si (Seigen Gyoshi, died 740). After Hui Neng's time, it was

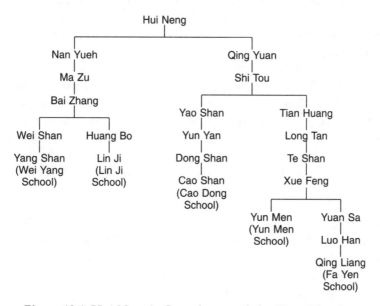

Figure 12.1 Hui Neng's Genealogy and the Five Schools

customary to prefix the name of the place where a Zen master taught to the master's own name. Thus, in the first name above, 'Nan Yue' was the place and 'Huai Rang' his name. An interesting convention arose in that a master was often better known by his place than his own name!

Nan Yue transmitted Zen to Ma Zu Dao Yi (Baso Doichi, 709–88), who in turn transmitted to Bai Zhang Huai Hai (Hyakujo Ekai, 720–814). Two outstanding disciples of Bai Zhang (or Po Chang) were Wei Shan Ling You (Yisan) and Huang Bo Xi Yun (Obaku, died 850). Wei Shan transmitted Zen to Yang Shan Hui Ji (Kyozan), and the school that derived from this time was called the Wei Yang School. Huang Bo's disciple, Lin Ji Yi Xuan (Rinzai, died 867), founded the Lin Ji School, or Rinzai sect in Japanese, which is well known for its extraordinary manner of awakening enlightenment.

Hui Neng's other disciple, Qing Yuan Xing Si, transmitted Zen to Shi Tou Xi Qian (Sekito Kisen, 700–90). Shi Tou means 'stone head', but this master's mind was exceptionally brilliant, and the other three Zen schools were derived from his genealogical line. One of his disciples was Yao Shan Wei Yan (Yakusan, 751–834), who transmitted Zen to Yun Yan Tan Sheng, who in turn transmitted to Dong Shan Liang Jie (Tozan), and then to Cao Shan Ben Ji. Dong Shan and his disciple Cao Shan founded the Cao Dong School, which spread to Japan as Soto Zen, which is now one of the two most popular styles of Zen in the world.

Another outstanding disciple of Stone Head was Tian Huang Dao Wu, which literally means 'Heavenly Emperor Awakening to the Way'. These names, incidently, serve as a reminder that in Zen we must always be humble in our search for cosmic reality, for even a 'Stone Head' can bring out a 'Heavenly Emperor'. Moreover, as we shall see presently, all the masters succeeding to Stone Head's genealogical line had very poetic names.

Tian Huang transmitted to Long Tan Chong Xin. Long Tan, meaning 'Dragon's Pool', transmitted to Te Shan Yi Jian (Tokusan, 780–865). Te Shan, meaning 'Virtuous Mountain', transmitted to 'Retaining Righteousness at Snow Summit' or, in Chinese, Xue Feng Yi Cun (Seppo Gizon, 822–908). One of Xue Feng's disciples, Yun Men Wen Yan (Ummon, died 966), founded the Yun Men school. In Chinese, Yun Men means 'The

Gate of the Clouds'. Another disciple of Snow Summit, Xuan Sa Shi Bei, transmitted Zen to Luo Han Gui Chen, whose disciple, Qing Liang Wen Yi, founded the Fa Yen school. Xuan Sa means 'Mystical Sand', Luo Han is an Arahant; Qing Liang means 'Pure and Cool', and Fa Yen is 'Spiritual Eye'. With such poetic names, it was no wonder that Zen had a great influence over the Confucian literati of the Song dynasty. The following lines from the great Song poet Lu You, for example, are indicative of Zen thought and experience:

> The mind is like the water of a pool,
>   tranquil without wind;
> Sitting silently for thousands of breaths;
> Midnight, but don't be surprised to see
>   whales making hugh waves
>   to welcome the sun at dawn.

If you can appreciate the above poem, you have acquired some basic understanding of Zen philosophy. The first line reminds us of what Hui Neng taught about the doctrine of non-thought in Zen meditation. Wind in Buddhist literature often represents the arising of thoughts. In his meditation, Lu You did not aim for a one-pointed mind, nor did he employ visualization; he attained a state of non-thought, and was subconsciously aware of his breathing – thousands of breaths – indicating that he had been meditating for some time and had attained a deep level of consciousness. But why did he see whales making huge waves in a tranquil pool, or the sun at dawn while it was still midnight? Realizing these lines may lead you to a Zen awakening.

VERBAL AND NON-VERBAL METHODS OF AWAKENING

Zen masters after Hui Neng used fantastic means to help their students attain awakening – means not found in any other Buddhist schools or any other spiritual cultivation. To the uninitiated, these methods are simply illogical, if not crazy. Hui Neng, for example, struck Shen Hui three times with a staff, and Ma Zu shouted at Bai Zhang until he was deaf for three days. Were the disciples offended? Not at all; they prostrated themselves to thank their teachers in all seriousness and sincerity for the compassion they had shown!

For convenience we may divide these fantastic means into the verbal and non-verbal. The following classification, as well as the four examples below, is culled from Cai Rong Ting's excellent analysis of the methods used by Zen masters to help their students experience awakening.[1] Her analysis is based on the 1,701 Zen stories describing enlightenment experiences found in *Transmission of the Lamp* (*Chuan Deng Lu*). Written by the Zen master Dao Yuan in about 1004 for the Song emperor, *Transmission of the Lamp* has become an evergreen classic of Chinese Buddhist literature. Two other classics describing stories of enlightenment are *Blue Cliff Record* (*Bi Yen Lu*) composed in 1125, and *Gateless Gate* (*Wu Men Guan*) composed a century later.

Verbal techniques may be classified into the following groups:

1 Quoting from the sutras
2 Direct reply based on
   a) daily activities
   b) student's weakness
   c) forceful affirmation
   d) examples
   e) paradoxes
3 Questions
4 Reversed conclusions
5 Impossible conditions
6 Interruptions
7 Irrelevant answers using
   a) hidden meaning
   b) denials
   c) questions
   d) orders
   e) quotations
   f) appellations

Non-verbal methods may be classified as follows:

1 Circles
   a) by themselves
   b) in combination with language

2 Sounds
   a) shouts
   b) nasal grunts
   c) anger
   d) breathing
3 Actions
   a) in combination with language
   b) in combination with objects
   c) in combination with students
   d) various combinations
   e) bodily movements
4 Silence
   a) for a long time
   b) for a short time

POINTING DIRECTLY AT THE MIND

The great poet of the Tang Dynasty, Bai Ju Yi (Po Chu I), asked the Zen master Niao Ke Dao Lin, 'What is the overall meaning of Buddhism?' Niao Ke ('Bird's Nest') quoted from the *Ekottaragama Sutra* to reply, 'Avoid all evils; do all good.' Surprised at the simple answer, Bai Ju Yi commented, 'Even a three-year-old child can understand this teaching,' implying there was not much depth to it. The Zen master replied, 'A three-year-old child may understand the teaching, but an 80-year-old person may not practise it.'

The significant aspect of Niao Ke's answer is the realization, from higher wisdom, that the goal in Buddhism is not the mere understanding of a teaching but the direct experience derived from putting it into practice.

An often quoted example of direct reply based on daily activities is provided by Tian Huang and his disciple Long Tan.

The student told the master, 'Sir, I have been here for a long time, but I have not received any teaching from you.' Tian Huang replied, 'I have been teaching you ever since you came here.' 'What kind of teaching?' the surprised Long Tan asked. 'Whenever you served me tea, I took it;

whenever you brought me food, I received it; whenever you greeted me, I responded. Where haven't I taught you?' Long Tan dropped his head to think. The master said, 'If you see it, you see it directly. If you think, you are mistaken.'

Thereupon, Long Tan attained his awakening.

What did Tian Huang teach? How did Long Tan achieve his awakening? The central point about Zen is direct experience. Instead of philosophizing on this central point, Tian Huang demonstrated it to his student directly in their daily living – when tea is served, drink it; when food is served, eat it – without fuss and without thinking. But direct experience of what? Is it merely the direct experience of drinking tea and eating food? Drinks and food are phenomena caused and conditioned by thoughts; when thoughts do not arise, these illusory phenomena disappear and we come face to face with ultimate reality. If you see cosmic reality, you see it directly. If you think about it, thoughts arise and you see only delusion. Long Tan grasped this point, and attained awakening.

The following gong-an between Zhao Zhou and his master Ma Zu illustrates the use of direct answers to point out the student's weakness as well as to affirm forcefully.

On arrival at Ma Zu's monastery, Zhao Zhou paid his respects to the master. Ma Zu asked, 'Where do you come from?'

'From the Great Cloud Monastery at Zhao Zhou.'

'Why do you come here?'

'To seek the Buddha's way.'

Ma Zu said, 'You didn't look after your own treasure but left your monastery to come here, for what? Here, I have not a single object; what Buddha's way do you seek?'

Zhao Zhou prostrated himself before the master and asked, 'Where is my treasure? I could not find it.'

'Now that which is asking me is your own treasure. It has everything it needs; it lacks nothing; its use is spontaneous,' the master affirmed forcefully. 'What for do you seek outside?'

Instantly, Zhao Zhou realized his own nature. He prostrated himself again to thank the master.

Ma Zu transmitted a cosmic truth directly to Zhao Zhou by means of forceful affirmation. Because Zhao Zhou had his own treasure, Ma Zu questioned why he had come to him, who had nothing. (Ma Zu had 'nothing' because, as an enlightened master, he perceived reality as undifferentiated.) Zhao Zhou's weakness was not knowing that he himself was the treasure; he himself was the Buddha's nature that he had been seeking. Ma Zu pointed this out to him directly, telling him to seek inside. This enabled Zhao Zhou to be awakened to the fact that he himself was an organic, integral part of cosmic reality.

Asking the student a question in return was a frequent technique used by the masters. The following gong-an concerns the very first teaching of the Sixth Patriarch after his enlightenment.

When Hui Neng left his teacher after being declared the next patriarch and receiving the cotton kasaya, he was pursued by a general. The Sixth Patriarch placed the kasaya on a boulder and sat on it. He told the general he could take the kasaya if he could move him from his seat. But the general, Dao Ming, prostrated himself before the master and said, 'I am here to seek the dharma, not the kasaya. Pray enlighten me.' The Sixth Patriarch said, 'Don't think of goodness; don't think of evil; at this instant, what is your original face?'

At this instant, the general attained his awakening.

How does Hui Neng's question help Dao Ming to attain awakening? Asking students what their original face looked like was a technique frequently used by the Sixth Patriarch, and asking them to think neither of goodness nor evil was a crucial approach of his meditation. At this instant of non-thought, cosmic reality reveals itself as being undifferentiated and tranquil, enabling the aspirant to realize his original face, which is the Buddha nature.

The above four gong-ans illustrate the use of language to help aspirants to attain enlightenment. It is worth noting here that language is not used to explain or describe, or to arouse an intellectual response in the seekers, but is used intuitively, to point directly at the mind. For the uninitiated, such use of language appears illogical because the stories are unintelligible.

SHOUTING TO AWAKEN ENLIGHTENMENT

Pointing directly at the mind is even more drastic when masters discard language in favour of non-verbal techniques, as illustrated by the following examples.

One of the most outstanding masters who used non-verbal methods with great originality and effectiveness was Ma Zu Dao Yi, meaning literally (and for fun) 'the one way of enlightenment of horses' ancestors'. Aspirants who attained enlightenment under his guidance and later became masters themselves numbered more than a hundred! Ma Zu had a wide range of techniques which he expertly employed to suit the aspirant's nature and ability, as well as the situation at that moment. He expounded that there is no Buddha beyond mind, and there is no mind beyond Buddha. (For those who may have missed this earlier in the book, 'Buddha' here does not refer to Siddhartha Gautama, the historical Buddha, but to the Eternal Buddha or the Supreme Reality.) Ma Zu stressed that the way to enlightenment is through the ordinary mind. In other words, Zen is found in every instance of our daily living; when we are enlightened, every moment that we regard as prosaic and dull in our deluded condition, is actually wonderful and divine.

Let us study one of Ma Zu's many gong-ans. It concerns his disciple, Bai Zhang, another great Zen master who later established the institution of Zen monasteries which were quite different from the other Buddhist monasteries of the vinaya tradition. He also established the tenet that 'a day without working is a day without eating'.

> Bai Zhang went to consult Ma Zu on his Zen development. In the interview, Ma Zu said nothing but stared at a feather duster hanging at a corner of his bed. Bai Zhang then commented, 'If we want to use it, we have to take it from its place.' The master retorted, 'If we take your skin from its place, what would become of you?' Apparently ignoring the master's retort, Bai Zhang went to the corner and held up the feather duster.
>
> Ma Zu then said, repeating Bai Zhang's words, 'If we want to use it, we have to take it from its place.' Notwithstanding this, Bai Zhang returned the feather duster to its original place. At this instant, Ma Zu gave a shout so loud

that Bai Zhang was deaf for three days. Later, when classmates asked him about his temporary deafness, he said,
'What deafness? After awakening, I just took a rest.'

Viewed from the level of ordinary knowledge, this gong-an may
suggest that Bai Zhang acted against the wish of his teacher,
who in retaliation shouted so loudly that the disciple became
deaf. Then, in quiet defiance, he said that his withdrawal from
his classmates for three days was not because of his temporary
deafness due to his teacher's punishment, but because he chose
to have a rest.

This, of course, is far from the truth when seen from the level
of higher wisdom. When Ma Zu gazed at the feather duster,
Bai Zhang knew that his teacher was testing his understanding
of Zen. So he said, 'If we want to use it, we have to take it from
its place', indicating the application and form aspects of cosmic
reality. In other words, cosmic reality is undifferentiated in form,
but manifested as countless phenomena in its application.

Ma Zu's question, 'If we take your skin from its place, what
would become of you?', was a further test of Bai Zhang's com-
prehension of cosmic reality, and was asking esoterically what
would happen if we separate application (phenomenal world)
from form (transcendental reality). To show that he had understood the unity of form and application, Bai Zhang held up the
feather duster as if he were about to use it.

The master's repetition of Bai Zhang's words, 'If we want to
use it, we have to take it from its place', was another test to see
if Bai Zhang realized that there is no difference between transcendental reality and the phenomenal world; their apparent
difference is not absolute but due to our deluded mind.

Bai Zhang understood, so he returned the feather duster to
its original place without using it. But his understanding was
not complete, so Ma Zu shouted to deafen him and this enabled
Bai Zhang to be enlightened![2] But why was Bai Zhang's understanding not complete? How did the deafening shout enlighten
him? If you wish to find your own answers, skip the next three
paragraphs and meditate on these two questions, or *huatou*. But
if you wish to satisfy your curiosity now, read on.

There were two areas where Bai Zhang's understanding was
not complete. Firstly, his understanding was intellectual, mainly
due to his attachment to Ma Zu's verbalized comment about

using the feather duster and taking it from its place. So he returned the duster to its place. Had his understanding been intuitive, he would have continued to use the duster. Since form and application are but two aspects of the same reality, using the duster (application) or returning it to its place (form) does not ultimately make any difference.

Secondly, using the feather duster would have been preferable to returning it to its original place, as this is consistent with Ma Zu's doctrine of attaining enlightenment through the ordinary mind. In other words, as the phenomenal world is not ultimately different from transcendental reality, and as we still exist in the phenomenal world, we can attain enlightenment here and now (symbolized by using the duster) rather than having to withdraw to a secluded place close to nature (symbolized by returning the duster to its hanging position). Moreover, the duster is meant to remove dust, which in Buddhist terminology means helping other beings to attain purity. This is in line with the Mahayanist spirit of Zen; withdrawing from society for self-cultivation is more akin to Hinayanist practice.

In Bai Zhang time, listening to a master's teaching and to the recitation of sutras, rather than reading books, was the main mode of receiving instruction. To be deaf was tantamount to being cut off from outside influence. Ma Zu's shout therefore effectively eliminated Bai Zhang's intellectual reasoning, which was activated by external stimuli. Once these were eliminated, there was no thought arising. This enabled Bai Zhang to look directly into his own mind and find his own Buddha nature. Later commentators described Ma Zu's shout as the Sword of Manjusri, used by a Bodhisattva to cut off defilement.

Throughout Zen history, the master most famous for his use of shouts was Lin Ji (Rinzai). The master himself said:

> Sometimes my shout is like the precious Sword of Manjusri, sometimes like a crouching lion, sometimes like a fisherman's testing pole; sometimes it is not used as a shout.[3]

In simple language, this means that Lin Ji applied his shout for any of the following uses: to cut off all intellectual and emotional explanation, to prevent any intellectual or emotional explanation arising, to test the student's development, to achieve other purposes. His use of shouting to awaken awareness was so successful that many of his students, as well as other people, imitated him. To prevent the misuse of this technique, Lin Ji once said:

> You all like to imitate my shouting. Now I ask you, if a person comes out from the eastern hall and another comes out from the western hall and they both shout together, can you tell the difference between the host and the guest, and how do you differentiate? If you cannot differentiate, then do not imitate my shout.[4]

'Host' and 'guest' are symbolic terms referring to two complementary aspects, like master and student, questioning and answering, initiating and responding, mind and awareness.

STRIKING TO AWAKEN ENLIGHTENMENT

While Lin Ji is noted for his shout, Te Shan (Tokusan) – who shared equal ranking with Lin Ji in Hui Neng's genealogy as both were 11th generation successors of Bodhidharma – is noted for striking his pupils with his staff. Hence, the Zen saying 'Lin Ji's shout; Te Shan's staff.'

> Once Te Shan told his disciples, 'Tonight I'm not answering any questions. Anyone who asks will receive 30 strokes of my staff.'
>
> A monk came forward to pay his respects to the master. Before he could say anything, Te Shan hit him with a staff. The monk said, 'I have not asked any questions; why do you hit me?'
>
> Te Shan asked, 'Where did you come from?'
>
> 'From Xin Luo.'
>
> Whereupon, Te Shan again hit him with his staff, explaining, 'Before you board a boat, you have to receive 30 strokes!'
>
> On another occasion, Xue Feng, who was later to become a famous Zen master, asked his teacher, 'From the supreme teaching, are students differentiated?'
>
> Te Shan struck him with his staff and asked, 'What did you say?'
>
> 'I don't know,' Xue Feng replied.
>
> 'There is no verbalization in our teaching,' Te Shan said, 'hence, there is not a single method to teach people.'

Hearing this, Xue Feng attained his awakening.

At the outset, we must realize that Te Shan's striking was not meant to hurt or punish; it was his special means to help students attain awakening. How? His advice to Xue Feng that 'there is no verbalization in our teaching' provides the best clue. Although he himself did not explain his use of striking, we can conclude that, like Lin Ji's shout, Te Shan's striking was used to eliminate existing thoughts, to prevent thought arising, to test students' development, and to achieve other relevant purposes. Therefore, before the monk opened his mouth to speak, which would necessitate thoughts, Te Shan struck him. When he answered the master's question, which also needed intellectual activity, Te Shan hit him again. What, then, should the monk do? He should give a non-verbal answer, such as breaking the staff or striking the master, as some awakened Zen students did and won the master's approval!

Western readers who are used to the supremacy of the intellect may find this Zen principle of non-thought baffling. It must be noted that Zen is not against the intellect per se: much of Zen philosophy is profound and involves deep thinking. The significant point is that if we want to attain Zen, to experience cosmic reality transcendentally, we must go beyond thought, beyond the intellect, because as soon as thought arises, the mind becomes defiled and we perceive illusion instead of ultimate reality. How does thought defile the mind? Through a number of transformational processes, explained by such doctrines as the Doctrine of Dependent Origination (see Chapter 5), thought transforms undifferentiated ultimate reality into the illusory phenomenal world.

A simple, prosaic example may be helpful. Suppose we have never eaten a mango, but would like to know what it tastes like. Obviously, no matter how much and deeply we think about a mango, read a description of it, or involve ourselves in any intellectual activity or verbalization concerning the mango, we cannot know its taste unless we eat it. In such a case, your teacher would ask you to eat the mango, not intellectualize or verbalize it. This, of course, does not mean that your teacher is against thinking or verbalization.

In the above story, Xue Feng's question about supreme teaching and student differentiation involves deep thinking.

If the purpose of Te Shan's teaching had been philosophical investigation into what constituted supreme teaching or why students should be differentiated, Te Shan would have expounded an elaborate discourse, perhaps quoting extensively from the sutras. But his purpose was not philosophy but spiritual realization, a direct experience of transcendental reality. So Te Shan hit Xue Feng in order to eliminate his thought process, and then asked him what he had said, to test his understanding.

Xue Feng realized the master's intention, and thus answered that he did not know, suggesting that he had eliminated the thought process. Yet his understanding was still not perfect, because by answering in words he was verbalizing. As was so characteristic of great Zen masters, Te Shan grasped this opportunity and directly pointed to his pupil's mind by telling him that in their teaching there is no verbalization, not a single verbal lesson to be given. So Xue Feng had to look into his own mind to find enlightenment, which he did.

13

ZEN GOES EAST TO JAPAN

Spiritual Cultivation Through Koans and Zazen

It is only a deluded mind that limits itself to a bodily prison. The aim of Buddhism is to liberate the mind from this self-imposed prison which is the result of ignorance.

EARLY INFLUENCE FROM CHINA

If you think that Zen masters are eccentric personalities who know nothing other than meditation and illogical answers to nonsensical questions, you will be in for a big surprise. In Japan, for example, Zen masters were frequently appointed as imperial advisers and heads of important departments of the Japanese civil service, especially in trade and foreign affairs. Zen touches every aspect of Japanese culture, including martial arts, poetry, painting, architecture, Noh drama, flower arranging and the tea ceremony.

Japan has contributed tremendously to the world's understanding of Zen, especially in the West – in fact so much so that some people think Zen is a Japanese product. Even the names of great Chinese Zen masters like Hui Neng, Ma Zu, Bai Zhang, Zhao Zhou, Lin Ji and Dong Shan are better known to Westerners in their Japanese transliterations: Yeno, Baso, Hyakujo, Joshu, Rinzai and Tozan. But although the word 'Zen' is Japanese, it is derived from the Chinese 'Chan'.

Zen was transmitted from China to Japan several times, both as a meditation practice of various Buddhist schools and as Zen Buddhism itself. The Japanese monk Dosho went to China in 654 to study under the great Chinese master, pilgrim and translator, Xuan Zang (Hsuan Tsang), and returned home to teach

Zen in Gangoji Monastery at Nara. Dao Xuan (Dosen in Japanese), a vinaya master who had practised Zen from Pu Ji, arrived at Nara in Japan to teach the northern school of Zen Buddhism in 710. Dao Xuan transmitted Zen to Gyohyo, who in turn taught Saicho, also known as Dengyo Daishi, the founder of the Japanese Tendai School. Zen of the southern school was propagated by the Chinese master Yi Kong (Giku) in Danrinji Monastery at Kyoto from 851 to 858. All these teachers enjoyed Japanese imperial support.[1] But Zen only really took root in Japan after its teachings were spread by the two native Japanese masters, Eisai and Dogen.

RINZAI ZEN

Eisai Nyoan (Ming An Rong Xi in Chinese, 1141–1215) first practised other forms of Buddhism on Mount Hiei. He was determined to visit China to further his Buddhist studies. After studying with Xu An Huai Min of the Chinese Lin Ji School, Eisai returned to Japan in 1191 as an enlightened Zen master, and founded the Japanese Rinzai Zen. He first taught Zen at Kamakura, where he was supported by the ruling Shoguns, and where Zen became popular among the samurais. Later he also taught Zen at Kyoto, where he built the Kenninji Monastery.

An influential treatise written by Eisai which had far-reaching effect was *Propagation of Zen for the Protection of the Country* (*Kozen Gokoku Ron*), in which he argued that Zen was beneficial for the welfare of the people and the security of the nation. In the preface to this treatise he said:

> Great is Mind. Heaven's height is immeasurable, but Mind goes beyond heaven; the earth's depth is also unfathomable, but Mind reaches below the earth ... Studying it [Zen], one discovers the key to all forms of Buddhism; practicing it, one's life is brought to fulfillment in the attainment of enlightenment. Outwardly it favors discipline over doctrine; inwardly it brings the Highest Inner Wisdom. This is what the Zen sect stands for.[2]

Besides introducing Zen to Japan, Eisai also introduced tea drinking, an aspect of Chinese culture that has become an essential feature of Japanese life. Eisai expounded that drinking tea not only refreshes the mind, but also promotes longevity. Tea drinking became a common practice among Zen practitioners, and the Japanese tea ceremony developed into an art form strongly influenced by Zen.

Two other great Rinzai masters were Takuan and Hakuin. Takuan (1573–1645) stressed that samsara is the same as nirvana, defilement the same as purity, and delusion the same as enlightenment. Their apparent difference is due to man's ignorance in mistaking phenomena for ultimate reality. His student, Yagyu Tajima no Kami, one of the greatest swordsmen Japan has produced, announced that the secret of his skill was his Zen training under Takuan. What has Zen to do with swordsmanship? Takuan gave this advice on the subject to his student:

> Where should your mind be kept? If your mind is not fixed anywhere, it will pervade throughout the body; then should the hands be in action, they will function to their fullest capacities. If your mind is fixed on a certain spot, it will be seized by that spot, and no activities can be performed efficiently ... In short, not to fix your mind anywhere is essential. Not fixed anywhere, the mind is everywhere. If the mind is fixed at any particular external point, the other points are left unguarded. When the mind is made so that it is not fixed at any point, it is able to pervade throughout the whole.[3]

Hakuin (1686–1769) is sometimes called the father of modern Rinzai Zen, because most Rinzai masters today trace their genealogical line back to him. He rejected formalistic and intellectual Zen, and advised practitioners not to discriminate between active and quiescent Zen practice. Active practice refers to the spirit of Zen in the arts and daily living, and in the solving of koans; quiescent practice is sitting meditation. Hakuin was not in favour of any syncretism between Zen and the practice of Amitabha-recitation (Nembutsu) of the Pure Land sect, although this was encouraged by many Lin Ji masters in China at this time.

In his autobiographical writings Hakuin cites numerous cases when he thought he was enlightened, only to be shown otherwise by his teacher Shoju Etan (1642–1721). On one occasion he presented a verse to his teacher to show the insight he thought he had gained from his enlightenment. Holding the verse in his left hand and extending the right hand to Hakuin, the teacher said, 'This is your intellectual insight; show me your intuitive insight!'

Hakuin's favourite technique was meditating on Zhao Zhou's Mu. Zhao Zhou (Joshu in Japanese) was asked whether a dog had Buddha nature. 'Wu,' the Chinese master replied. 'Wu' (meaning 'no') is 'mu' in Japanese. The problem was that in Zen philosophy, every being, including a dog, has Buddha nature. Why, then, did the master answer 'no'? This became a popular koan in Rinzai Zen.

Hakuin's way to solve the problem of Zhao Zhou's Mu did not involve thinking about the koan in order to find a logical or illogical answer. His method was to enter into sitting meditation and visualize that from his abdomen down to his soles he was Zhao Zhou's Mu. In time his whole body was nothing but Mu. Then, in a flash of illumination, even Mu disappeared, and he experienced the cosmic void. Hakuin's method of Zen cultivation through zazen, or sitting meditation, on Zhao Zhou's Mu may come as a surprise to those readers who thought that Rinzai Zen since Hakuin was devoted entirely to the study of koans.

SOTO ZEN

The other famous Japanese school is Soto Zen, founded by the Japanese pioneering master Dogen Eihei (Rong Ping Dao Yuan in Chinese, 1200–53). In many ways Dogen was a complete contrast to Eisai, the founder of Rinzai Zen. Born to a noble family with an emperor as an ancestor on his father's side and a prime minister on his mother's, Dogen was highly educated with a deep knowledge of Chinese studies. He declined the chance to be groomed for high office and instead devoted himself to a life of spiritual development.

In 1223 he went to China in search of Zen masters, but was deeply disappointed not to find any. In 1225, just before he was thinking of returning home, he met the great master Ru Jing of the Cao Dong (Tsao Tsung) School. During a meditation session, a classmate meditating beside Dogen dozed off. Their teacher Ru Jing reproached the dozing monk, exclaiming 'In Zen, body and mind are one. Why do you fall asleep?' Hearing this, Dogen suddenly attained awakening. Later on his enlightenment was confirmed by his teacher.

Dogen returned to Japan to establish the Japanese Soto Zen, which was later organized and popularized by Keizan Jokin (1268–1325). Unlike Eisai earlier on who had been ready to adapt his teaching to suit the demands of other Buddhist sects in Kyoto, Dogen refused to teach anything other than Zen. When under pressure from the Kyoto authority to change his ways, he chose to retire to the remote province of Echizen where he built the Eiheiji Monastery. According to legend, Dogen went to Kamakura to persuade the ruling regent Tokiyori to restore power to the emperor at Kyoto, but when the regent refused, instead of serving as an adviser to the illegitimate ruler, Dogen left Kamakura. This greatly impressed Tokiyori, who sent one of Dogen's students after the master with a generous offer of land. Dogen was so enraged that he not only drove the monk away at once, but also ordered the chair on which the monk had sat to be destroyed and the ground under the chair to be dug to a depth of 3 feet and the earth discarded!

The most significant difference between Dogen's and Eisai's teaching of Zen is in their approach to enlightenment. The latter's teaching, characteristic of Rinzai Zen, emphasized the use of koans while Dogen's teaching, characteristic of Soto Zen, paid great importance to zazen or sitting meditation.

These two approaches are the principal ways of spiritual cultivation in Zen, and are known respectively in Chinese as gong-an-chan, or 'public-case-Zen', and mo-zhao-chan, or 'silent-illuminating-Zen'. An example of each is given in this chapter and the details of how you can practise gong-an-chan and mo-zhao-chan will be described in later chapters.

Dogen's greatest work is the *Shobogenzo* (Treasury of the Correct Dharma-Eye), the first comprehensive Buddhist philosophical work written in Japanese. The following quotation from the *Shobogenzo* illustrates not only Dogen's compassion, but also a profound cosmic truth – and one which modern science is now beginning to accept.

> The truth is that the benefits of one's own sustained exertion are shared by all beings in the ten quarters of the world. Others may not be aware of this, and we may not realize it, but it is so. It is through the sustained exertions of the Buddhas and Patriarchs that

our own exertions are made possible, that we are able to reach the high road of Truth. In exactly the same way it is through our own exertions that the exertions of the Buddhas are made possible, that the Buddhas attain the high road of Truth. Thus it is through our exertions that these benefits circulate in circles to others, and it is due only to this that the Buddhas and Patriarchs come and go, affirming Buddhas and negating Buddhas, attaining the Buddha-mind and achieving Buddhahood, ceaselessly and without end. This exertion too sustains the sun, the moon, and the stars; it sustains the earth and sky, body and mind, object and subject, the four elements, and five compounds.[4]

INTELLECT AND EXPERIENCE

Despite its simple and clear language, some people may find the above quotation difficult to comprehend, because the concepts are profound. This passage again demonstrates that although intellectualization is generally discouraged in Zen cultivation, Zen thought can be very deep. How did Zen masters obtain such wisdom if they explicitly did not think? If you wish to explore the answer, and if you happen to believe in the supremacy of the intellect (a common belief in the West), you need first of all to be aware that this belief is only one of many possible beliefs, and it may or may not be the best belief. In Buddhist tradition, intellect (which by itself is highly valued by Buddhists) is generally regarded as inferior to direct experience. Interestingly, this is also the attitude implicitly accepted by modern scientists. All advances in science are accepted only after they have been confirmed by experiments, even though theoretical thinking may have initiated their investigation. Although the approach and emphasis are different, science and Buddhism both address the same question: what is reality? Unique among all religions, Buddhism has as its ultimate aim a direct experience of cosmic reality, not the assurance of a blissful afterlife. Perhaps for this reason more than any other, even kings and princes have been inspired to give up their luxurious lives to pursue Buddhism.

Buddhist masters obtained this wisdom or prajna not through intellectual speculation but through meditation. In the above quotation, for example, Dogen had access to cosmic wisdom not because he had thought about the topic deeply, but because he perceived it directly in his enlightened mind, which is eternal and infinite and not limited to his head, heart or any other part of his physical body. It is only a deluded mind that limits itself to a bodily prison. The aim of Buddhism is to liberate the mind from this self-imposed prison which is the result of ignorance. The principal aim of this book is to provide guidance in this noble endeavour through Zen: the first part of the book provides a basic understanding of Zen, the later part provides methods which you can practise to attain its direct experience.

KOANS – ILLOGICAL OR ILLUMINATING?

The koan, or gong-an in Chinese, is a Zen story esoterically illuminating a cosmic truth, usually recording the enlightenment of a master, and always incorporating a seemingly illogical situation. The three koans in the first chapter of this book are typical examples. In later chapters of the transmission of Zen from the First to the Sixth Patriarch, the koans that illustrated their enlightenment are described.

The koan is the principal technique used in Rinzai Zen to attain satori, or awakening. This is what the modern Rinzai master Daisetz Teitaro Suzuki says about satori:

> Samadhi alone is not enough. You must come out of that state, be awakened from it, and that awakening is Prajna. That moment of coming out of Samadhi, and seeing it for what it is, that is satori.[5]

The fact that many books written in English mention only the illogical situations which trigger satori, without explaining the necessary preparation in meditation training and their deeper meaning, gives rise to two common misconceptions: firstly, that the koan is the all-important and sole means of training for, as well as testing, satori – at least in Rinzai Zen if not in all other schools of Zen; and secondly, that awakening is a form of intellectual gymnastics for solving the koan riddle according to some esoteric paradigm.

Regarding the first misconception, Suzuki himself, who placed great value on the koan, says:

> This is where lurks the danger of the koan system. One is apt to

consider it as everything in the study of Zen, forgetting the true object of Zen, which is the unfolding of a man's inner life.[6]

The key to the unfolding of a man's inner life is meditation – in all schools of Buddhism, and particularly in Zen Buddhism, including Rinzai Zen. Zen Buddhism is so called not without reason – 'Zen' means 'meditation'. In every Zen monastery, meditation practice takes up several hours every day, as many as 18 on special days!

Traditionally, after a few years of daily meditation, a Zen student consulted his master concerning his development. The master would use incredibly ingenious methods to test or help the student (*see* Chapter 12), like shouting at him or hitting him. When the student attained an awakening, this encounter was recorded as a koan. Thus, a koan came at the end of a student's formal training. However, especially in Rinzai Zen since Hakuin, the koan was often used as a technique at the beginning, and sometimes in the middle, of Zen cultivation. But even when the koan was thus employed, it was never meant to be the sole or even the most important technique. We shall read more about this koan technique presently.

Regarding the second misconception, Alan Watts provides an illustrative example when he reports:

> One can perhaps understand why a man who had practised *za-zen* for eight years told R H Blyth that 'Zen is just a trick of words,' for on the principle of extracting a thorn with a thorn Zen is extricating people from the tangle in which they find themselves, from confusing words and ideas with reality.[7]

Zen is definitely not a trick of words. When a master used extraordinary methods, as described in koans, he used his words clearly and honestly; there was never an attempt to trick the student. For example, when Ma Zu repeated Bai Zhang's words 'If we want to use it, we have to take it from its place', or when Zhao Zhou told his student 'Go and wash your bowl', the masters were seriously and sincerely using words to help their students. If readers find these phrases puzzling, it is because they have not understood their deeper meaning.

Although words in a koan are often used to help students free themselves from confusing words and ideas with reality, especially when the koan is employed at the beginning of Zen training, this is not necessarily always so. For example, when Niao Ke told Bai Ju Yi that the overall meaning of Buddhism is avoiding evil and doing good, the Zen master was using words literally. When he further told the poet that the significance of the teaching is not mere understanding but actual practice, he was using language to express a great truth clearly and directly. Similarly, when Ma Zu forcefully affirmed for Zhao Zhou that 'Now that which is asking me is your own treasure. It has everything it needs; it lacks nothing; its use is spontaneous. What for do you seek outside?', the master was not using words to free Zhao Zhou from any confusion but was using words literally to point directly at Zhao Zhou's mind.

Moreover, a Zen master might use a non-verbal technique. Besides shouting and hitting, he might wave objects about, draw a circle in the air, or crawl on all fours growling like an animal!

ATTAINING SATORI THROUGH THE KOAN

Using koans to demonstrate the futility of intellectual thinking as a means to attain satori was typical of Rinzai Zen, and was established by Hakuin. This koan cultivation system was first developed by the Chinese Lin Ji master Da Hui Zong Guo (1089–1163). Hakuin organized the wide range of koans into six categories for systematic instruction to eliminate students' intellectualization so as to attain a direct experience of satori.

Hakuin's favourite koan to set students thinking was to ask them what the sound of clapping with one hand was. They were not allowed to discuss the problem with other people, nor try to find an answer from books; they had to find out themselves, on their own. What happened if some dishonest students cheated? They might know the answer intellectually, but they simply would not attain any satori – this is how the method works; just as if your art teacher teaches you an excellent method of painting but you ask a friend to reproduce a beautiful picture for you, you may become a good copy-cat but never a good artist.

So the students meditated on this koan during meditation day and night, as well as thinking widely and deeply about it at all other times. The koan became an integral part of them.

But eventually – after months or even years – the students would discover that no matter how much they intellectualized the problem they could not find a satisfactory answer, because there was no logical answer. They were at their wits' end and very frustrated. Then, in a flash of intuitive insight, sometimes when they least expected it, the 'logical' answer would shine in their mind. Different students might have different answers, but each one, if he was awakened, would intuitively know without any doubt that his answer was right. The Zen students would then, individually, consult their master in a personal interview known in Japanese as *sanzen* and present their answers, whereupon the master would confirm their satori.

A few better-informed students would try not to think about the koan problem, because they knew thinking would not produce the answer. Instead they would go into meditation and, when they reached a deep level of consciousness, or samadhi, throw their koan problem into the 'empty screen' of their mind, which had by then merged with the universal mind. At first nothing would happen, but gradually responses might appear. Usually students knew intuitively when these were not the right answer; they would realize, if they were well trained in their meditation, that these mental images were only manifestations of their thoughts. If they were not sure and presented these answers to their teacher, he would tell them so. But the time would come when they knew without a doubt that they had the right answer, for it would shine forth in celestial light.

Imagine that you are a Zen student working on Hakuin's koan of clapping with one hand. You may think about it or, if you are well versed in meditation, throw the problem into your subconscious mind. After much time and effort, you find an answer. You consult your Zen teacher and, after paying him due respect and other preliminaries, tell him that the sound of clapping with one hand is like a spring breeze wafting through fragrant roses. If he is gentle, as many modern masters are, he will smile and ask you to try again. If he resembles the masters of old, he will throw you out of the door, if not a window.

After more time and effort, you see your master again to present your answer. 'Clapping with one hand,' you say with confidence, 'is the sound of waves breaking on barriers.' Again, he smiles at you or throws you out of a window.

You work harder and longer on your koan. You are determined to have your satori; nothing else seems important to you. You see the master again. After the preliminaries, you say, 'You old fool, you can't even clap with two hands and yet you ask me to clap with one!' The master brims with joy and laughs heartily. He confirms your satori. If you are true to Zen tradition, you will prostrate yourself before him and thank him sincerely for his kindness in helping you to attain the highest goal humanity can ever aspire to.

But why can't the master, or anyone, clap with two hands? When you experience satori, you perceive reality as it ultimately is – undifferentiated and tranquil. In transcendental reality, there are no hands nor any sound of clapping.

ACHIEVING KENSHO THROUGH ZAZEN

While Rinzai Zen emphasizes the koan, Soto Zen emphasizes zazen. It must be remembered that this does not mean that zazen, or sitting meditation, is not important in Rinzai Zen, or that the koan is not used in Soto Zen. Because of the tremendous amount of material written in English on koans in Rinzai literature, albeit often without much explanation of their deeper meaning, it is easy for the uninitiated to believe that zazen is insignificant in Rinzai Zen.

To illustrate that this is not the case, I would point out that an applicant to a Rinzai Zen monastery customarily performs zazen outside the monastery gate while waiting to be called in, and has to do zazen for a few days in a waiting room before he is formally accepted into the monastery. During his stay there, irrespective of whether he is a novice or a master, zazen will constitute an essential part of his daily life.[8]

The modern Rinzai master Suzuki, whose writings are resplendent with descriptions of koans but contain few of zazen, says: 'As the most practical method of attaining spiritual enlightenment the followers of Zen propose the practice of Dhyana, known as *zazen* in Japanese.'[9]

On the other hand, concerning koans in Soto Zen, Katsuki Sekida, a modern Soto master, says:

Such a state of looking simultaneously both into one's own nature and into universal nature can be attained only when consciousness is deprived of its habitual way of thinking. Working on a koan is one way of doing this.[10]

This awakened state of looking simultaneously at oneself and the universe in the context of pure existence is known in Soto Zen as kensho, which is the same as satori in Rinzai Zen. According to the tradition of Soto Zen, although working on a koan is one way of attaining kensho, the best way is zazen. Indeed, Dogen, the founder of Soto Zen, expounded that zazen itself is enlightenment, and as long as the adept maintains a pure state of non-thinking in zazen, he is a Buddha.[11]

Katsuki Sekida advocates working on Zhao Zhou's Mu to attain kensho.[12] It is significant that this zazen method, greatly valued in Soto Zen, is similar to that of the Rinzai master Hakuin, suggesting that although Rinzai Zen and Soto Zen may superficially appear different in their approach to enlightenment, fundamentally they are similar. The methodology of both may be expressed as 'diligently working on zazen' – directly to attain awakening in Soto Zen, or supplemented with koans to trigger off awakening in Rinzai Zen.

There are three major stages in this working on the Mu in zazen, and they are all performed sitting in the lotus position. Throughout all stages the mind is kept free of thoughts.

Stage 1

Sit upright and fully relaxed in the lotus position, then close the eyes gently and be comfortably still. Breathe in deeply into the abdomen. (Abdominal breathing may be difficult at first; more detail on how this can be achieved is given in a later chapter.) Then breathe out deeply from the bottom of the abdomen, making the sound mu ... mu ... as you do so. The sound may be made softly or silently in the mind.

You must be able to perform Stage 1 well, and continue to practise it for some time, before proceeding to the next stage. 'Some time' may be a few months or a few years, depending on your ability, progress, needs, purpose, expectation, and time set aside for spiritual cultivation.

Stage 2

The posture in this stage is the same, but the breathing method is different. Exhale in a few short breaths instead of one continuous breath. But keep the breathing gentle and unforced. This is what Katsuki Sekida calls 'bamboo shoot breathing' – like a Japanese artist painting a bamboo shoot, with pauses at the joints in the stem. After a few of these short out-breaths, let the breath flow in naturally.

As you continue to practise Stage 2, you may unconsciously proceed to the next.

Stage 3

At this stage the periods when breathing almost stops become longer and longer, and your breathing becomes softer and gentler. Samadhi, or joyous tranquillity, has now begun. In this third stage, do only one thing – look into the *tanden*, or abdomen, with your mind with undivided attention. Eventually you will experience pure existence. When kensho occurs, you will find a radiant light illuminating your whole body, which by now has no boundary, and extends over the whole universe!

14

THE QUIET GRANDEUR OF VIETNAMESE ZEN

Where Kings Abdicated to Practise Buddhism

King Tran-Thai-Ton's preface contains golden advice for all of us – unfortunately, appreciated by many only when it is too late.

A GENTLE AND PEACE-LOVING PEOPLE

Numerous kings and princes have abandoned their thrones in their pursuit of spiritual development. The best example is our historical Buddha, Prince Siddharta Gautama. And Bodhidharma (who brought Zen Buddhism to China), Mahindra (who brought Theravada Buddhism to Sri Lanka) and Padmasambhava (who brought Vajrayana Buddhism to Tibet) were all princes who renounced their luxurious lives for Buddhism.

Vietnamese Buddhism provides many inspiring cases of royal renunciation for spiritual development. Numerous Vietnamese kings, for instance, abdicated in order to practise Zen full time. A religion with such a glorious history certainly deserves our close study.

The history of Vietnamese Buddhism reveals an aspect of the Vietnamese people of which many of us may not be aware. Because for much of the 20th century Vietnam has been a country ravaged by war, some of us may unfairly regard the Vietnamese as bellicose and aggressive, but a study of their involvement in Buddhism will reveal a gentle and peace-loving people. For further information about the history of Vietnamese Buddhism read *Buddhism and Zen in Vietnam*[1] by the Venerable Thich Thien-An, a former professor at the University of Saigon and the Director of the International Buddhist Meditation Center in Los Angeles.

The spread of Zen from China to Vietnam, where it is known as 'Thien', was even more significant than its spread to Japan, though this may not be so widely known. Jerrold Schecter reported that 'of Vietnam's population of 16 million, an estimated 12 million are Buddhist'.[2] While other Buddhist schools besides Zen are also eminent in Japan, 'the history of Vietnamese Buddhism is primarily an account of the development of various Zen sects in Vietnam.'[3] Zen Buddhism, naturally, has become ingrained in Vietnamese life.

As in China, there were five Zen sects in Vietnam: Ty-Ni-Da-Luu-Chi School, Vo-Hgon-Thong School, Thao-Duong School, Truc-Lam School, and Lieu-Quan School. These five Vietnamese sects are not the same as the five traditional Chinese sects, although four of them were directly derived from the Chinese.

ZEN OF EARLY PATRIARCHAL TRADITION

The first transmission of Zen from China to Vietnam was very early, about a century before Hui Neng taught Zen in China and six centuries before Eisai introduced Rinzai Zen to Japan. In AD 580 Vinitaruci, an Indian disciple of the Chinese Third Patriarch Seng Can, founded the first Vietnamese Zen school, which is named after him – Ty-Ni-Da-Luu-Chi in the Vietnamese language.

Vinitaruci had travelled widely in India to study Buddhism under various masters. Unsatisfied with his development, he journeyed to China for further Buddhist studies, arriving at Zhang-an (Chang-an) in AD 574, the year Emperor Wu of the northern Zhou dynasty (557–81) suppressed all religious activities. Despite these unfavourable conditions, he studied Zen under the Third Patriarch Seng Can and attained enlightenment. He then went to Guangzhou Province in south China where he translated various Buddhist texts from Sanskrit to Chinese. In 580 he crossed the border and settled at the Phap-Van Temple (meaning Temple of Dharma Clouds) in north Vietnam, where he met a Vietnamese monk called Phap-Hien.

'What is your name?' the Indian master asked the monk.

'What is your name?' the Vietnamese monk asked in return.

'So, you don't have a name?'

'Of course I have, but you can make a guess.'

'Why should I guess?' Vinitaruci shouted.

This shout, about 250 years ahead of the famous shouting technique of Lin Ji (Rinzai), triggered off the Zen awakening of Phap-Hien, whereupon the Vietnamese monk begged to be a disciple of the Indian Zen master.

Phap-Hien studied under Vinitaruci for about 15 years. In 594 Vinitaruci transmitted the mind-seal, or confirmation of Zen realization, to Phap-Hien, who succeeded him as the Second Patriarch[4] of the Ty-Ni-Da-Luu-Chi sect.

ZEN BEYOND LANGUAGE

Break Through Without Language – Wu Yen Tong in Chinese, Vo-Hgon-Thong in Vietnamese – was the name of the Chinese master who founded the second Zen school in Vietnam. Like the Sixth Patriarch Hui Neng, Vo-Hgon-Thong was a native of Guangdong, but from a wealthy family. He renounced his comfortable life and started to practise Buddhism at a young age far from home. Because he was intelligent and frequently understood profound Buddhist teachings intuitively, the other monks called him 'Break Through Without Language'. Yet he wanted to further his Buddhist understanding, so he travelled to Jiangxi to learn from the famous Zen master Bai Zhang.

Like Phap-Hien two centuries before him, Vo-Hgon-Thong attained his Zen awakening the very first time he met his Zen teacher. As he was ushered into the meditation hall of Bai Zhang's monastery, he heard a student asking the master to explain what Zen was. Bai Zhang said: 'When the mind attains its breakthrough, wisdom will radiate spontaneously like the sun.' Hearing this, Vo-Hgon-Thong was instantaneously awakened. His awakening was in line with Bai Zhang's teaching that:

> the perception of Buddha nature depends on the right moment, the direct cause and the intervening cause. When the time is ripe, one is like a deluded man suddenly awakened and one who forgets all about something which he suddenly remembers. Only then can his be the self-possessed nature which does not come from without.[5]

For Vo-Hgon-Thong, the right moment was when he entered the Zen hall and heard Bai Zhang's teaching; the direct cause was his realization that Zen, expressed as wisdom radiating spontaneously like the sun, does not abide at anything; and the intervening cause was the Buddhist insight he had acquired in his prior training.

How did Bai Zhang's description enable Vo-Hgon-Thong to realize Zen? The key word is 'spontaneously', pointing directly at his mind, breaking off all attachments due to delusion so that his mind or Buddha nature can shine forth like the sun and attain its breakthrough or Zen awakening.

Vo-Hgon-Thong studied under Bai Zhang for many years. Later he returned to his native province of Guangdong, and in 820 settled in north Vietnam at the Kien-So Temple, where he continued meditating against a wall, as had the First Patriarch Bodhidharma at Shaolin Monastery. A Vietnamese monk called Cam-Thanh prostrated himself before Vo-Hgon-Thong and asked to be his pupil. .

One day Cam-Thanh asked the Chinese master, 'Where is Buddha?'

'Everywhere!'

Cam-Thanh was puzzled. 'What, then, is Buddha Mind?' he asked.

'Undivided, undifferentiated, unlimited, unhidden,' Vo-Hgon-Thong replied.

Cam-Thanh was even more puzzled, but he thought over the problem deeply. When Cam-Thanh had exhausted all his intellectual powers and still could not find the reason why Buddha is everywhere, undifferentiated, unlimited and unhidden, the master taught him the famous lines from the *Flower Adornment Sutra* (*Hua Yen Jing*, or *Avatamsaka Sutra*):

> Mind, Buddha and sentient beings;
> There is no difference in the three.

He then understood intuitively, and attained his awakening.

Cam-Thanh became the Second Patriarch of the Vo-Hgon-Thong sect. One of the notable patriarchs of this sect was King Ly-Thai-Ton (ruled 1028–53), who spread Vo-Hgon-Thong Zen and built many temples, including the famous One-Column Pagoda in Hanoi.

ZEN MONARCHS WHO CARED FOR THE PEOPLE

The third Vietnamese Zen school, Thao-Duong Zen, is marked by many outstanding features. Its founder was a prisoner of war, but the king who had captured him not only became his disciple but later happily abdicated so as to become the next patriarch. The period when Thao-Duong Zen flourished was also the longest period of peace and prosperity for the Vietnamese people. During this time all the monarchs were strong patrons of Buddhism, and some abdicated to become patriarchs of the Thao-Duong sect. The recitation of Amitabha, a practice of Pure Land Buddhism, was incorporated and this had far-reaching beneficial consequences.

In 1069 the Chinese master Cao Tang (Thao-Duong in Vietnamese, meaning 'Hall of Grass'), who was teaching the syncretized Zen–Pure Land Buddhism in Champa, was among the prisoners of war captured by the Vietnamese King Ly-Thanh-Ton. The King assigned Thao-Duong to assist the Vietnamese Royal Head Monk. Later when the King knew that Thao-Duong was a great Zen master descended from Xue Dou Ming Jue (Tuyet-Dau Minh-Giac in Vietnamese) of the Chinese Yun Men (Ummon in Japanese) tradition, and after he had tested his deep understanding of Buddhism, the King appointed him as the Imperial Teacher.

Thao-Duong advocated the unified practice of Zen and Pure Land Buddhism, known by the Chinese doctrine of 'chan jing yi zhi' or 'the united attainment of Zen and Pure Land Buddhism', which was popular in China during the Song dynasty. Superficially, Zen and Pure Land Buddhism may appear diametrically opposite, as Zen appeals to the 'fast-wit' who depends on 'self-effort', whereas the Pure Land appeals more to the 'slow-wit' who depends on 'other-help'. In the philosophy of the Pure Land School, devotees who sincerely recite the name of Amitabha Buddha will be reborn in the Western Paradise of Eternal Bliss presided over by Amitabha Buddha. In these favourable conditions they can continue their spiritual cultivation to achieve perfect enlightenment. Zen practitioners depend on their own meditation to achieve spiritual realization.

When studied in greater depth, the Pure Land School and Zen represent the widest span of Buddhist methodologies, ranging from divine grace to self-effort. Hence, their combined practice offers people of greatly different aptitudes and abilities a comprehensive approach to attaining the same spiritual goal. Those people who may not be sufficiently spiritually developed to benefit from Zen directly, can gain much from the Zen–Pure Land combined approach: through the recitation of Amitabha, they can raise their spiritual level so that eventually they will be able to practise Zen and attain enlightenment in this life, or they will be reborn in the Western Paradise where they can continue to strive for enlightenment in a future life.

The Pure Land School and Zen also symbolize the two 'pillars' of Buddhism – *karuna* (compassion) and *prajna* (wisdom). Devotees reciting Amitabha are reborn in the Western Paradise because of the great compassion of Amitabha, a Buddha of a previous aeon who has vowed to save them whenever he is called; Zen practitioners are awakened to transcendental reality because of their realization of higher wisdom. Both approaches are united by meditation. 'The Pure Land method of "no stirring in the whole mind" (i-hsin pu luan) did not differ essentially from the Ch'an method of "meditating to the point of perfect concentration" (ch'an-ting).'[6]

The unified Zen–Pure Land approach may be practised in many ways, depending on the needs and developmental level of the follower. He may kneel before an image of Amitabha Buddha, focus on the image, or close his eyes and visualize the image, listen to no other sounds except his recitation, and recite the phrase 'Homage to Amitabha Buddha' ('Nan Mo A Mi Tuo Fo' in Chinese, 'Nammo A-Di-Da Pha' in Vietnamese, or 'Namu Amida Butsu' in Japanese) hundreds or thousands of times, until he and the recitation become one. This is known as Amitabha-recitation (Nien Fo in Chinese, Niem-Phat in Vietnamese, and Nembutsu in Japanese). Or he may sit in meditation, close his eyes gently, clear his mind of all thoughts, then recite softly or silently the phrase 'Namo Amitabha Buddha'. This is meditation on Amitabha. In this more advanced stage, he does not recite but instead focuses on Amitabha in his mind.

Basically, Thao-Duong's teaching is on emptiness. The following lines from his *Warning Statements*, a summary of his essential teachings on Zen–Pure Land Buddhism, illustrate the emptiness of phenomena and self:

> Regard the world as an air-flower,
> Unreal.
> See the body as though a vision,
> Without basis.
> All things change and are not dependable.
> Unless you seek the path of purification
> You live in illusion in many lives.[7]

Thao-Duong was a very popular teacher and large numbers of people from both Vietnam and China flocked to him. His successor and Second Patriarch of the Thao-Duong Zen School, King Ly-Thanh-Ton, was a most sincere Buddhist monarch, as the following passage shows.

> During the winter months his thoughts often dwelt on the suffering of the prisoners and poor people. Calling his attendant one bitter-cold day the king lamented, 'Here I am in the palace – warm clothes and shelter – yet still I feel cold. What of those in our prison cells who don't have enough to eat or enough to wear? How they must suffer from cold and hunger! And what of those suspects who have yet to be questioned – are we to assume them guilty and treat them like criminals? They would suffer unjustly merely waiting for interrogation which would be most pitiful. Surely we must do something about all this.' The king then ordered sufficient clothing, bedding, and food for all prisoners and suspects being detained by the state.[8]

Although King Ly-Thanh-Ton was not as well known in history as Asoka of India or Han Wu Di of China, he attained a higher spiritual level. Asoka and Han Wu Di were reborn in various heavenly realms because of their good karma, but Ly-Thanh-Ton, who had also performed good deeds, went further and attained enlightenment, thereby transcending the phenomenal realm.

King Ly-Thanh-Ton was not an isolated case: all the succeeding monarchs of the prosperous Ly dynasty followed his good example of caring for the people; two of these monarchs, King Ly-Anh-Ton and King Ly-Cao-Ton, also became patriarchs of Thao-Duong Zen. The former's appointment of the famous master Venerable Vien-Thong of Ty-Ni-Da-Luu-Chi Zen as the Imperial Teacher, illustrates his liberal attitude. It is not surprising that during the Ly dynasty, Confucianism and Taoism also flourished.

ZEN AND VIETNAMESE NATIONALISM

The history of Truc-Lam Zen provides many outstanding examples where men of fame and power, who had contributed much to society, renounced their worldly glories at the height of their careers for spiritual development. Truc-Lam Zen is also the only one of the five major Vietnamese Zen schools to be established indigenously. Of the three masters responsible for the founding of Truc-Lam Zen, two were kings and the other a general; all three were national heroes who not only halted the much dreaded Mongolian invasions of Vietnam but also brought peace and prosperity to the people. They were King Tran-Thai-Ton, the Venerable Tue-Trung and King Tran-Ngan-Ton.

King Tran-Thai-Ton (ruled 1225–58), who established the Tran dynasty, was one of the most respected monarchs of the Vietnamese people. Yet his greatest aim was to practise Buddhism. The preface to his *A Guide to Zen Buddhism* reflects the difficult choice he was faced with:

> On the one hand was the idea of responsibility toward human society and the nation, on the other hand was the idea of an eternal value, the basic meaning of the everchanging process of life and death. On the one hand, it was the call of the practical life, on the other was the call of a metaphysical universe.[9]

King Tran-Thai-Ton's preface contains golden advice for all of us – unfortunately, appreciated by many only when it is too late. You may consider the following lines trite or 'soft', but they come from the founder of a dynasty, from the soldier-king who pushed back a fierce Mongolian army that had earlier conquered the mighty Chinese empire.

> My thoughts dwelt constantly on the love which parents feel for their children and the great sacrifices they make to bring them up. During their whole lives, no matter how much they sacrifice, children can never repay this debt to their parents.

The great king continued, revealing his love for his people too:

I thought of how my father successfully dealt with the difficult task of ruling the country and bringing prosperity to the people. From the time I received the throne from him at a young age, I constantly worried and was never at ease. In the first place, I didn't have my parents to lean on; secondly, I was afraid I might not meet the expectations of my people.

One night the king left the palace secretly and climbed Mount Yen-Tu to Phu-Van Temple (Temple of Floating Clouds) to meet the master Truc-Lam (meaning 'Bamboo Grove'), 'to take the Buddhist vow to become a Buddha'. The master replied:

There is no Buddha in the mountain. Buddha is in the mind's heart. If your mind is calm and understanding, that indeed is Buddha; if you awaken to this mind you'll become Buddha. You needn't look elsewhere.

The prime minister leading the royal search party found the king and begged him to return. Truc-Lam told the king:

A successor to the throne must learn to identify himself with the will of the people and with each beat of their hearts. Now the people want you to return to the palace. How can you refuse? But in spite of your royal position and duties, always continue searching for spiritual truth.[10]

And that was what King Tran-Thai-Ton did. One night while reading the *Diamond Sutra*, he was struck by the following sentence: 'Attain a mind that abides nowhere.' The king meditated on this sentence and suddenly he was enlightened. He realized that nothing exists outside the mind. This was the same sentence in the *Diamond Sutra* that had enlightened Hui Neng, the Sixth Patriarch.

King Tran-Thai-Ton's accomplishments in state affairs were impressive, and he employed Confucian principles extensively in running the country. He believed that 'Buddhism needs the wisdom of Confucianism in order to function properly within human societies.' He revamped the administrative system, introduced social reforms to benefit the people, and peacefully settled all differences with neighbouring Champa. He also encouraged Taoism. He was known as the Great Monk-King. In 1258, a year after defeating the Mongols and making sure his country was prosperous, he gave up the throne to devote his time to Zen Buddhism. His son and successor, King Tran-Thanh-Ton (ruled 1258–78), followed his benign example.

In many ways, King Tran-Thanh-Ton's son, Prince Kham, was like his grandfather. He showed keen interest in Buddhism at an early age, and declined his appointment as crown prince. But his father insisted that he should rule for the benefit of the people. Later he ran away from the palace to Dong-Cuu Temple on Mount Yen-Tu, but was brought back by a search party and soon after crowned as King Tran-Ngan-Ton (ruled 1278–1308).

Like his grandfather the Great Monk-King, King Tran-Ngan-Ton ruled his country with compassion. But in the evening he would retire to Tu-Phuc Temple to practise meditation under the Imperial Teacher, the famous Zen master Tue-Trung Thuong-Si. Tue-Trung himself was a prince and general who had voluntarily renounced worldly glories for spiritual life. He was noted for his directness and the Taoist doctrine of naturalness. Once, when a student asked him about birth and death, he replied:

> Why bother to worry about a bubble in the ocean,
> Clouds flying with the wind across an evening sky?

After successfully repulsing fierce Mongolian attempts to conquer Vietnam in 1285 and 1287, King Tran-Ngan-Ton devoted his time to national unity and prosperity, including the formulation of the Vietnamese national script, Chu-Nom, by organizing Chinese characters according to the sound and meaning of the Vietnamese language. By this time, 'Vietnamese Buddhism and Vietnamese nationalism were one and the same, not two.'[11]

The king trained his son for five years to take over his monarchical duties, then, after his abdication in 1287, he became a monk and wandered from place to place to teach Zen. Later he built the Ngoa-Van Temple (Temple of Reclining Clouds) on Mount Yen-Tu, where he was known as Truc-Lam Dai-Si, meaning 'Great Teacher of the Bamboo Grove'. (The Zen master who enlightened his grandfather the Great Monk-King on this mountain was also called Truc-Lam.) Here Truc-Lam codified the doctrines and established the practice of the school of Zen known as Truc-Lam Zen.

The teaching of Truc-Lam Zen incorporates the thoughts of three masters: the Buddhist compassion combined with Confucian pragmatism of King Tran-Thai-Ton, the Buddhist concept of emptiness expressed in the Taoist naturalness of Tue-Trung, and the doctrine of dynamic engagement in the daily world of King Tran-Ngan-Ton. In the resultant Truc-Lam doctrine, Zen is not practised separately from the world of affairs. Yet, despite its active and effective involvement in daily life, its spirit of spontaneous joy and detachment is unmistakable, as illustrated in the following lines of its First Patriarch, King Tran-Ngan-Ton, an accomplished poet:

> The willows trail such glory that the birds are struck dumb.
> Evening clouds balance above the eave-shaded hall.
> A friend comes, not for conversation,
> But to lean on the balustrade and watch the turquoise sky.[12]

WHERE DOES ONE RETURN TO?

The fifth major Zen sect in Vietnam is Lam Te, which is the Vietnamese term for the Chinese Lin Ji and the Japanese Rinzai. However, as Thich Thien-An points out, Lam Te Zen is not necessarily the same as Lin Ji Zen or Rinzai Zen, because although both the Vietnamese and the Japanese versions originated from China, when Lin Ji Zen was brought to Vietnam in the 17th century it had evolved to encompass aspects of Pure Land, Tian Tai and Hua Yen doctrinology and practice, and was different from the Lin Ji Zen brought to Japan in the 12th century. He says that the Obaku Zen that was introduced from China to Japan in the 17th century resembles modern-day Vietnamese Zen, which is mainly derived from Lam-Te Zen.[13]

Lam-Te Zen was introduced from China to Vietnam by the Chinese master Yuan Shao, or Nguyen-Thieu in Vietnamese (died 1712), who arrived in central Vietnam by sea in 1665. Before his parinirvana, he left the following verse for his students:

> No image disturbs the mirror's nature;
> No dust dulls the diamond splendour.
> Dharmas being present as no dharmas,
> Tranquil sunyata is not empty.[14]

The gatha reveals that the master was not only advanced in meditation but also learned in the scriptures, especially the

Lankavatara Sutra and the *Wisdom Sutras*, as the content of the poem reflects the philosophy of these texts. This combination of meditation practice and canonical studies was a prominent feature of Buddhist masters during the Ming dynasty.

Nguyen-Thieu was succeeded by another Chinese master, Ming Huang Zi Rong (Minh-Hoang Tu-Dung in Vietnamese) as the Second Patriarch of Nguyen-Thieu Zen. One of Ming Huang's students was a Vietnamese monk, Thiet-Dieu Lieu-Quan, who had studied Buddhism from a young age under various teachers. After questioning Lieu-Quan on his previous training, Ming Huang decided that Lieu-Quan would best benefit from koan practice. So he taught him to meditate on the koan 'All dharmas return to One; where does One return to?'

Day after day and month after month Lieu-Quan worked on the koan. But he got nowhere; he became disappointed, even ashamed of his own ignorance. Then one afternoon, eight years later, while reading *Transmission of the Lamp*, he came across the following lines:

> Using objects to transmit the mind of Zen,
> This is beyond the comprehension of ordinary people.

Suddenly Lieu-Quan realized that neither objects nor thoughts obstruct the unfolding of prajna which results in the liberation of the mind. He had found out where the One returns to; he had attained enlightenment. Looking back he realized that the eight years spent on the koan were the most rewarding years of his life. He felt so grateful that he set out to seek his teacher to thank him. When Ming Huang saw the enlightened Lieu-Quan, the master asked:

> 'Buddhas have succeeded one after the other, as have the patriarchs. So what did they transmit among them?'
>
> 'Are you asking how long the bamboo sprout grows on the piece of stone, or would you like to know the weight of a turtle-feather broom?' Lieu-Quan replied.
>
> 'Water flows uphill, horses race in ocean depths, a boat floats on the mountain,' Ming Huang said.
>
> 'The unstrung guitar made music the whole day through; the horn-broken earthen oxen roared the night long,' Lieu-Quan added.[15]

The master was very happy. He transmitted the mind-seal to his disciple and named him his successor. Being a Vietnamese, Lieu-Quan was able to incorporate many Vietnamese features into his teaching. The resultant Zen school, known as Lieu-Quan Zen, is the most popular Buddhist sect in Vietnam today. The school that issued from the other disciples of Nguyen-Thieu continues to be called Nguyen-Thieu Zen.

To the unenlightened, the above statements by Lieu-Quan and his teacher are nonsensical. How can water flow uphill, or an unstrung guitar make music the whole day through? Yet these lines are not riddle, or jokes, or a play on words. Once you have found out experientially that all dharmas return to One, and where One returns to, you will have attained a state of mind where all the above statements become meaningful.

The later part of this book provides methods which you can incorporate in your training to attain Zen awakening, and even enlightenment. You will need to put in a lot of time and effort: Lieu-Quan spent eight years on his koan; Gautama Buddha spent six years meditating, and Bodhidharma nine. It is certainly unreasonable and unrealistic for lesser minds to expect a similar result in any shorter time.

15

UNDERSTANDING ZEN IN ARTS AND CULTURE

The Cosmic Dimension in Martial Arts and Poetry

You yourself have probably had many encounters with Zen without consciously knowing it.

ZEN IN DAILY LIVING AND CULTURE

Zen influence in our everyday life is extensive, though it is often so subtle that most people may not be aware of it. All the great discoveries and inventions in the arts, science and philosophy have been made under the influence of Zen, which is in this case a deep meditative state of awareness different from ordinary consciousness. For example, when Michelangelo created his masterpiece, when Crick and Watson visualized the double helix of DNA, or when Plato wrote the *Republic*, their minds were all in contact with cosmic reality in a state rightly described as Zen.

Even ordinary people encounter Zen in various degrees, such as when a student is oblivious to all other things while writing examination answers, when a trader buys and sells amidst the chaos of a busy dealing room, or when a performer perfects a difficult technique in a demonstration. You yourself have probably had many encounters with Zen without consciously knowing it. When you savour your food, immerse yourself in a hobby, get wrapped up in your work, admire a beautiful sunset, are captivated by music, moved by a touching scene, feel the wonders of nature, or experience a deep communication with God, you are in a state of Zen.

For many Eastern societies, Zen has become an inseparable part of their culture. When Japanese industrialists emphasize the directness and effectiveness of their products, or when Vietnamese peasants long for the rustic joy of their rice fields and water buffaloes, they express in different ways, often unconsciously, the role Zen has played and the effects Zen has brought to their cultural matrix.

In some cases, the effects of Zen are more discernible, though many people may still be unaware of them. Anyone who reads both modern Chinese – or *bai hua wen* (colloquial language) – and classical Chinese – or *wen yen wen* (literary language) – can readily tell the difference between these two styles of the same language. Modern Chinese, with its simple, direct expression, developed from the gong-ans or public records of Zen stories.

Today, when we talk of Chinese painting, many people think of Chinese watercolour 'mountain-stream' (or landscape) painting, but this is only one of the numerous genres of Chinese painting. It is also a product of Zen influence. The Venerable Jin Ming says:

> Because of the transcendental mind of Zen, the green vastness of mountains and flowing purity of streams merge easily into one body with Zen; there exists another world in the mountain-stream painting so that the spirit of the painting and the heart of Zen are one.[1]

The influence of Zen on these cultural patterns and products, on the instances of cosmic glimpses resulting in extraordinary creations, as well as on subtle Zen encounters in our daily lives, are too extensive and complex to be discussed in this chapter; they are mentioned here in passing to show the pervasive influence of Zen in daily life, even in people who may not have heard of the term 'Zen'. The arts where Zen influence is more direct and remarkable are varied and numerous: they include the martial arts, painting, literature, architecture, interior decoration, flower arranging, Japanese Noh drama, and the tea ceremony.

It is helpful to note that although some of these arts can be used as a supplementary, and sometimes even as the main, means to attain a Zen awakening, this is not the primary purpose of the people who practise these arts; nor are these arts, with a few exceptions (*see* page 162), normally used by

Zen practitioners in their spiritual cultivation. For example, the famous 'one-brush technique' of Chinese painting (another genre much influenced by Zen) and the Japanese tea ceremony are both imbued with Zen, but the painters or the tea drinkers, even though they may be Zen monks, are not generally painting or drinking tea as part of their Zen practice.

For convenience, the influence of Zen on the arts can be said to be one of philosophy, approach or spirit. For example, the rise of neo-Confucian literature was greatly influenced by Zen philosophy, the efficiency of the Samurai by Zen approach, and the plot of a Noh play by Zen spirit. This threefold division is arbitrary: not only is there often much overlapping in the various aspects of Zen influence, but the decision as to which aspect is most prominent is sometimes difficult to make. Nevertheless, accepting such a convenient division may enable us to solve some seemingly contradictory problems. For example, it is often asked how it can be said that a Samurai, whose sole purpose was to kill his lord's enemy without question, was greatly influenced by Zen, which is unequivocally against killing. The answer is that the Samurai embraced the Zen approach of directness and effectiveness, but not necessarily the Zen philosophy of not taking life.

SHAOLIN KUNGFU AND TAI CHI CHUAN

Historically as well as methodologically, the arts that are most intimately connected with Zen are Shaolin Kungfu and Shaolin Chi Kung.[2] In fact, Kungfu (Chinese martial arts), Chi Kung (the art of energy) and Zen are the three treasures of Shaolin. When the First Patriarch Bodhidharma taught Zen at Shaolin Monastery, he found the monks too weak to practise meditation. So he first taught them two invaluable sets of exercises known as Eighteen Lohan Hands and Sinew Metamorphosis, which later evolved into Shaolin Kungfu and Chi Kung. The practice of these two arts is actually preparation for Zen, leading to spiritual awakening and enlightenment; they are therefore the earlier mentioned exceptions which can be employed directly for Zen cultivation.

However, both Shaolin Kungfu and Shaolin Chi Kung have developed so much on their own, and have served other purposes so effectively, that most people regard them as independent of, or even unrelated to, Zen. Indeed, even among Shaolin Kungfu and Chi Kung masters today, very few are aware of the intimate relationship between these three Shaolin arts, or of the fact that the original primary aim of Shaolin Kungfu and Chi Kung was not to improve fighting skills or health, but to strengthen the Shaolin monks – physically, emotionally and mentally – so that they bettered their chance of attaining spiritual fulfilment. It is worthwhile remembering that Bodhidharma, whom exponents of Shaolin Kungfu and Chi Kung as well as Zen regard as the First Patriarch, was a Bodhisattva whose mission in the Shaolin Monastery was to help people not merely to become good fighters, nor even just to have good health, but to attain the highest, greatest achievement humanity can ever aspire to – the actualization of their cosmic reality. Shaolin Kungfu and Shaolin Chi Kung will be explained in greater detail in separate chapters.

Closely related to Shaolin Kungfu and Shaolin Chi Kung in matters concerning Zen are Taiji Kungfu and Taiji Chi Kung, although many people who practise the latter two may be surprised at this statement, and some may vehemently protest. 'Taiji', which is Romanized Chinese, is more commonly spelt as 'Tai Chi' in English; and Taiji Kungfu and Taiji Chi Kung were generally practised together as Tai Chi Chuan ('Taijiquan' in Romanized Chinese), although nowadays most people practise only the outward form of Tai Chi Chuan, neglecting both the kungfu and the chi kung aspects. In other words, most people today merely perform Tai Chi movements, but they do not know how these movements can be used for fighting or developing internal force.[3]

Traditionally, Tai Chi Chuan is considered a Taoist art. How could it, then, be connected with Zen, which is usually associated with Buddhism? The answer is twofold. Firstly, Zen is used here to mean a glimpse, or even the actualization, of cosmic reality (see Chapter 1); it is not used to mean Zen Buddhism. Secondly, Zen Buddhism – despite being called Buddhism – transcends religious delineation! Any person of any religion can practise and benefit from Zen Buddhism without unfavourably affecting his religious beliefs. So, even if we use the term 'Zen' to mean Zen Buddhism, there is a lot of Zen in Tai Chi Chuan. Actually the two interpretations are similar; the apparent complications, if any, are due to the inadequacies of language to express the intended meaning clearly and concisely.

How is Tai Chi Chuan related to Zen? In the case of Shaolin Kungfu, we can gain a better perspective if we examine its history. Tai Chi Chuan was invented by the Taoist master Zhang San Feng (Chang San Foong) towards the end of the Sung dynasty in China. Zhang San Feng was a Shaolin disciple, expert in Shaolin Kungfu, Shaolin Chi Kung and Zen Buddhism, although he himself was a Taoist. He retired to Wudang Mountain to continue his Taoist cultivation, where he also modified Shaolin Kungfu and Shaolin Chi Kung into Wudang Kungfu and Wudang Chi Kung, which together with Taoist meditation were collectively known as the Wudang art. Later, during the Ching dynasty, the Wudang art was renamed Tai Chi Chuan by Chen Wang Ting, an accomplished scholar-general. Like Bodhidharma, Zhang San Feng was a great master; the art he invented was not just for fighting to decide mundane quarrels, it was for attaining the Tao, which in Buddhist terms is called Zen.

The fundamental philosophy of Tai Chi Chuan is based on the principle of yin-yang. Yin and yang harmonize to form the Tai Chi (Taiji), the 'Grand Ultimate', also known as Cosmos, Supreme Reality, God, Brahman, the Tathagata, and Zen. At the ultimate level, practising Tai Chi Chuan leads to the attainment of this Tai Chi.

Have you ever wondered why Tai Chi Chuan is usually performed slowly, gently and gracefully? It is because this is one of the best ways to engender energy flow, and to attain harmony of body, breath and mind. This dynamic or 'yang' aspect of Tai Chi Chuan is complemented by the quiescent or 'yin' aspect in meditation, known as jing-zuo or 'silent-sitting', which is zazen in Zen terminology. When body, breath and mind of the Tai Chi Chuan exponent are harmonized into one organic whole and are no longer three separate parts, he merges the organic whole of his person into the organic whole of the cosmos. He thus attains the Tao, which is the actualization of cosmic reality where the phenomenal difference between the exponent and the environment, between the knower and the known, disappears. Hence, Tai Chi Chuan is also an art which can be used directly for Zen cultivation, more commonly known as cultivating the Tao. However, most Tai Chi Chuan practitioners today, including Tai Chi instructors, do not consider this spiritual (but not religious) aspect, and practise Tai Chi Chuan primarily for health.

The philosophy and approach as well as the spirit of Tai Chi Chuan are similar to those of Zen, especially Zen as practised in the Shaolin tradition. Nevertheless, it is difficult to say how much, if at all, Zen Buddhism (and not just Zen in the sense of cosmic realization) has influenced Tai Chi Chuan. The philosophy of yin-yang, the practice of jing-zuo and the spirit of attaining the Tao were all in Taoism long before Zen Buddhism came to China from India. But there is no doubt that the Shaolin arts have directly and greatly influenced Tai Chi Chuan; after all, Tai Chi Chuan was developed from Shaolin. However, if some Tai Chi Chuan practitioners feel slighted by this reference to the Shaolin origin of their art (perhaps due to provincial loyalty), they can take comfort that, in my opinion, because Shaolin Kungfu has moved so far away from its original aim – and which even many Shaolin masters seem to have forgotten – for most people Tai Chi Chuan is probably a more efficacious vehicle than Shaolin Kungfu for attaining an experience of Zen awakening.

ZEN AND THE ARTS OF BUSHIDO

It is interesting to compare the influence of Zen on Shaolin Kungfu and Tai Chi Chuan with its influence on Bushido, or the Japanese Way of the Warrior. The intimate connection between Zen and the Japanese warrior class, or the Samurai, began soon after Eisai introduced Rinzai Zen to Japan. There is a Japanese saying that 'The Tendai is for the royal family, the Shingon for the nobility, the Zen for the warrior classes, and the Jodo for the masses.'[4]

There were good reasons why the Samurai was devoted to Zen. The Zen principles of directness, simplicity and effectiveness promoted qualities that were particularly useful to him in combat. The Zen teaching on detachment from life and death enhanced his determination and fearlessness when facing a deadly opponent. The Zen emphasis on intuition and experience, and disinterest in intellectual speculation, fulfilled the Samurai's needs as a warrior. Zen meditation provided the Samurai with not only relaxation (much needed in his stressful life), but also a refreshed mind and the ability to react intuitively (exceedingly useful in combat).

Hence, the modern Japanese martial arts like jujitsu, kendo, judo and karate that are derived from classical Bushido, also value Zen highly. Zazen constitutes an important aspect in the training of these martial arts, and is particularly useful in checking aggressiveness which tends to develop unwittingly in such arts as kendo and karate.

There is, however, a crucial, though subtle, difference between these Japanese arts and the Chinese martial arts of Shaolin Kungfu and Tai Chi Chuan. The last two, though they are in their own right excellent for combat, were originally developed as a means to enhance Zen cultivation; whereas Zen cultivation was originally employed to enhance Bushido, the fountain-head of the Japanese martial arts. In other words, in Japanese martial arts the relationship with Zen is reversed. A Shaolin disciple, for example, progresses from kungfu to Zen; whereas a karate-ka progresses from Zen to his martial art. A Shaolin disciple starts from kungfu, but at the highest level, he discards this fighting art and attains spiritual enlightenment. A karate-ka starts from karate, and at the highest level uses Zen to enhance his martial art so as to become a formidable fighter. The difference, however, is so subtle that even many martial arts masters themselves may not be aware of it, especially when they have lost sight of the fact that originally Shaolin Kungfu and Tai Chi Chuan were meant to aid the quest for spiritual enlightenment. Thus it is that many Shaolin and Tai Chi Chuan masters employ Zen in their arts only to enhance their fighting skills and for health, neglecting the spiritual aspect.

In this connection it is illuminating to note that in his book *Zen in the Art of Archery*, Eugen Herrigel unequivocally regards his art as a spiritual, and not a martial, training. The ultimate aim of his master, Kenzo Awa, was not merely to produce an expert archer, but to help his pupil realize the 'Great Doctrine', which is Zen, or the actualization of cosmic reality. Indeed, in my opinion, Herrigel's description of his archery training is probably more helpful to uninitiated readers than many of the current Zen books in English. While these books (including some by Zen masters) talk about Zen in a language uninitiated readers would not understand, or repeat verbose platitudes that will not directly help them in their Zen practice, Herrigel's book suggests a concrete way in which to approach Zen.

However, it is unfortunate that throughout Herrigel's book there is no clear indication that he himself realized the meaning or significance of the Zen he was seeking, or that he attained a Zen awakening at the end. He became a changed, but not necessarily an awakened or enlightened, person. His not being awakened is evident from such statements as: 'When I asked the Master how we could get on without him . . .' and when his master told him 'Perhaps you have hardly noticed it yet . . .'[5] If he was awakened, he would have had no doubts about the nature of cosmic reality and how he should continue his cultivation to attain enlightenment. Because he was unsure of what he was seeking, even if he were to continue his archery practice faithfully and become a master archer, he would take a long time to attain a Zen awakening – if at all. He would arrive at an experience of Zen more quickly if he had a prior understanding of what Zen is.

ZEN IN NEO-CONFUCIANISM

It may come as a surprise to some people that, Zen is a prominent feature in many martial arts. In Chinese culture, an ideal person is well versed in the arts of both the warrior and the scholar. Many people may be even more surprised to learn that Confucius himself was not only a great sage but also an expert in archery and horsemanship. Many Shaolin monks who were expert in martial arts were great poets and painters too. As well as being an essential ingredient of both Shaolin Kungfu and Tai Chi Chuan, the two most famous Chinese martial arts, Zen also greatly influenced the rise of neo-Confucianism during the Sung dynasty.

It is interesting to note that the great Tang poets – such as Bai Zhu Yi (Po Chu I), Wang Wei and Meng Hao Ren of the Tang dynasty – and virtually all the great scholars responsible for the revival of Confucianism during the Sung dynasty – such as Au Yang Xiu, Wang An Shi, Su Dong Bo (Su Tung Po), Lu You and Zhu Xi (Chu Hsi) – studied Zen. Some of them made a point of spending some time each year in Zen monasteries to practise Zen.

In the following lines, the Tang poet Wang Wei (701–61), who was a good friend of the Zen master Ma Zu, is actually describing Zen philosophy:

> Once defiled thought arises,
> Physical body will abound.
> That's the illusion of aggregates;
> Where can true self be found?[6]

According to Buddhist philosophy, a person is a transient collection of five aggregates: form, perception, ideation, activity and consciousness. These five aggregates – which we ordinarily regard as a person – are actually an illusion, not his true self. The objective of Zen is to realize the true self, which in reality is the Buddha nature.

During the Sung dynasty, Zen as meditation was such an important practice among Confucian scholars that Zhu Xi's advice to 'spend half the day on meditation, and the other half on study' became a Confucian axiom. The poem 'Non-Action' of the great Sung reformer, Wang An Shi (1021–86), reads like a Zen gong-an:

> In non-action, good deeds we practise;
> With ignorance, phenomena will flow.
> Every being is born, abides and ceases;
> As thought arises, concepts will grow.
> If free from attachment you can achieve,
> The robes of monks you need never receive.[7]

Zen philosophy on cosmic reality, where form is emptiness and emptiness is form, also had a remarkable influence on Confucian philosophers and scientists (or rationalists). The Confucian philosophy that the universe can be explained by the two primordial concepts of 'chi' (energy) and 'li' (principle) was a result of the Buddhist philosophy of emptiness and form. Lu Xiang Shan (1139–93) said: 'The cosmos is my mind; my mind is the cosmos.'[8]

Confucian philosophers and scientists did not merely speculate on the cosmos. Through the practice of Zen meditation and the study of Taoist thought, they discovered astonishing facts that were not known to modern science until many centuries later. For example, Zhou Dun Yi (1017–73), often regarded as the father of Confucian physics, systematically described the structure of the cosmos using the Taoist Taiji concept in terms which modern scientists would interpret as the constant integration and disintegration of energy and matter. His contemporary, Shao Yong (1011–77), described the subatomic world using the Taoist Bagua (Pakua) concept in terms now used in computer science and to explain DNA![9]

HAIKU AND ENGLISH POETRY

Of the numerous genres of Japanese literature, the haiku is probably the closest to the philosophy, approach and spirit of Zen. A haiku is a Japanese poem of 17 syllables, with five, seven and five syllables respectively in its first, second and last line. The following is a celebrated example, written by Basho (1643–94), who is considered as the founder of the haiku.

> Furu ike ya
> Kawazu tobikomu
> Mizu no oto.

Its translation is as follows:

> Ah! the old pond
> A frog jumps in
> The water's sound.

Although the translation of a poem in any language loses much of its original beauty, luckily there is still enough left for us to see how the above haiku is related to Zen. An obvious feature is its simplicity of content. Readers familiar with the religious poetry of John Donne and George Herbert, or the classical poetry of Milton, may wonder what a frog jumping into an old pond and making a sound has to do with Zen Buddhism.

The close relationship between Zen and the haiku can be explained as follows. Like Zen, the above haiku is simple, direct and effective. It does not need, for example, to elaborate on the complexity of man's weakness or the prolixity of Greek gods and goddesses, as in English religious or classical poetry, in order to convey effectively the beauty and wonder of the Supreme Reality.

What the poet seeks to convey is not mere information concerning the mundane world. Neither is it his intention to present

l discourse or philosophical speculation. If this
poet would probably choose to use prose rather
lable haiku. What Basho wishes to convey is an
an inspired glimpse into cosmic reality; and this
corporates an intense feeling as well as an insight
into a transcendental truth.

The feeling here, as I interpret it, is one of childlike awe and
bewilderment. An old pond may be prosaic to most people,
but to the poet its serenity, indicative of the tranquillity of
transcendental reality, brings forth a feeling of awe, even rever-
ence, as suggested by his exclamation of 'Ah!'

Suddenly, amidst the tranquillity, a frog – considered by
ordinary people as a common, lowly creature – jumps in,
breaking the serenity and making a sound which resonates
throughout the previously quiet surroundings. A spiritual
aspirant, if he is ready at this moment, may experience a sudden
merging of the sound, frog, pond and himself into one organic
unity, in an inspiring flash of Zen awakening. If this happens,
he has a direct experience of cosmic reality, even for an endless
moment. But even if this does not happen, because he is intuitively aware he will still acquire an insight into cosmic reality
though it is not a direct experience at this time – and an understanding of the interpenetration of everything in the universe.
In an illuminating instant, he will realize that the phenomena
he ordinarily sees are an illusion; he will intuitively understand
a great cosmic truth.

Of all the English poets, William Blake and William Wordsworth come closest to Zen, yet their treatments, beautiful in
their respective ways, are different. Let us examine the last three
stanzas of Blake's famous poem, 'The Tyger'.

> What the hammer? what the chain?
> In what furnace was thy brain?
> What the anvil? what dread grasp
> Dare its deadly terrors clasp?
>
> When the stars threw down their spears,
> And water'd heaven with their tears,
> Did he smile his work to see?
> Did he who made the Lamb make thee?

> Tyger! Tyger! burning bright
> In the forests of the night,
> What immortal hand or eye,
> Dare frame thy fearful symmetry?

Like Basho, William Blake is not concerned with merely conveying literal information. And, like a Zen koan, the literal meaning of his poem may be illogical. What, for example, had the hammer or the chain to do with the tiger's brain? Blake is an enlightened poet; he conveys to us a glimpse of cosmic reality in a language that ordinary people may find hard to comprehend. The difficulty is twofold: his symbols are profound, and his cosmic experience is inexplicable (in the sense that even if he had described it exactly, others who never had this kind of experience would not understand him).

Blake's expression of Zen is different from that of Basho. Basho is simple and direct, whereas Blake is deep and symbolic. Because of its simplicity and directness, Basho's poem may act as a catalyst for ready aspirants to attain their awakening. Blake's poem requires some introspection. A Zen aspirant meditating on it as a koan may one day suddenly be awakened to its cosmic truth. It can be said, then, that Blake's poem is imbued with the philosophy and spirit of Zen.

Although both Zen and Blake express the underlying interconnection and oneness of the universe, and the grandeur of the Supreme Reality, their approach is different. Zen is simple and direct, Blake arcane and symbolic.

While Blake's 'Tyger' is fiery, the opening lines of Wordsworth's 'Prelude' evoke a serene yet joyful environment characteristic of Zen:

> O there is blessing in this gentle breeze
> That blows from the green fields and from the clouds
> And from the sky: it beats against my cheek,
> And seems half-conscious of the joy it gives.
> O welcome messenger! O welcome friend!
> A captive greets thee, coming from a house
> Of bondage, from yon city's walls set free.

The philosophy, approach and spirit of these lines are similar to those of Zen. Here Wordsworth expresses a philosophy of spontaneity and naturalness, using a simple, direct and effective approach that brings out the spirit of universal consciousness. All these qualities are also highly valued in Zen.

Yet it is not as clear here as in Blake's case, that Wordsworth has achieved a Zen awakening. Reading Blake's poem, a Zen master could tell that Blake had been awakened to transcendental reality; but he could not be so sure in Wordsworth's case as shown in the above lines. When Blake mentions shaping the tiger's brain with a hammer or a chain, or framing its fearful symmetry with immortal hand or eye, a Zen master knows for sure that Blake has had a direct experience of cosmic reality as tranquil and undifferentiated, because his descriptions are transcendental.

On the other hand, Wordsworth's descriptions and his references to the breeze as a messenger and friend, and himself as a captive, are still in the phenomenal dimension. Hence, Wordsworth's philosophy, approach and spirit are Zen, but he has not entered Zen. Wordsworth comes very close to Zen, but his understanding of it is still not complete.

UNDERSTANDING AND EXPERIENCE

Imagine you are a Zen master, and your pupil Wordsworth comes to you with the above lines for a Zen assessment. How would you help him to attain a Zen awakening, or even an enlightenment?

You may, for example, say that the breeze comes not from the green fields or the clouds or the sky, but from your backside. If he looks puzzled, you can help him further by whacking his backside and telling him that now the breeze comes from there. If he realizes that the breeze can come from anywhere, he could have a Zen awakening.

Or, you can ask him what made him a captive? If he repeats that it was a house from yon city's wall, you cut him short by asking if he is still a captive once he has been set free from the house. If his answer is 'yes', ask him what is holding him captive. If his answer is 'no', ask him what is still holding him captive. Hopefully he will be awakened to what is actually holding him prisoner, so that he can liberate himself.

If you can appreciate the deeper meaning behind the hypothetical Zen interview with Wordsworth, you have a sound understanding of Zen; you may even have had some experiences of Zen awakening already. But even if you have not, this understanding will provide a very good foundation for Zen training. This understanding indicates that you have the appropriate 'spiritual roots' for Zen cultivation.

Up to this point in this book we have been concerned mainly with understanding Zen. From the next chapter onwards we shall start our practical cultivation, beginning with an explanation of general principles, followed by the actual methods that we can practise to experience Zen. It must be emphasized that in Zen the onus is on direct experience, not the mere acquisition of knowledge. Nevertheless, some prior understanding is exceedingly helpful. If a person plunges blindly into Zen, without knowing what he is seeking, what methods are available, why he follows them, and what signs to look for to ensure he is progressing properly, he is not likely to achieve good results. Without such understanding, the aspirant is not ready, and his condition may be interpreted as not having the necessary spiritual roots.

For some reason, most current books in English on Zen seem to avoid telling readers clearly and directly what Zen is, and what they should be seeking when they embark on its cultivation. This situation is rather strange, especially when the subject is amply explained in Chinese, the language of the land where Zen developed and blossomed. Moreover, since simplicity and directness are characteristics of Zen, it is ironic that these writers in English should shroud Zen in a veil of mystery.

One possible reason why these writers are cryptic is their confusion over the difference between explaining koans and explaining Zen, with the result that their books resemble a huge koan which uninitiated readers find incomprehensible. Zen is clear and direct: if you hold a rose and ask a Zen practitioner what it is, he will say it is a rose – not something like 'If I call it a spade it would smell as sweet.' On the other hand, koans appear cryptic, but this is not because they are purposely made to be so but because the listener or reader misses their intended meaning. For example, when a student asks a master 'Where is Buddha?', and he answers 'Buddha is everywhere', he means exactly what he says. His intention is to help the student realize that cosmic reality (Buddha) is omnipresent, found in minute atoms as well as infinite stars and all the space in and between

them. But if an ordinary person not connected with Zen cultivation asked the master a similar question, he would give a
clear, direct answer like 'There's a statue of the Buddha in the
hall', 'You can read about him in the scriptures', or whatever
information that person is seeking.

When a Zen master uses a koan as a testing or teaching tool
for his student to solve, it is obvious that he will not tell him
the answer; doing so would defeat the object of the exercise. In
other situations – when an explanation would help students to
understand Zen, or when Zen is being read for fun or knowledge – it is useful to explain the koan, especially to those who
do not have the advantage of a master's personal guidance.
Some readers may find it reassuring to know that koans are
clearly explained in both classical and modern Zen books in
Chinese.

It is also surprising that most Zen books in English provide
little or no help with practical Zen cultivation, despite their
frequent assertion that Zen is an experiential and not an intellectual discipline. I hope the following chapters will help to
overcome this shortcoming.

16

PREREQUISITES FOR ZEN TRAINING

Preparing for a Long but Rewarding Journey

Life becomes more meaningful and beautiful as you work towards the realization of your own innate immortality.

REVIEW OF ESSENTIAL INFORMATION

After understanding what Zen is, we are now ready for practical training to experience Zen directly. This chapter marks the start of Zen cultivation proper; all previous chapters are only preparatory. But before we practise the techniques, we should be familiar with a certain amount of essential information. We need to have asked ourselves the following important questions:

1 What is Zen?
2 What exactly do we aim to attain in our cultivation?
3 What are the other benefits we can get from our training?
4 What effective methods can we use?
5 What are the principles behind these methods?
6 How much time is needed?
7 What are the pitfalls we should try to avoid, and what signs indicate that our training is progressing properly?
8 What are the essential principles of Zen cultivation?

ZEN AND ITS CULTIVATION

What Zen is, is covered in detail in Chapter 1. The following is a brief summary.

Zen has many meanings, all of them relevant to our training. Basically, Zen means 'meditation'. In this meaning Zen is an eminent aspect of Yoga, Taoism, Confucianism and mysticism, and is also found in the inner or higher cycles in Christianity, Islam and other religions. It is essential to all schools of Buddhism. Yet Zen, or meditation, is non-religious. It is also employed in parapsychology to acquire extra-sensory perception. Zen may also refer to a meditative state of mind.

Due to a heightened or deepened state of consciousness as a result of meditation, we often experience reality differently. This too is called Zen. Some religious teachers regard such an experience as a communication with God; others as a glimpse of the Ultimate Absolute. Zen Buddhists refer to this experience as looking into your original face, or into Buddha nature.

Zen may also refer to the Ultimate Absolute or Supreme Reality itself. It is 'ultimate' because there is nothing beyond it; it is 'absolute' because it is the same to every sentient being. The Ultimate Absolute is known by various names, such as God, Allah, Brahman, Tao, and the Tathagata. Buddhists call this direct experience of cosmic reality, enlightenment.

'Zen' is also used as a short form of Zen Buddhism, a school of Mahayana Buddhism. Mahayana Buddhists believe that every sentient being has Buddha nature, and can therefore become a Buddha. According to most Buddhist schools, attaining Buddhahood takes a long time and requires spiritual cultivation over numerous reincarnations. Buddhahood may be interpreted as a direct experience of organic oneness with the Ultimate Absolute, in other words, the actualization of cosmic reality. Zen Buddhists believe that this experience – also known as nirvana, bodhi, enlightenment, or jue in Chinese – can be attained here and now.

The aim of Zen cultivation is to attain Zen, which may be interpreted in any one of the above meanings. At the lowest level, Zen cultivation may mean practising meditation, for spiritual or other purposes. For example, an ordinary lay person may cultivate Zen by sitting comfortably or lying down, closing the eyes gently, and keeping fairly still in order to relax.

At a higher level, cultivating Zen may refer to training to attain a state of mind which enables one to have a glimpse of cosmic reality, or be receptive to cosmic wisdom. In parapsychology this awakening to a cosmic glimpse may be an instance of telepathy, clairvoyance or some other extrasensory perception. Hallucinations, delusions, epileptic visions and other abnormal experiences due to drugs or mental disorders are categorically not Zen.

At the supreme level, Zen cultivation means dedicatedly working towards a spiritual realization of the Supreme Reality. This is the objective of all religions and is known by various terms: finding God's kingdom within, returning to Allah, union with Brahman, merging with the Cosmos, becoming the Buddha, or simply 'going home'.

If Zen is intended as a short form for Zen Buddhism, then Zen cultivation is practising Zen Buddhism. The practice may be directed towards any one or more of the above aims, or to other objectives. For example, it may mean meditating on a gong-an (koan), or consulting a master on a spiritual matter.

OTHER BENEFITS OF ZEN TRAINING

Besides realizing our aims in Zen cultivation, there are many other benefits, as discussed in some detail in Chapter 3. Here, for convenience, they can be categorized as physical, emotional, mental and spiritual benefits.

Zen cultivation will improve our physical health, especially if approaches like Shaolin Kungfu and Tai Chi Chuan are also incorporated into the training. So-called incurable diseases may be relieved, especially if chi kung is practised. Dr Hasekawa Zaburo, MD, reports that Zen meditation is an effective remedy for nervousness, excess gastric acid, abdominal distension, tuberculosis, insomnia, indigestion, chronic ptosis, atony, chronic constipation, dysentery, gallstones and high blood pressure.[1]

It is generally well known that Zen practitioners are calm and cheerful. Their emotional stability and optimistic attitude have been acquired as a result not of extrinsic moral instruction from their masters, but of the intrinsic process of their Zen training. Practising Zen is therefore an excellent way to overcome emotional disorders, which in Chinese medical philosophy include psychiatric and neurological problems.

Zen training is the best method of mind expansion, a claim that has been amply substantiated throughout history by the fact that virtually all the great works of art, science, literature, philosophy, religion and other disciplines were accomplished when their creators were in a meditative state of mind. Venerable Sheng-Yen says:

> the practice of Ch'an will continually provide you with a means to excavate your precious mine of wisdom. The deeper the excavation, the higher the wisdom that is attained until eventually you obtain all the wisdom of the entire universe.[2]

This is not an exaggeration. In Zen the practitioner's mind taps into the all-knowing Universal Mind and perceives reality as it really is. Some Zen practitioners find within their abilities what ordinary people would term supernormal powers.

The greatest achievement of Zen lies in its spiritual dimension. A Zen practitioner irrespective of his religion, or even the lack of it, will develop an awareness of spirituality as he progresses in his cultivation. Developing from within rather than being instructed from without, he becomes morally upright, tolerant and compassionate, and experiences a sense of inner peace. He becomes aware that there is more to living at the physical level and, as he catches glimpses of his own divine spark or Buddha nature, life becomes more meaningful and beautiful as he works towards the realization of his own innate immortality.

CULTIVATION METHODS AND PRINCIPLES

Short of training under a Zen master in a monastery, the methods provided in the following chapters constitute probably the most comprehensive programme for Zen cultivation, especially for those attempting Zen cultivation without the advantage of a personal master. The methods follow the Shaolin tradition taught by Bodhidharma, the First Patriarch of Zen, and they consist of Shaolin Kungfu, Shaolin Chi Kung, and meditation. The kind of meditation taught by Bodhidharma involves meditating on the void, known as Patriarch Zen. As meditation on the void is quite difficult for beginners, the other major method of meditation, meditation to attain a one-pointed mind, or Tathagata Zen, is also introduced.

Although there are gong-ans (koans) about Bodhidharma using extraordinary verbal and non-verbal means to help students attain Zen awakening, the use of gong-ans as a systematic method of Zen cultivation was developed by Da Hui Zong Guo (1089–1163) more than 500 years later. Hence, the gong-an method, which is characteristic of Lin Ji (Rinzai) Zen, is not normally used in the Shaolin tradition as an active means to train Zen, though it is sometimes used to test students' understanding or experience of Zen. The Shaolin Monastery did not adhere to any particular school of Zen, and its abbots came from various Zen schools, including Lin Ji; but the school that was most often practised and that had supplied the most abbots was Cao Dong (Soto) Zen. Nevertheless, as the gong-an method is popularly used by many Zen practitioners today, it is also explained fully in a later chapter.

Many people may wonder why kungfu and chi kung are included in Zen cultivation, thinking that meditation alone is sufficient. Certainly, one can attain awakening and enlightenment by practising only meditation; meditation is essential – in fact, in this respect, Zen is meditation. Even if a person uses the gong-an method as the sole means of Zen cultivation, he still has to practise meditation. But while kungfu and chi kung are not essential, they are extremely useful. To meditate correctly and persistently is a very difficult and demanding task, but it can be made easier and more pleasant if we start with kungfu and chi kung. Indeed, for some people it can be said that kungfu and chi kung are essential, in the sense that if they start meditation immediately, without preliminary training in kungfu or chi kung, they will not be able to achieve a Zen awakening in this life. Further, some people may attain a Zen awakening by practising kungfu or chi kung alone, without performing formal meditation.

Why are kungfu and chi kung so useful to Zen cultivation? Why is it possible for some people to achieve an awakening by practising only kungfu or chi kung, when it has been said that practising meditation is essential?

The path of meditation is the path to spiritual fulfilment, which is the apex of a person's development, and attainable only when he is healthy and fit physically, emotionally and mentally. A handicapped person, someone who has lost an arm, say, can still cultivate for spiritual development as long as he is healthy and fit. But spiritual cultivation would be very difficult, if not impossible, for those who are chronically sick – physically, emotionally or mentally – such as someone suffering from frequent physical pain, manic-depression or imbecility.

Practising meditation can help to relieve these conditions, although in some situations if it is not carried out properly it can aggravate an illness. But even if these conditions can be helped by meditation, it would be an uneconomical use of time and effort. For example, a person suffering from a psycho-somatic disease like asthma, diabetes or hypertension, could practise meditation for many years, yet he might not have any inkling of Zen awakening – though he may feel calmer and refreshed and his symptoms may be relieved – because the benefits derived from his meditation practice have gone into his physical, emotional and mental development, with little left for spiritual progress. He would attain similar or more effective results, and in a shorter time, if he first practised kungfu and chi kung.

Often an aspirant is not clinically sick, but he may have insidious health problems that are not serious enough to warrant formal medication but serious enough to hamper his spiritual cultivation. For example, certain meridians (or energy pathways) inside his body may be blocked. If he persists in meditation practice for a long time, not only will he not progress spiritually but he may also experience harmful consequences. For instance, prolonged meditation practice will increase his vital energy, but if his meridians are blocked, the increased energy is unable to flow smoothly and may press against his internal organs and cause serious problems. Practising kungfu and chi kung are excellent ways to overcome such problems.

Most people find it difficult to keep their mind 'empty' or focused on one point even for a few seconds. If they stubbornly attempt sitting meditation for half an hour, they will encounter mental chaos, which may be harmful. A better approach is to first learn to keep the mind empty or focused. This can be effectively accomplished in kungfu and chi kung practice. Only when this essential skill of mind control has been acquired, should sitting meditation be attempted.

Breath control is equally important in meditation. Kungfu and chi kung are very effective means to acquire various types of breath control. (If you have practised kungfu or chi kung but have no knowledge of breath control, then you have missed some important aspects of your art.) Many meditation masters stress the importance of abdominal breathing; some consider the *dan tian*, or the central energy field located at the lower abdomen, as the source of spiritual power. If you breathe slowly and deeply during sitting meditation, as many teachers recommend, you may, if you are lucky, develop abdominal breathing after many years. If you learn abdominal breathing in kungfu or chi kung, an example of which is explained on page 223, you can acquire abdominal breathing in a few months.

Practising Shaolin Kungfu and Shaolin Chi Kung not only contributes greatly to the practice of meditation, but we may attain a Zen awakening or even enlightenment by practising Shaolin Kungfu or Shaolin Chi Kung alone, though the process will be faster if we allot time specifically for practising sitting meditation. This is because meditation is an integral aspect of Shaolin Kungfu and Shaolin Chi Kung. In fact, in the Shaolin tradition kungfu, chi kung and meditation were integrated; they were classified into three arts for convenience. However, the subsequent development of these arts led them further apart, with the result that today many people practise them separately.

HOW MUCH TIME IS NEEDED?

Depending on the purpose, Zen cultivation may be practised for a few minutes or for a whole lifetime. If all you want is to be able to relax after a taxing activity or before an important engagement, you can just lean back on your seat, close your eyes gently and follow your breathing with your mind for a few minutes. But for those who have renounced material wealth and power and wish to liberate themselves from the chains of birth and death to attain cosmic realization, Zen cultivation is a life-long mission. For most of us, it will lie somewhere between these two extremes.

How much time you put into Zen training will depend on numerous factors, such as your aims and objectives, environment and facilities, needs and time available, abilities and developmental stages. Even if you were prepared to spend an hour a day for six years, this is a very small price to pay for the tremendous benefits that you would definitely receive. It is permissible, though not advisable, to miss a day or two in training, but on the whole training must be regular. If you practise every day for a few weeks, stop for one or two weeks, then continue off and on for a few months, you are not likely to get good results.

During the first year of a six-year programme the emphasis would be on kungfu, for the next two years on chi kung, and the last three years on meditation. This does not mean that the three arts are practised separately; kungfu, chi kung and meditation are practised every year, but progressively the emphasis is shifted. If you can commit yourself only to a shorter period for cultivation, say 15 minutes daily for six months instead of an hour daily for six years, then you have to adjust the time allocation proportionately: the first month for emphasizing kungfu, the next two months for chi kung, and the final three months for meditation.

Of course the effect of a six-month practice is vastly different from one of six years. If you have a chronic illness, for example, two months of emphasis on chi kung may not be sufficient to relieve you of that illness. But if you are generally healthy and fit, this short programme can give you a feel of what Zen cultivation is like.

The progression from kungfu to chi kung to meditation is only a suggestion, though this suggested procedure is ideal according to the Shaolin tradition of Zen cultivation. For various reasons, you may wish to modify the programme to suit your needs. For example, if you cannot find a kungfu instructor and are not able to follow the kungfu description in this book, you can skip the kungfu part and practise only chi kung and meditation. If you suffer from a chronic disease for which conventional medication is not helpful, you may wish to spend more time on chi kung before focusing on spiritual cultivation. If you are already following a suitable programme of Zen cultivation, then from the various techniques presented in this book choose only those you think will complement your own programme. In short, there is no hard and fast rule: make whatever modifications seem sensible.

PITFALLS AND ENCOURAGING SIGNS

For each technique of Zen cultivation described in this book, the specific pitfalls to avoid, if any, are also explained. Here we examine some important advice applicable to all techniques generally. Pitfalls as well as encouraging signs for meditation practice are also found in Chapter 4.

In all three aspects of Zen cultivation – kungfu, chi kung and meditation – it is extremely important to progress gradually. Results hastily obtained may often be injurious rather than beneficial. A useful guideline to bear in mind is 'When in doubt, it is always better to under-train than over-train.' If your training is insufficient, you may obtain little benefit but you are unlikely to hurt yourself. You will therefore take a longer time to achieve your objective. If you over-train, the result may be so overbearing that your body or mind may not be ready to accept it. This can sometimes be serious. Nevertheless, you will be given adequate warning in the form of pain, tiredness or great discomfort. If you heed the warning, and perform appropriate remedial exercises like Self-Manifested Chi Movement (*see* page 218), your harmful side-effects can be eliminated.

Do not overdo the number of times you repeat an exercise. Know when to stop. In this way, you will always feel fresh and pleasant at the completion of the exercise, knowing that you could have continued for longer without any undue stress had you wanted to do so. You must never proceed with any exercise to such an extent that at its completion you feel tired.

Your mind should be emptied of irrelevant thoughts when you perform the exercises. They will all help you to attain an 'empty' or a focused mind, but if sometimes your emotions or thoughts are overwhelming, it is better not to practise at that time.

Besides pitfalls to avoid, there are encouraging signs to indicate that you are progressing properly. In all three aspects of cultivation, if you have practised the exercises correctly, you should feel fresh, energetic and full of vitality.

If you have not been exercising recently, practising kungfu may initially cause you to feel some muscular pain, but this is normal. As you progress, the bodily pain will soon disappear, to be replaced by a feeling of agility and alertness. Your appetite may increase, but do not worry; the extra food you eat will be transformed into extra vital energy and if you do acquire any extra flesh it will be allocated to the right places.

As you progress with your chi kung practice, you may find that your hair and finger nails grow faster and healthier. This is because your harmonious energy flow has transported nutrients to the extremities of your body. Some people may find that their breathing becomes heavier, their body smells slightly, and they pass wind frequently. These are just some of the ways in which the body disposes of toxic waste as a result of proper chi kung practice. These symptoms – a small price to pay for cleansing your body of rubbish – will disappear shortly.

As you progress in your meditation, you will find that you are not so easily irritated. Your mental concentration and thinking power will certainly improve, and you will become more appreciative of both your environment and the people around you. You will become more intuitive, and may find inspiring thoughts popping into your head at odd times.

You will become aware of all these welcome signs of progress if you put in some time and effort to cultivate Zen. But before the dedicated cultivation begins, let us review some of the essential principles of Zen Buddhism.

CHARACTERISTIC FEATURES OF ZEN BUDDHISM

The following principles were spoken by Sakyamuni Buddha to Mahakasyapa, but because later they became a popular part of Bodhidharma's teaching, these words are often mistakenly accredited to him:

> Not recorded in language and words,
> Transmission beyond the tradition,
> Directly pointing at the mind.
> Entering Buddhahood in an instant.

These lines also represent the four special features which distinguish Zen Buddhism from other schools.

Bodhidharma emphasized that in spiritual cultivation the onus is on direct experience, not book learning. It is illuminating to note that around this time there was a hugh controversy in Sri Lanka over whether practice or learning was the more important. The Dhammakathikas who favoured learning won the argument and thus influenced the whole character of Sri Lankan Buddhism, which is now virtually Theravada.

Nevertheless, stressing practical work and direct experience does not mean denying the importance of book learning. The Zen doctrine 'Not recorded in language and words' refers to the transmission of Zen, meaning that it is transmitted from heart to heart, and cannot be obtained from language or words. It does not mean that Zen teaching cannot be written in or conveyed through books. As will be explained in more detail later, instant enlightenment as advocated in Zen Buddhism is for those who are spiritually ready; book learning is helpful in developing that readiness.

'Transmission beyond the tradition' refers to the methods of Zen cultivation that are different from the traditional ways practised in other schools of Buddhism. Hence, traditional methods like the cultivation of moral purity (as in Theravada), devotional worship of the Buddha and Bodhisattvas (as in many Mahayana schools), and the use of mantras (as in the Vajrayana tradition) are seldom found in Zen Buddhism. Even the all-important practice of meditation, essential in all schools, is quite different in Zen meditation. Here the meditator focuses on the void, whereas other schools use the traditional method from Indian Buddhism where the meditator trains his mind to be one-pointed.

The Zen doctrine 'Directly pointing at the Mind' emphasizes the direct and practical training which is necessary to purify the mind for awakening and enlightenment. This aspect of Zen Buddhism contrasts sharply with other famous Mahayana schools that were flourishing at about the same time, such as the Wei Shi (Ideation) School which analyses the consciousness in great detail, the Tian Tai (Lotus) School which philosophizes on the syncretism of all major schools, and the Hua Yen (Garland) School which investigates in depth the interpenetration of countless worlds.

The doctrine of 'Entering Buddhahood in an instant' in Zen Buddhism is unique among all Buddhist schools. It postulates that if you actualize transcendental cosmic reality now, you become a Buddha instantaneously! This represents a glaring contrast to, or as some scholars suggest a protest against, the numerous lifetimes an aspirant may need to progress to enlightenment along the path of Theravada or some Mahayana schools.

But such a instantaneous approach to enlightenment is not easy, nor is it necessarily the fastest route, especially if the aspirant is not spiritually ready.

In Buddhist philosophy, everything is subject to the law of cause and effect. The fact that you are reading this book indicates that your karma has brought you to this opportunity for spiritual development, irrespective of your religion. If you are ready, turn to the next chapter for the long but exceedingly rewarding journey of Zen cultivation.

17

ZEN OF STRENGTH AND MOVEMENT

Shaolin Kungfu for Zen Cultivation

When a one-pointed mind is attained in the
process of practising a kungfu set, some
practitioners may experience a Zen awakening or
satori during the final standing meditation.

THE GREATEST MARTIAL ART IN THE WORLD

Many people rightly believe that Shaolin Kungfu is the greatest martial art in the world. This claim, which devotees of other styles may vehemently dispute, can be substantiated from many angles. Historically, Shaolin Kungfu is the most senior martial art in the world, with a continuous history of 1,500 years, while some martial arts have barely 100. From the perspective of technique, Shaolin Kungfu contains virtually all the techniques found in all the world's major martial arts: all the punches in karate, all the kicks in taekwondo, all the throws in judo, all the locks in aikido, all the holds in wrestling, all the jabs and hooks in Western boxing, all the elbow and knee strikes in Siamese boxing, all the subtle twists and turns in Malay silat. Its range of weapons, totally absent in some modern martial arts, is bewildering.

The principles guiding the application of techniques in combat are both deep and extensive. For example, while some arts advocate meeting force with equal force (which is not usually appropriate when women fight hefty men), or aim to strike the opponent in the shortest time (which may in certain situations be disadvantageous), Shaolin fighters are guided by useful principles to assess all relevant conditions so as to select the best moves to meet the particular situation. At the same time they are able to provide themselves with the best possible cover in case their opponent goes for a sudden or all-out counter attack with no concern for his own safety, which can result in mutual injuries.

In force training, while some martial arts aim at breaking bricks and planks, the accomplishments of Shaolin force training are astounding: smashing granite blocks with the head, withstanding punches, kicks and weapon attacks on the body without sustaining injury, and affecting internal damage on an opponent with a palm or finger without leaving any external mark.

Yet the greatest benefits of Shaolin Kungfu are not fighting skills. Aesthetically, a demonstration of Shaolin Kungfu is beautiful to watch. It is poetry of strength, agility, gracefulness and artistic patterns in motion – very different from a demonstration of other martial arts. From the perspective of health, Shaolin Kungfu is excellent for promoting physical, emotional and mental well-being, whereas the practice of some martial arts is actually detrimental to health – when an internal injury sustained during sparring is not treated satisfactorily, becoming aggressive due to the nature of the training itself, and taking punishment to the head which can impair mental faculties!

It is mainly for its excellent health-promoting qualities, as well as for introducing mind control, that Shaolin Kungfu is presented here as a prelude to Zen meditation. Hence, its features as a fighting art, for which Shaolin Kungfu is perhaps better known, are not described.[1] Moreover, as the kungfu patterns presented in this chapter are elementary, readers looking for techniques similar to those found in other martial arts, may not find them here.

Because of space constraints, how the patterns are to be performed is only summarily described. Readers who have no martial arts background may find it hard to follow the brief descriptions, and they are advised to seek instruction from kungfu or other martial arts masters. However, if this is not feasible, they are advised to follow the illustrations and descriptions as best they can, and not become unduly worried that they are not performing the form exactly. The inaccurate performance of form can be disastrous if the kungfu patterns are being practised for combat purposes, but it is permissible here because they are practised for Zen cultivation.

A SHAOLIN KUNGFU PROGRAMME

This programme for Zen cultivation consists of the following four parts:

1 Stances, especially the Horse-Riding Stance
2 Leg exercises
3 A kungfu set
4 Standing Meditation

Learn and practise the exercises according to the sequence described in this chapter, though if you have a particular reason you may alter the suggested sequence, or skip one or more exercises. Practise for about half an hour in the morning and for another half hour in the evening or at night.

Basic Stances

Horse-Riding Stance

The most important stance in Shaolin Kungfu is the Horse-Riding Stance (figure 17.1). It is a very tiring stance which, when

Figure 17.1 Horse-Riding Stance

performed correctly, most beginners will not be able to hold for more than a minute.

Once you are in the proper position, remain still; do not raise your body when you begin to feel tired, as most beginners do. Your body should be upright but totally relaxed. Clench your fists and place them at the waist. Breathe naturally. Clear your mind of all thoughts and 'place' your mind at your abdomen – do not worry about how to do it, just do it. Your eyes may be open or closed.

Bow and Arrow Stances

From the Horse-Riding Stance, if you turn your right foot about 45 degrees and your left foot about 60 degrees to your right, with your right (front) leg bent at the knee and your left (back) leg straight, you change to the right Bow and Arrow Stance. Similarly, if you turn to the left, you form the left Bow and Arrow Stance (figure 17.2).

Figure 17.2 Bow and Arrow Stance

False-Leg Stances

From the left Bow and Arrow Stance, bring your left (front) leg backwards and place your left toes about 12in (30cm) in front of your right (back) leg, with your left heel off the ground. Your weight is now mainly on your slightly bent right leg. This is called the left False-Leg Stance (figure 17.3). The reverse is the right False-Leg Stance.

These are the three main stances in Shaolin Kungfu. After practising them, with emphasis on the Horse-Riding Stance, proceed to the leg exercises.

Figure 17.3 False-Leg Stance

Leg Exercises

Three Levels to the Ground

Stand with feet about a shoulder width apart, and take both arms out to the sides at shoulder level, with fingers pointing out and palms facing down (figure 17.4a). Without lifting your heels, and keeping your arms outstretched throughout the exercise, bend your knees and lower your body fully, breathing out through your mouth in the process (figure 17.4b). Then bring your body back to the 17.4a position, breathing in through your nose at the same time. Repeat about ten times.

Figure 17.4a and b Three Levels to the Ground

Dancing Crane

Stand with feet about three shoulder widths apart, with arms outstretched at the sides (figure 17.5a). Without lifting your heels, and keeping the arms outstretched, bend your right knee and lower your body down, keeping your left leg straight and breathing out through your nose in the process (figure 17.5b). Then bring your body back to the 17.5a position, breathing in at the same time. Repeat bending on the right side about ten times. Then repeat bending on the other side the same number of times.

Figure 17.5a and b Dancing Crane

Touching Toes

Stand with feet together (figure 17.6a). Without bending your knees, bend over to touch your toes with your fingers, breathing out at the same time (figure 17.6b). Then stand upright in the starting position, breathing in simultaneously. Repeat about ten times. When your leg muscles are sufficiently stretched so that you can easily touch your toes with your fingers, change to touching your toes with your clenched fists, and later with your palms flat. Although the name of this exercise may be prosaic, it is very important in preparing your legs for performing the lotus position in sitting meditation.

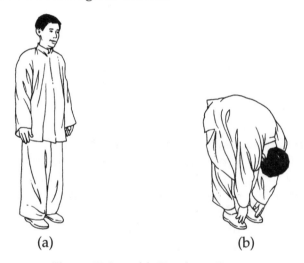

(a)   (b)

Figure 17.6a and b Touching Toes

Lohan Taking Off a Shoe

Place one foot on a support, such as a table, at about waist height (figure 17.7a). Both legs should be fairly straight, though it is permissible to bend the standing leg slightly. Bend your body forward to touch the toes of the supported foot with your fingers, and later, when you are more flexible, the knee with your forehead (figure 17.7b). Then straighten your body to the starting position. Breathe out as you bend forward, breathe in as you straighten. Repeat about ten times for each leg.

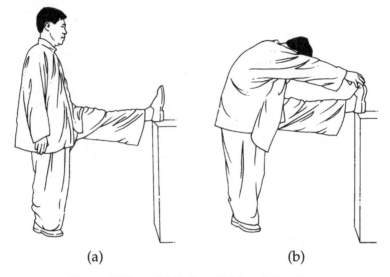

(a)   (b)

Figure 17.7a and b Lohan Taking Off a Shoe

Saint Clasping Feet

Sit on the ground with both legs stretched out in front of you. Keep your legs close together and the knees straight (figure 17.8a). Without bending your knees, bend forward and clasp both feet with your hands and later, when you are more flexible, bring your forehead to your knees (figure 17.8b). Breathe out as you bend forward. Then straighten your body to the starting position, and breathe in. Repeat this exercise about ten times.

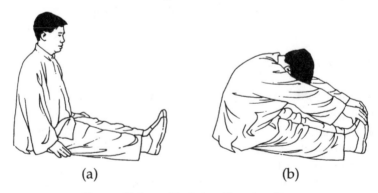

(a)   (b)

Figure 17.8a and b Saint Clasping Feet

Dragonfly Plays with Water

Sit on the ground with legs spread apart and knees straight (figure 17.9a). Without bending your knees, bend forward so that your outstretched hands touch your toes, and later your face and chest touch the ground (figure 17.9b). Repeat about ten times. Breathe out as you bend, and breathe in as you straighten up. Be careful that you do not hit the ground hard with your face or head. You may, if you wish, bend your head to one side then the other so that the side of your face instead of your nose gently touches the ground. Initially your outspread legs can form a letter V, but gradually you should be able to open them out so they are in a fairly straight line.

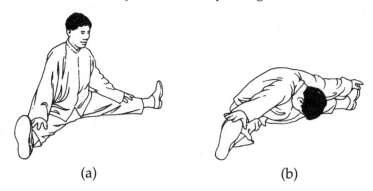

(a)   (b)

Figure 17.9a and b Dragonfly Plays with Water

All these exercises are very important and should be performed every day if you want your legs to be flexible enough for the lotus position. Because I paid much attention to the Horse-Riding Stance when I first started kungfu training, my stance was firm but my legs became very stiff – so stiff that I could not even sit cross-legged, let alone in the lotus position. Years later my Shaolin master Sifu Ho Fatt Nam gave me some priceless advice. He said, 'If you want to soar to the greatest heights in kungfu, you must practise chi kung; if you want to soar to the greatest heights in chi kung, you must practise meditation.' Realizing my weakness in my stiff legs, I asked my master, 'Can I practise meditation by sitting on a chair?' 'You can,' he said 'and may reach very high levels and attain fantastic psychic powers, but if you wish to attain the greatest height, spiritual fulfilment, you must meditate in the lotus position, at least the single lotus.' I always aimed for excellence, and was ready to pay the price. I practised those leg-stretching exercises daily for two years before I could meditate in the lotus position.

The importance of footwork in Shaolin Kungfu – an aspect not often appreciated by many students – is reflected in the fact that we have to spend considerable time making our legs strong and flexible by practising the above exercises before we learn any kungfu patterns.

Dragon in Zen – a Simple Kungfu Set

The following Shaolin kungfu set is made up of 28 kungfu patterns. It was specially invented by me for this book and is named Dragon in Zen. (In Chinese culture, the dragon is a majestic, divine being.)

A kungfu pattern is the particular way a kungfu exponent poses or executes a movement or series of movements. A series of kungfu patterns are linked together to form a kungfu set. Kungfu sets and patterns are usually meaningfully and poetically named in Chinese, though much of their poetry is often lost in translation.

Kungfu patterns are generally used for effective fighting, but as our primary purpose here is the practice of Shaolin Kungfu for Zen cultivation, we shall pay little attention to their combat functions and focus instead on how they can help us in our spiritual development. Some people may see a conflict between kungfu for fighting and kungfu for spirituality. In fact, there is no contradiction. As explained earlier, Shaolin Kungfu was initially developed for spiritual training, and it serves this purpose very well.

The kungfu patterns in this set are typical Shaolin kungfu movements which have been passed down through generations. Since it is difficult to learn kungfu movements accurately from a book, if possible seek the service of a kungfu instructor, but if this is not feasible, practise the movements as best you can.

1 No-Ego Stance

Stand upright but relaxed, with feet fairly close together, and effortlessly drop both arms to your sides (figure 17.10). Your eyes may be gently closed, half-closed, or gently open. Forget all cares and worries. Forget even yourself. If you are relaxed enough, you may feel your own vital energy flowing inside you. If you can forget your own ego, you may feel that you are an integral part of the cosmos.

Figure 17.10 No-Ego Stance

2 Dragon and Tiger Appear

Hold your two fists at your waist. First move your right leg, then move your left leg in front into the left False-Leg Stance (figure 17.3). Simultaneously hold your left palm and right fist close together in front of your chest in a typical Shaolin greeting (figure 17.11).

3 Two Tigers at the Ready

Move back to the starting position with your fists at your waist (figure 17.12). In kungfu patterns, any hand not in use is usually

Figure 17.11 Dragon and Tiger Appear

Figure 17.12 Two Tigers at the Ready

clenched at the waist. Do this in the patterns below, unless indicated otherwise.

4 White Snake Shoots Out Energy

Move your left leg forward into the left Bow and Arrow Stance (figure 17.2) with the body leaning slightly forward. Simultaneously strike out a right finger-thrust (formed by keeping the fingers close together, hooking in the thumb, and thrusting

Figure 17.13 White Snake Shoots Out Energy

the palm forwards with the tips of the fingers as striking points) at throat level (figure 17.13).

5 Precious Duck Swims Through Lotus

Without moving from your position turn your body to your right side to sit on the Horse-Riding Stance (figure 17.1), and simultaneously strike out a left punch at navel level (figure 17.14). Focus your eyes on your left punch.

Figure 17.14 Precious Duck Swims Through Lotus

6 Black Tiger Steals the Heart

Without moving from your position, turn your body to the front to the left Bow and Arrow Stance and strike out a right punch at chest level (figure 17.15). Focus your vital energy on your abdomen, your eyes on your right punch, and your mind on

Figure 17.15 Black Tiger Steals the Heart

your movement. Attempt to get these three focuses in the same instant, so that the three become one. In this way you attain unity of mind, energy and body.

7 White Snake Shoots Out Energy

Move your right (back) leg forward into the right Bow and Arrow Stance with your body leaning slightly forward. Simultaneously strike out a left finger-thrust (figure 17.16). This is the same as pattern 4, except that left and right are reversed. When you move your right leg forward, try not to feel that you are physically moving your right leg; rather, be aware that your whole being (including your leg, body, finger-thrust, energy and mental focus) is flowing effortlessly forward.

Figure 17.16 White Snake Shoots Out Energy

8 Precious Duck Swims Through Lotus

Turn your body to your left side into the Horse-Riding Stance, and simultaneously strike out a right punch at navel level (figure 17.17). This is the reverse of pattern 5, Precious Duck Swims Through Lotus, *see* figure 17.14. Your movement must be smooth and 'effortless'. Focus your whole being on the punch. Eventually you may find that your consciousness is not in your head, but in your punch!

Figure 17.17 Precious Duck Swims Through Lotus

9 Black Tiger Steals the Heart

Turn to the front into the right Bow and Arrow Stance and strike out a left punch at chest level (figure 17.18) – all in one smooth, effortless movement. This is the reverse of pattern 6,

Figure 17.18 Black Tiger Steals the Heart

Black Tiger Steals the Heart, *see* figure 17.15. You have now forgotten about your own body; your consciousness is in the punch.

10 Beauty Looks at Mirror

Without moving from your position, but only the angles of your feet as appropriate, make a 180-degree turn to the left to form the left Bow and Arrow Stance. Move your left hand to block at face level, with your right hand placed near the left elbow (figure 17.19). Feel the whole movement as one harmonious flow of mind, energy and form.

Figure 17.19 Beauty Looks at Mirror

11 False-Leg Hand Sweep

Move the left (front) leg back slightly, but keep it in front of the right (back) leg to form the left False-Leg Stance, with your body facing to the right. Simultaneously sweep your left hand down from above your right shoulder to a position in front of your left leg (figure 17.20). Focus your mind on the hand sweep – feel that you are the sweep itself.

Figure 17.20 False-Leg Hand Sweep

12 *Green Dragon Shooting Across a Stream*

Move your left leg forward into the left Bow and Arrow Stance and strike out your right palm at chest level (figure 17.21). Feel the energy at your right arm shooting out like a green dragon.

Figure 17.21 Green Dragon Shooting Across a Stream

13 *Golden Dragon Plays with Water*

Move the left leg a short step back, but keep it in front of the (back) right leg to form the left False-Leg Stance, with your body facing diagonally to your right side, and 'thread' out your left hand in a dragon-form. The 'thread' is an arc movement with fingers pointing forward, as if pulling a needle and

Figure 17.22 Golden Dragon Plays with Water

thread. The dragon-form here is formed by bending the little finger, the fourth finger and the thumb, keeping the middle finger and the index finger fairly straight (figure 17.22). Imagine you are that dragon.

14 *Yellow Oriole Drinks Water*

Kick out your right leg, with your right instep as the striking point. Simultaneously move your right hand, in dragon-form, in front at eye level, keeping your left hand, still in dragon-form, near your right elbow (figure 17.23).

Figure 17.23 Yellow Oriole Drinks Water

15 Happy Bird Hops up a Branch

Place your right foot on the ground in front, turn your body to the right and execute a left side-kick (figure 17.24). Focus the mind on your kick.

Figure 17.24 Happy Bird Hops up a Branch

16 Reverse Hanging of the Golden Lotus

Place your left foot on the ground to form the left Bow and Arrow Stance, and swing your left fist, with the knuckles as striking points, from near your right temple to out in front of you (figure 17.25). Place your right palm near your left elbow. Focus your mind on your left fist.

Figure 17.25 Reverse Hanging of the Golden Lotus

17 *Beauty Looks at Mirror*

Make a 180-degree turn to the right to form the right Bow and Arrow Stance, appropriately adjusting your feet position as you turn, and use your right arm to block, with your left palm at your right elbow (figure 17.26). This is the reverse of pattern 10, Beauty Looks at Mirror, *see* figure 17.19.

Figure 17.26 Beauty Looks at Mirror

18 *False-Leg Hand Sweep*

Bring the right (front) foot back half a step but keep it in front of your left foot to stand in the right False-Leg Stance. Sweep your right palm down (figure 17.27). Visualize yourself as your

Figure 17.27 False-Leg Hand Sweep

sweeping hand. This is the reverse of pattern 11, False-Leg Hand Sweep, *see* figure 17.20.

19 Green Dragon Shooting Across a Stream

Move your right leg forward into the right Bow and Arrow Stance and simultaneously strike out your left palm (figure 17.28). Let your consciousness flow with your left striking hand. This is the reverse of pattern 12, Green Dragon Shooting Across a Stream, *see* figure 17.21.

Figure 17.28 Green Dragon Shooting Across a Stream

20 Golden Dragon Plays with Water

Bring your right (front) leg back half a step but keep it in front of your left leg to form the right False-Leg Stance, and 'thread' out your right hand in a dragon-form (figure 17.29). Visualize yourself to be a golden dragon. This is the reverse of pattern 13, Gold Dragon Plays with Water, *see* figure 17.22.

21 Yellow Oriole Drinks Water

Kick out your left foot with your instep as the striking point. Simultaneously 'thread' your left dragon-form forward with your right dragon-form at your left elbow (figure 17.30). Place

Figure 17.29 Golden Dragon Plays with Water

Figure 17.30 Yellow Oriole Drinks Water

your mind at your kicking leg. This is the reverse of pattern 14, Yellow Oriole Drinks Water, *see* figure 17.23.

22 *Happy Bird Hops up a Branch*

Place your left foot just in front of your right foot, turn your body to the left and execute a right side-kick (figure 17.31). Focus on your kicking leg. This is the reverse of pattern 15, Happy Bird Hops up a Branch, *see* figure 17.24.

Figure 17.31 Happy Bird Hops up a Branch

23 *Reverse Hanging of the Golden Lotus*

Place your right leg in front to form the right Bow and Arrow Stance, and 'hang' your right fist forward (figure 17.32). Place your left palm near your right elbow. Focus your attention on your right fist. This is the reverse of pattern 16, Reverse Hanging of the Golden Lotus, *see* figure 17.25.

Figure 17.32 Reverse Hanging of the Golden Lotus

24 *Single Dragon Emerges from the Sea*

Bring your right foot back and stand momentarily in the right False-Leg Stance, simultaneously pulling back your right fist close to your chest. Then instantly shoot out your right leg into the right Bow and Arrow Stance and at the same time thrust

Figure 17.33 Single Dragon Emerges from the Sea

out a right punch, with your left palm near your right armpit (figure 17.33). Visualize yourself as the dragon shooting forward.

25 *Tranquillity of One-Finger Zen in the Whole Cosmos*

Take a big step back with your right (front) leg so that you are now sitting in the Horse-Riding Stance, with your body facing to the right and your face looking forward. Stretch out your left arm in front at shoulder height, in line with your gaze. Your left hand makes the typical Shaolin sign of One-finger Zen, ie your index finger straight and pointing skyward, your thumb and other fingers bent at the *second* joints (not the knuckles), and the palm held at right angles to the wrist. Hold your right fist firmly at your waist (figure 17.34). Relax totally, despite the tension in this pattern, and experience yourself immersed in Zen. Focus your eyes on the tip of your upright index finger.

Figure 17.34 Tranquillity of One-Finger Zen in the Whole Cosmos

Empty your mind of all thoughts and remain in this pose for a few seconds.

26 Dragon and Tiger Appear

Bring the left leg close to the right leg, adjust the position of the feet to stand in the left False-Leg Stance. Simultaneously place your left palm and right fist together in front in the Shaolin greeting (figure 17.35). This is the same as pattern 2, Dragon and Tiger Appear, *see* figure 17.11.

Figure 17.35 Dragon and Tiger Appear

27 Two Tigers at the Ready

Move back to the standing position with your two fists at your waist (figure 17.36). This is the same as pattern 3, Two Tigers at the Ready, *see* figure 17.12.

28 Standing Meditation

Drop both arms to your sides with the palms facing backward. Close your eyes and empty your mind of all thoughts (figure 17.37). Remain in this meditative pose for a few minutes. You will be surprised at how wonderful this feels. Then complete the exercise by rubbing your palms together to warm them,

Figure 17.36 Two Tigers at the Ready

Figure 17.37 Standing Meditation

dab the centres of your palms on your eyes as you open them, massage your face, and walk about briskly.

The above kungfu set helps us to train the mind. When a one-pointed mind is attained in the process of practising a set, some practitioners may experience a Zen awakening or satori during the final standing meditation. The complete set of patterns forming Dragon in Zen is repeated at the end of the book.

18

ZEN FOR HEALTH, INTERNAL STRENGTH AND VITALITY

Zen Training Through Shaolin Chi Kung

These methods of Zen cultivation were taught by Bodhidharma himself, and have been preserved throughout the centuries in the Shaolin tradition.

THE ZEN TRADITION OF BODHIDHARMA

When the First Patriarch Bodhidharma taught Zen at the Shaolin Monastery, he found the monks too weak for long hours of meditation. To help them overcome their weakness, the great master taught them two very special sets of exercises, Eighteen Lohan Hands and Sinew Metamorphosis. It is reputed that he also taught them Marrow Cleansing, but no direct record exists of these exercises at the Shaolin Monastery, or anywhere else. There are some arts called Marrow Cleansing being practised today, but it is generally believed that they were later inventions, and not genuinely transmitted by Bodhidharma. Nevertheless, from indirect records, we may postulate that if Bodhidharma did teach the Marrow Cleansing exercises, they were similar to the advanced form of visualization exercises in Self-Manifested Chi Movement, where vital energy is channelled to flow within the bones. Self-Manifested Chi Movement, which is also called Induced Chi Flow, constitutes a part of our Shaolin arts. Eighteen Lohan Hands and Sinew Metamorphosis are still widely practised today.

Later in the Shaolin Monastery, Eighteen Lohan Hands developed into the Eighteen Lohan Fist, a famous kungfu set which constitutes the foundation of Shaolin Kungfu. Sinew

Metamorphosis provided the basic principles and methods for many Shaolin Chi Kung techniques to train internal strength and vitality. In this chapter we shall study and practise some selected exercises from Eighteen Lohan Hands, Sinew Metamorphosis and Self-Manifested Chi Movement, as well as an effective method of Abdominal Breathing, not only for health, internal strength and vitality but also for Zen cultivation.[1]

Some Zen practitioners of other systems, whose main cultivation method is either koan solving or sitting meditation, may question whether the methods described in this chapter are actually a part of Zen. Let them be assured that these methods of Zen cultivation were taught by Bodhidharma himself, and have been preserved throughout the centuries in the Shaolin tradition. In my chi kung classes in different parts of the world, many students who had practised Zen or other meditative training systems for years with little result, were amazed at how quickly and effectively the methods described in this chapter brought about a Zen experience or awakening.

Standing Zen

Lifting the Sky – from Eighteen Lohan Hands

To many people, and for various purposes, the best exercise in Eighteen Lohan Hands is the first one, Lifting the Sky. It is an excellent exercise for inducing an overall energy flow within the body, learning breath control, developing visualization ability, attaining a one-pointed mind, and experiencing the void that many practitioners find so hard to achieve sitting in the lotus position. Of course, as in all mystical or spiritual training, it is not just the mechanics of the technique that are crucial but the personal initiation or transmission of the desired effect from master to student.

Stand upright and relaxed with feet fairly close together. Place both hands in front, with the palms face down and the fingers pointing towards each other (figure 18.1a). Keeping your arms straight throughout the exercise, raise your palms in a *continuous* arc forward and upward until they face the sky, simultaneously breathing in *gently* through your nose. Push your palms up

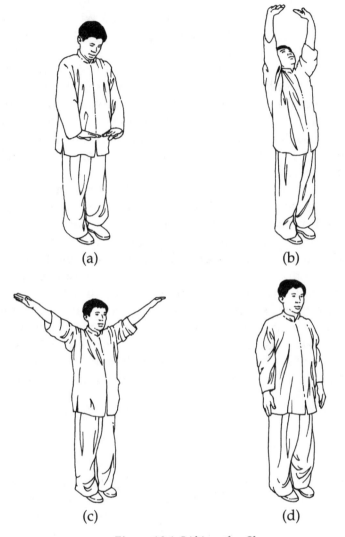

(a)

(b)

(c)

(d)

Figure 18.1 Lifting the Sky

against the sky, and then pause (in breathing as well as action) for a second or two (figure 18.1b).

Next, lower your arms to your sides in a continuous movement (figure 18.1c), breathing out gently through your nose at the same time, until they come to rest near your thighs (figure 18.1d). Pause for a second or two. Repeat the procedure about 10 to 20 times.

For the first few repetitions of the exercise, gently focus on your breathing so that it is well co-ordinated with your move-ment. When you have attained a unity of mind, breathing and movement, you have entered a state of Zen. Continue your exercise in this state of Zen. Then, as you breathe in, visualize good cosmic energy flowing into you, and as you breathe out feel the energy flowing down your whole body and out through your feet into the ground. In this wonderful experience you will feel yourself as an integral part of the cosmos, with the harmonious cosmic energy flow linking you organically with heaven and earth.

After you have repeated the exercise as often as you feel necessary (between 10 and 20 times), drop your arms effortlessly to your sides, close your eyes gently if you have not spon-taneously closed them earlier, stand comfortably upright and relax. Remain in Standing Zen (*Zhan Chan*) for some time (5 to 15 minutes or more) and enjoy the peace and tranquillity. If you are 'ready', you may attain a Zen awakening or satori.

Complete the exercise by rubbing your palms together, dabbing your warm palms on your eyes as you open them, shake yourself loose and then walk about briskly. This is the normal way of ending chi kung and meditation exercises, and this routine should be performed after all the exercises described in this chapter.

Changing Muscles and Tendons

Comparatively speaking, the exercises in Eighteen Lohan Hands are gentle and those in Sinew Metamorphosis forceful. In some respects the terms 'gentle' and 'forceful', being rather poor equivalents of the Chinese *rou* and *gang*, are misleading. Some of the exercises in Eighteen Lohan Hands, for example, can develop tremendous internal strength, and the forceful exercises in Sinew Metamorphosis should be practised in a relaxed manner.

Lifting Heels – from Sinew Metamorphosis

There are twelve exercises in Sinew Metamorphosis, including the one described here known as Lifting Heels.

Stand upright with feet fairly close together and relax. Visualize your body being charged with good cosmic energy. Place the tip of your tongue behind your upper teeth throughout the exercise.

Raise both arms above your head, with your elbows straight but not locked and your upper arms just a few inches from your ears. With the base of your hands facing forwards, clench your fists.

Bend your elbows as if you are pulling yourself up, clenching your fists fairly tightly; feel the power of your arms but do not tense your chest. Simultaneously breathe in gently through your nose and slowly raise your heels to stand on your toes as you pull yourself up (figure 18.2a).

Then slowly lower your heels and straighten your arms; simultaneously breathe out through your mouth, loosen your grip slightly but still maintain a clenched fist (figure 18.2b).

This exercise should be performed 49 times, but initially repeat only about 5 times, then gradually build up. It is very important that you do not strain yourself.

After repeating a suitable number of times, lower your arms to your sides, release your fists, gently straighten your fingers, and with your feet flat on the ground stand comfortably upright with your eyes gently closed. Be totally relaxed. Do not think

(a)   (b)

Figure 18.2 Lifting Heels

of anything, but feel yourself merged with the cosmos. You may feel internal force at your fingers or in other parts of your body, but although you are energized, you are tranquil and at peace. Remain in this Standing Zen position for some time, 5 to 15 minutes or more.

Many students are surprised that such an apparently simple exercise can generate so much internal force and inner peace. If you practise it daily for a few months you may feel that you have changed all your muscles and tendons (which in fact is true, because the cells of your muscles and tendons are being replaced every second).

THE ART OF FLOWING ZEN

Self-Manifested Chi Movement or Induced Chi Flow, known as *Zi Fa Dong Gong* in Chinese, is a genre of chi kung exercise which should be attempted only under the supervision of a master, or at least a competent instructor. Chi kung is the art of training intrinsic energy, and is an excellent introduction to and preparation for spiritual cultivation.

It is not easy for the uninitiated to believe that a form of chi kung such as Self-Manifested Chi Movement is possible. Do you, for example, believe that you can, in full consciousness and with your consent, move without your own volition, or perhaps make comic actions or funny noises? In line with Zen philosophy, you are requested not to accept anything on faith alone, but to have an open attitude and give yourself a chance to experience for yourself one of the marvellous methods of maintaining health and practising Zen.

But before you attempt the self-induced chi flow exercise below (under supervision), it is helpful to be aware of the following three points. One, you will probably be very surprised at your experience and will find it very pleasant. Two, you must not stop your movement abruptly; always bring it to a halt gracefully. Three, there is nothing occult or spiritualistic about this exercise; your movement is due not to an outside force or spirit but to your relaxed condition and your own energy flow. Energy, like blood, is constantly flowing inside you, though you are normally unaware of it; in this exercise your energy flow is enhanced and your perception sharpened.

This set of Self-Manifested Chi Movement consists of three patterns: Turning Head, Green Dragon Presents Claws, and Double Dragons Emerge from the Sea. Practise them in a safe place, away from sharp drops, high windows and pointed corners.

Turning Head

The first pattern consists of three parts. In all three, let your breathing be spontaneous, and keep your mouth slightly open.

Stand upright and relaxed with feet fairly close together. Without moving your shoulders, turn your head to one side as far as comfortably possible, and then turn to the other side (figure 18.3a). Gently visualize that your turning head is gently leading your vertebrae one by one. Perform this horizontal turning three times.

Then, with your head facing to the front and without moving your shoulders, drop your head down as far as possible, and then raise your head back as far as possible, opening your mouth wide as you look upwards and back (figure 18.3b). Gently visualize that every one of your vertebrae is opening and closing gently as you move your head down then up and down three times.

In the third part of this pattern, rotate your head in as big a circle as possible (figure 18.3c), ensuring that you do not move your shoulders. As you rotate your head, gently visualize that your nervous system, which is hanging down like a bunch of roots from your head, is being given a good shake so that all the rubbish falls away. Rotate your head three times to one side, then another three times to the other side.

After completing the three parts of Turning Head, continue with the next pattern.

Green Dragon Presents Claws

Stand with your legs apart in the right Bow and Arrow Stance, and take your left arm forward and your right arm back (figure 18.4a). Imagine that you are holding a ball in each hand, with your left fingers pointing to the front and your right fingers

(a)

(b)

(c)

Figure 18.3 Turning Head

pointing to the back. Breathe out gently through your mouth as you stretch your arms, visualizing that chi or vital energy is flowing out from your fingers.

Next turn to the left and take up the left Bow and Arrow Stance, gently breathing in through your nose. Stretch your right arm out with the fingers pointing forward, and your left arm back with the fingers pointing backward, as shown. Simultaneously breathe out and visualize that chi is flowing out from

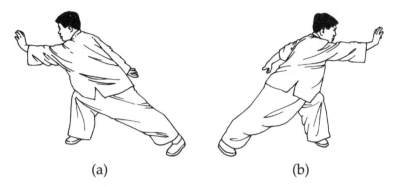

(a)   (b)

Figure 18.4 Green Dragon Present Claws

your fingers (figure 18.4b). Repeat this movement about five to ten times on each side, alternately. Then continue with the next pattern.

Double Dragons Emerge from the Sea

With your feet fairly close together, place your palms, with fingers pointing forward, at your sides at breast level. Stretch both arms forward, with fingers pointing forward, and at the same time bend your body and head forward and breathe out gently through your mouth (figure 18.5a).

Next, bring your palms back to your sides at breast level by bending your elbows back (not sideways), with fingers still pointing in front. Simultaneously bend your body and head backward and breathe in gently through your nose (figure 18.5b). Repeat this movement – pushing your palms forward and bringing them back, together with the accompanying body and head movements and appropriate breathing out and in – about 15 to 20 times.

Then, after pushing your hands forward, drop your arms, stand upright, close your eyes gently and relax. Do not think of anything, but simply let yourself go. You will feel your chi or vital energy flowing inside you. Soon, if you are sufficiently relaxed and let go of everything, the energy flowing inside you may move your body. Do not resist or go against this bodily movement. Just relax and let your body move spontaneously; it is a most pleasant and wonderful experience, and if you are 'ready' you may attain a Zen awakening.

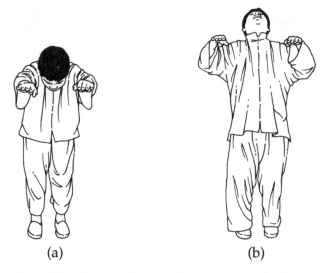

(a)   (b)

Figure 18.5 Double Dragons Emerge from the Sea

Most people sway gracefully in this Self-Manifested Chi Movement exercise; some may even progress to a gentle dance not of their own volition. In some cases, and for various good reasons, practitioners move vigorously or make noises, some of which may be comical or unsettling to the uninitiated, but these reactions are actually manifestations of the cathartic or cleansing effects of the Self-Manifested Chi Movement exercise. However, if a master or a competent instructor is not around, and unless you are already familiar with this kind of chi kung exercise, it is not recommended that you progress to this stage. Thus, if you find that your self-manifested movements are becoming vigorous, you should control them. This can be easily done: just tell yourself gently but firmly to slow down. Your body will obey your mind – this is a cosmic truth.

As with any Self-Manifested Chi Movement exercise, do not finish abruptly. Gently tell yourself to slow down and then come to a graceful stop. With your eyes closed, remain still for some time (which may range from a few seconds to a few minutes), then rub your palms together, warm your eyes with your palms as you open your eyes, and conclude the exercise by walking about briskly.

ABDOMINAL BREATHING

Of the many types of breathing techniques in chi kung training, Abdominal Breathing is the most important because it builds a pearl of energy at the dan tian, or abdominal energy field, which acts as a reservoir from where this energy can be channelled to other parts of the body for various useful purposes. Indeed many experts whose activities require large amounts of energy, like top-class martial artists, runners, swimmers and singers, often develop Abdominal Breathing unconsciously. Abdominal Breathing is also employed in many kinds of religious or mystical disciplines, as in Buddhism and Taoism.

It is advisable that you practise this exercise under the supervision of a master, or at least a competent instructor. You are likely to get more benefits, and in a shorter time, if you learn Abdominal Breathing in stages.

Stage 1

Stand upright with feet fairly close together. Relax totally and clear your mind of all thoughts. Loosen your jaw so that your mouth hangs loosely. Close your eyes gently and smile from your heart. You may continue this Abdominal Breathing exercise with your eyes open or closed.

Place one palm on your abdominal dan tian, (the energy field about 3in below your navel), and place the other palm on top. Gently press down with both palms to deflate your abdomen. Your pressing must be smooth and *continuous*. At the first stage, let your breathing be spontaneous, but do not breathe in as your deflate your abdomen – many people tend to breathe in as they deflate their abdomen, which is a mistake in Abdominal Breathing.

Pause for a second or two after deflating your abdomen. Then gently and *continuously* release the pressure of your palms so that your abdomen rises. Pause for a second or two. Repeat this falling and rising of your abdomen about ten times. Then drop your arms naturally at your sides and gently close your eyes (if you have not already closed them). Do not think of anything during this Standing Meditation, which should last for about five to ten minutes. Complete the exercise by rubbing your palms together to warm them, placing them on your eyes, and dabbing your eyes as you open them. Gently massage your face and then walk about briskly. As you progress you can gradually increase the number of times your abdomen rises and falls, and the length of time for your Standing Meditation.

After you have practised Stage 1 daily for at least a week, but preferably longer, you may proceed to the next stage.

Stage 2

This is the same as the first stage except that as you deflate your abdomen, visualize negative energy flowing out from your abdomen and other parts of your body through your mouth. Then, as you let your abdomen rise, visualize good cosmic energy flowing into your abdomen and other parts of your body through your nose. Your breathing should be spontaneous, but you must ensure that you do not breathe in as you deflate your abdomen. If you make this mistake, not only will you not succeed in Abdominal Breathing, but you may develop unwanted side-effects. Conclude the exercise with Standing Meditation, including its proper completion as described above.

After practising the second stage for at least a week, preferably longer, you may proceed to the final stage.

Stage 3

In this stage, as you deflate your stomach, breathe out gently through your nose, and as you let your abdomen rise, breathe in gently through your mouth. Gently follow your breathing in and out with your mind. In other words, as you breathe out be aware that you are breathing out, and as you breathe in be aware that you are breathing in.

From the perspective of Zen cultivation, this gentle awareness of your breathing in and breathing out is the most important aspect of the exercise. This requirement seems simple, but most people find it one of the hardest things to do. So, after three years of daily practice, if you can accomplish a fairly sustained period of awareness of your gentle breathing in and breathing out, you have accomplished much. This attainment would be an excellent example of 'profundity in simplicity'. As a form of encouragement for your practice, you can take it from me, in my capacity as a Shaolin grandmaster, that if you have mastered this one technique and nothing else – which exemplifies the difference between qualitatively training your mind and quantitatively putting information into your head – you have accomplished more in Zen cultivation than if you had read all the books on Zen put together.

CHI KUNG AND ZEN

Those used to thinking that Zen cultivation involves only sitting meditation or solving gong-ans, may be surprised to learn that practising chi kung is also practising Zen. As has been mentioned many times in this book, the term 'Zen' can be interpreted at three levels: meditation, a cosmic glimpse, or the Supreme Reality. Irrespective of which level we aim at, Zen can be realized through any one of the Shaolin Chi Kung exercises described above.

To be in meditation, the lowest meaning of Zen, is a crucial feature in chi kung practice, although many chi kung students may be ignorant of this important fact. Without 'entering meditation', known as *ru jing* in classical chi kung nomenclature, or *qigong zhuang tai* (chi kung state of mind) in modern chi kung terms, a practitioner cannot achieve good results in any chi kung practice. For example, in the Lifting the Sky exercise described earlier, he would be unable to tap cosmic energy and let it flow down his body; his chi kung would become a mere physical exercise. In the Self-Manifested Chi Movement or Induced Chi Flow exercise, if a practitioner is not in a meditative state of mind, it would be difficult for his vital energy to flow harmoniously.

The training of energy and the training of mind in Shaolin Chi Kung have a mutually beneficial effect: when a practitioner is in a meditative state, his energy effects are enhanced; conversely, the good effects of his energy training lead him to deeper levels of consciousness where he may have glimpses of cosmic reality. As he progresses to the highest level of chi kung, he may achieve cosmic realization.

This becomes clearer and more meaningful if we reflect that, after all, we and everything else in the universe are, in scientific terms, an undifferentiated spread of energy, which may be described variously in different religious terms as emptiness, the great void, Buddhahood, the Ultimate Reality, the Tathagata, Tao, Brahman, or the omnipresent and omniscient (but not the anthropomorphic) God. If energy flow is blocked, in either the micro scale of the human body or the cosmic scale of infinity, its tranquil and undifferentiated nature is interrupted. Chi kung is the art of energy, and its hallmark is harmonious energy flow. Manifested on the human micro scale, it promotes good health; manifested in the cosmic dimension, it breaks down the illusory boundaries caused by human delusion and allows us to attain Zen.

19

THE ZEN OF HIGHEST ATTAINMENT

Meditation of One-Pointedness and of No-Mind

> *In Zen Buddhism and other spiritual disciplines,*
> *training the mind in meditation is used for*
> *supramundane attainment, but many people use*
> *meditation for more mundane purposes.*

MUNDANE AND SUPRAMUNDANE FUNCTIONS OF MEDITATION

Although many people, including many Buddhists, may not be aware of this, meditation is the most important practice in Buddhism because it is the essential path to nirvana. The modern Theravada master, the Venerable Sri Dhammananda, expresses the extensive range of the benefits of meditation as follows:

> The immediate purpose of meditation is to train the mind and use it effectively and efficiently in our daily life. The ultimate aim of meditation is to seek release from the wheel of Samsara – the cycle of life and death.[1]

The beauty and conciseness of the above quotation is better appreciated when we realize that it points the way to the highest attainment in both the mundane and the supramundane dimensions. In our mundane daily life, a trained mind would be more efficacious than an untrained mind for an artist, for example to produce a masterpiece, for a scientist to produce research of far-reaching consequences, or for a philosopher to realize some awe-inspiring truth. Even for ordinary people, a trained mind allows them to achieve better results in whatever mundane tasks they perform.

In Buddhism as well as other religious or spiritual disciplines, a devotee aims to transcend the mundane to attain the supramundane. A trained mind is not only advantageous but often essential for significant supramundane attainment. At lower levels, sometimes it may be possible for a devotee without any mind training to experience the supramundane in, say, a deep feeling of affinity with nature or the presence of God. But to reach higher levels of the supramundane, a trained mind is necessary.

It is important to note the difference between training the mind and merely adding information to the brain. In fact it could be said that the whole of modern, especially Western, education focuses mainly on increasing knowledge rather than mind development! It is common for modern educators to point out that if you want to strengthen your body, you do physical exercise; if you want to strengthen your mind you must do mental exercise. Typically, in the West physical exercise consists of running, stretching and lifting weights, and mental exercise involves studying such disciplines as logic, mathematics and law. From the Shaolin perspective, as well as the perspective of many Eastern traditions, that is putting the cart before the horse. The ability to run, stretch and lift weights is the result of physical strength, not the cause of it; similarly, a trained mind enables a person to do well in the study of such disciplines as logic, mathematics and law, but not the reverse.

It is also useful to realize that a person knowledgeable in mundane or even supramundane matters is not necessarily one with a mind trained for supramundane development. The following saga, which is popular in both the Christian and the Muslim traditions, serves as a good illustration.

A priest, or an imam, sailed to an isolated island and after months of dedicated teaching converted the natives to his religion. Then he sailed home, but as he looked back fondly across the sea at the island he was surprised to see three bright lights skimming over the water towards his boat. As the lights came nearer, he made out three of his most devoted converts. But they were running across the sea towards him!

When they were close to the boat they said, 'Our Holiness, we have forgotten whether to say Amin or Amen after our prayers to the Lord. Please teach us before you go back so that we can say our prayers correctly.' Touched to the point of tears by their devotion, his Holiness said, 'My good men, don't worry whether it is Amin or Amen, but continue to pray in the way you have been for you have attained a spiritual level much higher than I have.'

How can we train for spiritual development? Through meditation. Meditation is the training of the mind to reach higher states of reality where the meditator becomes aware that he is more than his physical self. It is not necessarily practised while sitting in a lotus position, although many spiritual disciplines, such as Buddhism, Taoism and yoga, recommend this for the highest achievement. There are two principal aspects in mind training: focusing the mind, and letting the mind expand. In Zen Buddhism as well as other spiritual disciplines, training the mind in meditation is used for supramundane attainment, but many people use meditation for more mundane purposes.

FAILURE TO UNDERSTAND THE SUPRAMUNDANE

The failure to differentiate between the supramundane and the mundane functions of meditation has led to much confusion among scholars and scientists. It is surprising, for example, that A V Grimstone, the editor of Katsuki Sekida's highly recommended book, *Zen Training: Methods and Philosophy*, should say:

> The aim of Zen training is not markedly different from what has been identified by some Western writers as the correct object of moral effort.[2]

If this were true, people, including kings and princes, would not need to renounce their mundane lives to practise Zen. (Indeed, it could be said that the powers of kings contribute to the cultivation and spread of moral values, which are in the mundane dimension.) It is surprising for Grimstone to believe that 'Zen training is a means of enabling us to live our ordinary lives supremely well'[3] and nothing more, because there are many instances in Katsuki Sekida's book to indicate that Zen training aims beyond ordinary lives and mundane morality:

> By stilling the activity of our mind, a state is reached in which time, space, and causation, which constitute the framework of consciousness, drop away. We call this condition 'body and mind fallen off.'[4]

> Such a state of looking simultaneously both into one's own nature and into universal nature can be attained only when consciousness is deprived of its habitual way of thinking.[5]

As Grimstone is aware of these statements of the Zen master, probably he does not realize that a state 'in which time, space, and causation, which constitute the framework of consciousness, drop away', and 'when consciousness is deprived of its habitual way of thinking', refers to a supramundane dimension very different from our everyday mundane world.

But what is the supramundane? It refers to ultimate reality, which is of course beyond the mundane, everyday, phenomenal world perceived by ordinary consciousness. This is what the distinguished parapsychologist, Lawrence LeShan, called 'clairvoyant reality', as distinguished from our everyday sensory reality. In the former, according to Einstein's general relativity and unified field theory:

> the entire universe appears as one elemental field in which each star, each atom, each wandering comet and slow-wheeling galaxy and flying electron is seen to be but a ripple or tumescence in the underlying space-time unity.[6]

Yet Lawrence LeShan says:

> A person cannot live fully consciously aware of the Clairvoyant Reality for any length of time. One would not survive biologically in this way for very long. To live completely consciously unaware of it, however, makes man less than he can be, and robs him of much of his potential.[7]

Lawrence LeShan believes that no one could survive for long in clairvoyant reality because there is no differentiation into separate entities, and time and space do not exist. Perhaps, had he known that in Zen teaching, what he calls clairvoyant reality is ultimate reality, the realization of which represents the supreme aim of Zen practitioners and many other spiritual cultivators, Lawrence LeShan would have felt able both to survive biologically in the mundane dimension and to attain his full potential in the supramundane.

Tomio Hirai, who has spent 20 years studying the scientific basis of Zen meditation, and who concludes that 'Zen is a rich source of emancipation from the severe social conditions of modern times for the layman as well as for the priest',[8] says, rather amazingly:

> I do not believe that Zen meditation alone can lead to an enlightened condition. Under no religious faith or tenet can enlightenment, once achieved, be universal . . .
>
> Enlightenment is personal and can be many things to many different people. The state that Henry David Thoreau experienced as a result of his more than two years by Walden Pond can be called enlightenment, as can the reflection of reality of the Hippies. Professor Kouji Sato has described the ecstatic state experienced by people who use the alcaloide compound known as LSD 25 as identical to Zen enlightenment. If this is true, the formula Hippy life + LSD 25 could equal a shortcut to the ultimate goal of Zen.[9]

It is obvious that Dr Tomio Hirai not only fails to understand the purpose of Zen meditation and the meaning of Zen enlightenment, but is also unfamiliar with the basic teaching of Zen Buddhism. Everyone, including Dr Tomio Hirai, has a right to an opinion, but it is sweeping to say that all Zen monks who insisted on having reached enlightenment were deluded. In the first place, the onus of Zen Buddhism is on practice, not research. Hence if Dr Tomio Hirai were to ask a Zen master whether he knew the pattern of his brain waves (which happens to be the doctor's research topic), a typical answer to help the doctor attain an awakening might be 'Go and wash your face!'

While a knowledge of brain-wave patterns or any research may be useful to someone for mundane purposes, it is not only unnecessary but even detrimental to Zen meditation practice, for it binds the mind or brain to the phenomenal, mundane world which he aims to transcend. It is indeed interesting to note that while many scientists as well as ordinary people regard our phenomenal world as objectively real, and Zen practitioners and other spiritual cultivators as victims of delusion, in actual fact it is the other way round. The latest discoveries (or rediscoveries) in physics, psychology and other sciences have confirmed that our phenomenal world is an illusion, a creation of our mind according to a set of conditions. Meditation provides the essential means for Zen practitioners and other spiritual cultivators to be emancipated from this delusion and realize ultimate cosmic reality.

It is irresponsible and misleading to suggest, as Dr Tomio Hirai does elsewhere, that ego and greed cannot be surpassed; in fact a primary objective of the teaching of Zen and all other Buddhist schools is the overcoming of ego and greed, because these two factors hinder a cultivator in his realization of cosmic reality. Enlightenment is the term used to describe this cosmic realization, and it is universal, for unlike the phenomenal world which appears differently to different beings according to their different conditions, ultimate reality transcends the knower and the known and is the same to all enlightened beings. Dr Tomio Hirai, evidently, has failed to distinguish the supramundane from the mundane.

VARIOUS TYPES OF BUDDHIST MEDITATION

Buddhism is exceedingly rich in meditation methods that lead to the supramundane. The ultimate goal of meditation is always the same, that of attaining enlightenment, but since aspirants have many differences – background, environment, development stages, training facilities and so on – the appropriate meditation method varies. Generally speaking, of the three traditions of Buddhism, Theravada places emphasis on achieving a one-pointed mind, Mahayana on focusing on the void, and Vajrayana on visualization. But these are broad generalizations: a Theravadin, for some particular reason, may use more visualization in his meditation than a Vajrayanist.

For the convenience of better understanding, Buddhist meditation, irrespective of whether it is from the Theravada, Mahayana or Vajrayana tradition, is frequently divided into two principal kinds: samadha or tranquil meditation, and vispasyana or insight meditation. The main objective of the former is to concentrate the mind, and of the latter to employ the concentrated mind to investigate cosmic reality. Masters have always said that this division is made purely for convenience, and can sometimes be arbitrary: there is actually only one meditation, with the mind first passing through a calm and concentrated state in samadha, then experiencing direct insight of the ultimate in vispasyana.

Zen meditation is in some ways different from either samadha or vispasyana meditation, and also different from the attaining of a one-pointed mind, the focusing on the void, or the visualization techniques of mainstream Theravada, Mahayana and Vajrayana schools. Zen meditation aims at no-mind, which is actually all mind. It is often said that Zen cultivation is outside the tradition (of Theravada, Mahayan or Vajrayana) and points directly at the mind (without first going through samadha and vispasyana). Hence Zen's method is the fastest and most direct and is often regarded as 'attaining Buddhahood in an instant', but, of course, the aspirant must be ready. If he is not ready, it would be better for him to use other methods, of which there are many.

When is a person ready for Zen meditation in order to attain the supramundane, the highest spiritual achievement? When he is able to focus his mind. If his mind is still prone to wandering, as are most untrained minds, his time could be better spent on practising meditation to calm and concentrate the mind. But even before this, if he is serious about meditation for spiritual cultivation, he should be physically and psychologically healthy, with a sound understanding of what he is aiming at. In addition he should be morally and spiritually upright, which includes, among other things, never harbouring any evil intentions towards others or using his spiritual powers to harm any beings. It is a universal truth that if a person is not morally and spiritually upright, the more powers he acquires from meditation, the more likely he is to ruin himself. If he is not ready, even if his intention is genuine and sincere, his progress on the spiritual or supramundane path will be slow, although he will derive much benefit in the mundane dimension.

An understanding of these various types of Buddhist meditation is helpful in our cultivation, but we should remember that the classification into various types is for convenience only, and sometimes there is much overlapping. Actually the word 'meditation' is not a good choice for it often has connotations of employing the mind to think of something. In Chinese, what is referred to here as 'meditation' is zuo-chan, rendered into Japanese as zazen, both of which mean 'sitting in the lotus position to cultivate towards the realization of cosmic reality'. Probably because of the linguistic and cultural differences of these words, Philip Kapleau comments:

> Such mind exercises as counting or following the breath cannot, strictly speaking, be called meditation since they do not involve visualization of an object or reflection upon an idea. For the same reasons koan zazen cannot be called meditation. Whether one is striving to achieve unity with his koan or, for instance, intensely asking, 'What is Mu?' he is not meditating in the technical sense of this world.[10]

ATTAINING A ONE-POINTED MIND IN TATHAGATA ZEN

The best way to practise meditation is to train under a master, and the best way to gain information on meditation is to study the teachings of various masters. The following teaching on attaining a one-pointed mind – taught by the greatest master, the Buddha himself – is recorded in the *Satipatthana Sutta*, or Scripture on the Foundation of Mindfulness,[11] and is highly valued in Theravada Buddhism:

> Bhikkhus, this is the direct path for the purification of beings, for the surmounting of sorrow and lamentation, for the disappearance of pain and grief, for the attainment of the true way, for the realisation of Nibbana – namely, the four foundations of mindfulness.
> What are the four? Here, bhikkhus, a bhikkhu abides contemplating the body as a body, ardent, fully aware, and mindful, having put away covetousness and grief for the world. He abides contemplating feelings as feelings, ardent, fully aware, and mindful, having put away covetousness and grief for the world. He abides contemplating mind as mind, ardent, fully aware, and mindful, having put away covetousness and grief for the world. He abides contemplating mind-objects as mind-objects, ardent, fully aware, and mindful, having put away covetousness and grief for the world.

The four famous foundations of mindfulness used by many Buddhists to attain the highest spiritual goal are mindfulness of the body, mindfulness of feelings, mindfulness of mind, and mindfulness of mind-objects. In the *Satipatthana Sutta*, the

Buddha continues to explain how these four foundations can be attained:

> And how, bhikkhus, does a bhikkhu abide contemplating the body as a body? Here a bhikkhu, gone to the forest or to the root of a tree or to an empty hut, sits down; having folded his legs crosswise, set his body erect, and established mindfulness in front of him, ever mindful he breathes in, mindful he breathes out. Breathing in long, he understands: 'I breathe in long'; or breathing out long, he understands: 'I breathe out long.' Breathing in short, he understands: 'I breathe in short'; or breathing out short, he understands: 'I breathe out short.'

In other words, in his meditation practice, the aspirant gently focuses his attention on his breathing. In the process of his natural breathing during the meditation, when he breathes in or breathes out a long or a short breath, he is mindful of what he is doing. In this way he attains a one-pointed mind, he accomplishes the objective of samadha meditation.

He should maintain this samadha or mindfulness state not only in his formal sitting meditation, but also when he is walking, standing and lying down:

> Again, bhikkhus, when walking, a bhikkhu understands: 'I am walking'; when standing, he understands: 'I am standing'; when sitting, he understands: 'I am sitting'; when lying down he understands: 'I am lying down'; or he understands accordingly however his body is disposed.

With his one-pointed mind derived from samadha meditation, the aspirant now progresses to investigate his body in vispasyana meditation. He contemplates on the various parts of his body, such as hair, nails, teeth, skin, flesh, bones, marrow and internal organs, as well as on the four 'elements' of 'earth', 'water', 'fire' and 'air' that make up the body. Hence the aspirant is mindful of his body as a body.

In the same way, the aspirant becomes mindful of his feelings, mind and mind-objects. When a pleasant or a painful feeling arises during meditation, or his daily life, he is aware of that particular feeling. When his mind is affected, or unaffected, by lust, hate or delusion, for example, he is aware of it. When objects or images arise or are extinguished in his mind, the aspirant is aware of them. These mind-objects include the five hindrances (sensual desire, ill will, sloth and torpor, doubt, and distraction), the five aggregates (form, feeling, perception, activity and consciousness), the six bases (eye and form, ear and sound, nose and odour, tongue and taste, body and feeling, mind and consciousness), the seven enlightenment factors (mindfulness, investigation, effort, bliss, tranquillity, concentration and equanimity), and the Four Noble Truths (of suffering, of the origin of suffering, of the cessation of suffering, and of the Eightfold Path leading to the cessation of suffering).

When an aspirant in his samadha meditation is mindful of his body, feelings, mind and mind-objects, and in his vispasyana meditation acquires the insight that all these are ultimately transient and illusory, he will attain enlightenment. According to the Buddha, if a person practises these four foundations of mindfulness for seven years, or even for seven days, 'one of two fruits could be expected for him: either final knowledge here and now, or if there is a trace of clinging left, non-return'. That is, either he attains *anuttara-samyak-sambodhi* or the realization of ultimate cosmic reality here and now, or, if there is a trace of desire in him which results in him being reborn, he will return not to our human realm but to some heavenly or higher realms where he can continue his spiritual quest. This type of meditation to attain cosmic reality, as taught by the Buddha to most people, is known as Tathagata Zen.

SEEING THE ORIGINAL FACE IN PATRIARCH ZEN

The type of meditation practised in most Zen monasteries is not Tathagata Zen but Patriarch Zen, taught by the First Patriarch Bodhidharma. But before a person embarks on Patriarch Zen, he should have attained a one-pointed mind; if he has not, it is recommended that he practise mindfulness in breathing as taught by the Buddha and described above. The crucial point about Patriarch Zen is pointing directly at the mind, or 'looking straight at the original face', which is a Zen phrase for attaining a realization of cosmic reality without the prior need to investigate or to eliminate thoughts, because if an aspirant is without the delusion caused by arising thoughts (which in turn differentiate him as a separate entity), he is actually the undifferentiated cosmic reality. That is why the great Japanese Zen master Dogen

stresses that when you practise Patriarch Zen, you are not cultivating to become a Buddha; you are a Buddha.

One of the best pieces of advice on seeing the original face,
or attaining enlightenment, was given by the great 14th-century
Rinzai master, Daito Kokushi (1281–1337), to the Japanese
Emperor Hanazono:

> All Zen students should devote themselves at the beginning to *zazen*
> (sitting in meditation). Sitting in either the fully locked position or
> the half-locked position, with the eyes half-shut, see the original
> face which was before father or mother was born. This means to
> see the state before the parents were born, before heaven and earth
> were parted, before you received human form. What is called the
> original face will appear. The original face is without colour or
> form, like the empty sky in whose clarity there is no form.
>
> The original face is really nameless, but it is indicated by such
> terms as original face, the Lord, the Buddha nature, and the true
> Buddha. ['Original face' is a Zen term for enlightenment.] The sev-
> enteen hundred koans or themes to which Zen students devote
> themselves are all only for making them see their original face. The
> World-honoured One sat in meditation in the snowy mountains for
> six years, then saw the morning star and was enlightened, and this
> was seeing his original face. When it is said of others of the ancients
> that they had a great realization, or a great breaking-through, it
> means they saw the original face. The Second Patriarch stood in the
> snow and cut off his arm to get realization; the Sixth Patriarch heard
> the phrase from the Diamond Sutra and was enlightened. Reiun
> was enlightened when he saw the peach blossoms, Kyogen on
> hearing the tile hit the bamboo, Rinzai when struck by Obaku,
> Tozan on seeing his own reflection in the water.[12]

But how do you practise to see the original face? The master
explains:

> Every time a thought arises, throw it away. Just devote yourself
> to sweeping away the thoughts. Sweeping away thoughts means
> performing zazen. When thought is put down, the original face
> appears.[13]

It is not easy to find another teaching that is more simple and
direct, or more effective. Indeed, it is so bafflingly simple that
many people find it hard to believe. A lot has been written on
Zen meditation, but the essence of its practice is this: 'Sit in the

lotus position and keep the mind free from all thought.' This was what my own master told me when he taught me Zen meditation. Even if you forget everything else in this chapter, just practise this 'essence'. It takes less than a minute to read, less than five minutes to be fully understood, yet may take more than ten years or ten lifetimes to accomplish. But if you are ready, it can be realized in an instant. The essence of Zen meditation is to cut off thought. There are many ways to achieve this objective, but they can be generalized into two principal methods: silent-illuminating-Zen and public-case-Zen (or koan Zen). Koan Zen will be discussed in the next chapter; the following method of silent-illuminating-Zen is taught by the modern Soto Zen master Takashina Rosen, who is also the current president of the Japanese Buddhist Association:

> There are several methods, but the Zen method is to sit in the meditation posture and swell with our breath and vitality what is called 'the field of the elixir' [the abdomen below the navel]. In this way the whole frame is invigorated. Then we meditate, discarding body and mind. Now the delusions which are the impure heart come up without ceasing. We should make these fancies, coming one after another, the koan [theme] of our meditation. What, after all, is this thought? Where did it come from? We penetrate with the spear-point of our meditation to the source of the successive fancies.
>
> When we practise sitting in this way regularly and make progress in meditation, then of itself the meditation becomes deeper and fuller until there is no room for the fancies to show their heads. The practice is quite unrestricted, and the entry into the experience of truth is also unrestricted; in the end appears the glory of the true self, where the practice *is* the realization. This is called seeing one's true face, and it is said that nine out of ten people can achieve it [in this very life].[14]

There are two parts in the above method. Firstly, focus the breathing at the abdomen. This will calm and concentrate the mind, attaining the objective of samadha meditation. When thoughts arise, investigate them with the calm, concentrated mind. Ask what these thoughts are, and where they come from. This will result in insight, which is the objective of vispasyana meditation.

Secondly, when you have made progress in samadha and vispasyana meditation, continue the meditation practice spontaneously, without any thoughts arising. This is what is called *shikan-taza*, which means in Japanese 'merely sitting in meditation', a technique the great Dogen learned in China and popularized in Japan. When the time is ripe, the glory of your true self will appear – you will attain a Zen awakening or even an enlightenment.

20

ILLOGICAL ZEN – OR SO IT SEEMS

Zen Cultivation Through the Gong-Ans

The gong-ans are an ingenious technique uniquely employed in Zen to break down the illusion in order to realize ultimate reality.

RECORDS OF ILLOGICAL ZEN ENCOUNTERS

There is a misconception, especially in the West, that Zen is nothing but gong-ans which involve giving illogical answers to logical questions – or so it seems. If a Zen student asks a Zen master 'Where is the Buddha?', he may answer with: 'Three pounds of flax', or 'Your mouth is the opening of suffering', or 'If I see him I will kill him'! These formidable puzzles are made even worse by the fact that many books on Zen in the West not only never explain the significance of the gong-an but are themselves like gigantic gong-ans. See if you can make any sense of the following quotation from Daisetz Teitaro Suzuki's *An Introduction to Zen Buddhism*, one of the most influential books on Zen in the West, but which tends to mystify rather than explain Zen.

> A monk asked, 'According to Vimalakirti, one who wishes for the Pure Land ought to have his mind purified; but what is the purified mind?' Answered the Zen master: 'When the mind is absolutely pure, you have a purified mind, and a mind is said to be absolutely pure when it is above purity and impurity. You want to know how this is to be realized? Have your mind thoroughly void in all conditions, then you will have purity. But when this is attained, do

not harbour any thought of it, or you get non-purity. Again, when this state of non-purity is attained, do not harbour any thought of it, and you are free of non-purity. This is absolute purity.[1]

Here the Zen master, Yuan Wu (Yengo in Japanese) has given an exceptionally clear explanation on purity, and Suzuki has translated it exceptionally well. If you have read my book up to this point, you should have no difficulty understanding the above quotation; in fact, this realization of purity, or no-mind, was described in some detail in the previous chapter. But for most people it would be bewildering. Why, for example, does your purified mind become impure when you harbour any thought of purity, and why does this state of non-purity become free from non-purity when you do not harbour any thought of it? The quotation is not even a gong-an, as it seeks to explain something simply and clearly.

A gong-an is also stated simply and clearly. As Suzuki says, 'There is no quibbling, no playing on words, no sophistry. Zen is the most serious concern in the world.'[2] The crucial difference between a gong-an and the above quotation on purity and non-purity is that a gong-an is directed to the intuition and is meant to trigger off a Zen awakening, whereas the quotation, like most other writings, is directed to the intellect and is meant to explain something. A gong-an is never meant to explain anything.

When a master gives seemingly illogical answers, it is never his intention to tell the enquirer where, who or what the Buddha is; his intention is to awaken the student to a glimpse of cosmic reality. When the master says 'Three pounds of flax', his intention is to provoke the student's mind into realizing that the answer could be five pounds, 200 pounds or any unit of measurement of flax, jute or anything; it can be anything or everything. In other words, the Buddha is everywhere.

By saying 'Your mouth is the opening of suffering' the master wants to provoke a realization that the onus of Zen is on direct experience, not intellectual discussion. As soon as the student opens his mouth to speak, he uses words and this results in ideas, therefore perpetuating the process of the phenomenal world of suffering. The aim of Zen is to attain the mind of non-thought, and this is accomplished through dedicated practice, not intellectualization.

The Buddha manifests in three bodies: the transformational

body, the reward body and the spiritual body. The transformational body of the Buddha refers to the myriad individual entities of the phenomenal world which are actually an illusion. The reward body is the divine form of the personalized Buddha in the astral realm, seen by spiritually advanced persons as a reward for their cultivation. It corresponds to the anthropomorphic image of God in Christianity and other theistic religions. Although it is supramundane, it is still in the phenomenal dimension. The spiritual body of the Buddha is the ultimate cosmic reality, tranquil and undifferentiated, the realization of which is the supreme aim of Buddhism. Thus, 'when I see the Buddha, I will kill him' means that I will earnestly cultivate so that rather than seeing the transformational or reward bodies of the Buddha I will experience the Buddha's spiritual body – that is, cosmic reality as undifferentiated without any visible form.

One should understand that such Zen encounters were not directed to just anybody, but to Zen students who had spent years in a Zen monastery, meditating and listening to daily sermons of Zen masters. In other words, the students were well prepared, and such seemingly illogical sayings represented an ingenious technique on the part of the master to help them attain an awakening. The sayings were never meant to give a literal answer to where, who or what the Buddha was, because the students already knew the literal answer very well. These encounters between masters and students were recorded by special clerks, and have been passed down to posterity as gong-ans.

ZEN ENCOUNTERS THAT ARE NOT GONG-ANS

If a layman, without the preparation of a Zen student, asks a Zen master a similar question, he is unlikely to receive a gong-an type of answer. For example, Emperor Soon Zong of the Tang dynasty asked the Zen master Ru Man, in poetic style:

> From where did the Buddha come,
> To where did the Buddha go?
> If the Buddha is still around,
> Where can be the Buddha found?

The master replied in the same style:

> From non-activity the Buddha came
> To non-activity the Buddha disappeared.
> Cosmic reality his spiritual body is,
> In no-mind the Buddha will appear.

The emperor was himself well versed in Buddhist teaching. He further asked:

> Great mountains, rivers and seas,
> Heaven and earth, sun and moon.
> Who says there is no birth and death?
> For even these meet their end soon.

The Venerable Ru Man replied:

> Birth is also before birth,
> Death is also before death.
> If you have attained no-mind,
> Naturally there will be nothing left.[3]

Although the above questions and responses seem Zen-like, and are not easily understood by many people, they are not gong-ans, because they were intended not to trigger intuitively a Zen awakening in the emperor, but to explain to him intellectually where the Buddha can be found, and why ultimately there is no life and death. The master's answer, typical of Zen, was simple, direct and effective, and phrased to suit the listener and the occasion. But if you do not understand the answer, it is because it was not meant for you. If someone without the background knowledge of the emperor had asked the master the same question, he would have given the same answer but in different words, perhaps as follows:

Cosmic reality in its ultimate nature is when no activities of the phenomenal world have started to arise. In other words, ultimate reality exists before the myriad phenomena of the universe have been formed. But how are phenomena formed? They are formed when human minds create them. Thus, as soon as thoughts which generate activities arise, ultimate reality disappears and manifests as the phenomenal world. Ultimate cosmic reality is called the spiritual body of the Buddha. It is the same cosmos, but manifested in two dimensions, namely the phenomenal and the ultimate. When there are thoughts giving rise to myriad phenomena, we experience the cosmos as the phenomenal world. When there is no mind, or no thoughts arise, we experience the same cosmos as ultimate reality.

When we see mountains, rivers and seas, heaven and earth, the sun and the moon, we experience the phenomenal world, which is actually an illusion. The mountains, rivers, seas, heaven, earth, sun, moon and all other phenomena are only relatively real, not ultimately real. These phenomena which appear relatively real to us, may not appear to other beings who also inhabit our universe at the same time, but who operate in a different set of conditions, such as having different types of eyes or minds, that is, if they ever have eyes or minds at all. Similarly, when these mountains, seas and other phenomena disappear in due time, their disappearance is only meaningful to us relative to our sensual perception. To other beings with a different nature or range of sensual perception, the disappearance of these phenomena would never have happened. All these phenomena are creations of the mind. If you attain the state of no-mind, these phenomena will not occur or exist; you would experience the same cosmos as ultimate reality, where there is no difference between the subject and the object, no difference between the knower and the known.

GONG-ANS AND PARADOXES

Gong-ans are not paradoxes, although they may appear to be so. A paradox is a statement that appears absurd or contradictory although it is based on truth, such as 'the child is the father of the man' or 'a man's stomach is outside his body'. A gong-an is a direct statement of cosmic truth without any conscious attempt to make it appear absurd or self-contradictory, although it may sometimes appear paradoxical to the uninitiated. There is, however, nothing paradoxical in the reply 'Three pounds of flax' to the question 'Where is the Buddha?', although it appears non-sensible to many people.

It is illuminating to compare gong-ans with paradoxes to understand what gong-ans are not. Among the Chinese philosophical schools, the *Ming Jia* or Dialecticians, who flourished during the period of Warring States (480–221 BC), were well known for paradoxes. Ming Jia means the School of Names, for their dialectics depended mainly on the play of names or words, as the following examples illustrate:

1 Different things are the same; similar things are different.
2 The sun at noon is the sun declining; the creature born is the creature dying.
3 A dog may be a sheep.
4 A white dog is black.
5 A fowl has three legs.
6 The shadow of a flying bird never moves.

These paradoxes are often mistaken for Taoist sayings because Chuang Tzu, the great Taoist master of the 4th century BCE, mentioned some of them in his book, also called *Chuang Tzu*. Some people, having only a superficial knowledge of the paradoxes, cite them as forerunners of the gong-ans, in support of their mistaken claim that Zen was developed from Taoism. But a deeper investigation will show that they are very different.

The Dialecticians' paradox relies on the use, or more appropriately the abuse, of language, whereas the Zen gong-an explicitly distrusts the use of language, regarding verbalization as at best only an imitation of reality. As examples of the first paradox type above, the Dialectician may argue that because a table and a chair both have four legs, a table is the same as a chair. Or, a cat has a tail, a cat has a head; a tail is different from a head; therefore a cat is different from a cat. Such logic, of course, is never used in Zen. Indeed, Zen often considers logic, which places much value on verbalization and intellectualization, a waste of time. If a student were to argue with a Zen master that a table is a chair, or a cat is not a cat, the master would probably strike him or shout at him to stop him from further verbalization.

As evident from the above, the Dialecticians' argument is often shallow, sometimes unreasonable, and therefore their statements cannot be strictly called paradoxes, but it is difficult for their opponents to refute them. Zen gong-ans, on the other hand, are often too deep even for highly intelligent people, and the question of argument never arises. But it would be wrong to believe that the Dialecticians themselves or their listeners were unaware of the shallowness or unreasonableness of the argument, because many of the Dialecticians were scholars and scientists of high repute. The crucial point is that they argued just for the sake of argument.

Chuang Tzu criticized his friend and rival, Hui Shi, who was a famous Dialectician, saying that although Hui Shi's scholarship was extensive, the logic of the paradoxes could only stop people's mouths from further argument but could not convince their hearts. If they argued in this way, they would come to no conclusion even if they argued their whole life long.[4]

Let us look briefly at the Dialecticians' logic. When the sun reaches its highest point at noon, it starts to descend; when any creature is born it will one day die. Therefore the sun at noon is the sun declining, and the creature born is the creature dying. A dog has skin, and fur grows on its skin; a sheep has skin, but wool grows on its skin. Therefore a dog may be a sheep, or it may not be. A white dog has black eyes; its eyes are black; the dog's eyes are black, not white or blue or green. Therefore the dog is black, and since it is a white dog, a white dog is black. Speaking of 'a fowl's legs' makes one, which added to its two legs makes three; thus a fowl has three legs. The shadow of a flying bird never moves: it is the flying bird that moves, not its shadow.

Hence, the Dialecticians use words and paradoxes to mislead and discredit their opponents; Zen masters avoid using words. Unlike Confucianists who regard names as important, Zen Buddhists say that at their best words and names give only an imperfect concept. If paradoxes in the form of gong-ans are used, they are meant to enlighten.

Perhaps the most important difference, though it is not easily noticeable, is that paradoxes deal with the phenomenal world, whereas gong-ans point towards ultimate reality. The sun, the dog, the fowl, the flying bird and all other entities used in the paradoxes are phenomena, an illusion, but the Dialecticians and their opponents treat them as objectively real. The gong-ans are an ingenious technique uniquely employed in Zen to break down the illusion in order to realize ultimate reality.

GONG-ANS AS A TRAINING TOOL

Initially the gong-an was used by a master as the catalyst to trigger a Zen awakening in a student or to test whether he was already awakened. Thus, in 527, when asked by Emperor Liang Wu Di who he was, the great Bodhidharma said 'Don't know!' The emperor, despite his tremendous blessings accumulated by his numerous good works in promoting Buddhism, was not ready, and therefore missed the opportunity provided by Bodhidharma to have a glimpse of cosmic reality. But at the Shaolin Monastery when Hui Ke asked Bodhidharma to calm his mind, the master said, 'Bring out your mind and I'll calm it' Hui Ke was ready, and so he had a Zen awakening.

It was much later that the Song dynasty Zen master Da Hui Zong Guo (1089–1163) developed the gong-an as a training tool. After being dissatisfied with the silent-illuminating-Zen of the Cao Dong (Soto) school which he first practised, Da Hui turned to the Lin Ji (Rinzai) school where he meditated on the *huatou* (*mondo* in Japanese), or crucial point, of various gong-ans. Regarding how an aspirant could use a gong-an to attain a Zen awakening, Da Hui says:

> Push intellectualization and delusion right to the bottom of your heart; all thought and differentiation to the bottom of your heart; the desire to live and the fear of death to the bottom of your heart; opinions and explanations to the bottom of your heart; silliness and activity to the bottom of your heart. At once push all down; nothing else but just push them down; then look at the *huatou*, or crucial point. A monk asked Zhao Zhou: Has a dog Buddha nature or not? Zhao Zhou said no. This single word 'no' is the tool that breaks down countless instances of intellectualization and distraction.[5]

Thus, Gong-an Zen, or Koan Zen in Japanese, is also known as kan hua-tou, which means looking at the crucial point of the gong-an. It is the hua-tou or crucial point that is important; the gong-an, or public case history of a Zen encounter when, usually, someone experiences an awakening, merely serves as a background. For example, in the all-important gong-an of Zhao Zhou's No, who the enquirer or Zhao Zhou was, where or when the encounter took place, or why they referred to a dog and not an elephant or a table, is not significant. It is not even significant why Zhao Zhou's answer was 'no', or what would have happened had he said 'yes'. All these things are unimportant, all that matters is that the aspirant, both during his meditation and at all other times, must put his whole mind, his whole life, into 'no'.

As masters constantly advised, the aspirant must *not* attempt to reason or use his intellect in any way; he should not think, but intensely look 'psychically' at the hua-tou. Many people, especially those used to the Western concept of the supreme intellect, wonder why intellectualization cannot be used; Western philosophy, they may argue, is virtually intellectualization. The simple yet profound answer is that any form of intellectualization will bind the aspirant to the phenomenal world, which Zen cultivation aims to transcend. As soon as any thought arises, it will activate the process of transforming the undifferentiated ultimate reality into differentiated ideas and entities.

When an aspirant continues to look at the hua-tou, he will develop doubt. The modern Chinese master, the Venerable Sheng Yan, who had part of his training at Shaolin Monastery and now teaches Zen in America, says:

> When we use *hua-tou* to cultivate, we want to find out what it is that existed before spoken or written language or symbol is used to describe it. At the start of cultivation there is no doubt to talk about. It is only when you have used this method well to cultivate, that doubt arises in you. When your cultivation becomes more and more intense, your doubt becomes bigger and bigger. In such a situation, you become unaware of your own body, become unaware of everything in the world. There is only one thing left, and that is doubt, the great doubt. When people have great doubt, and if they also have good spiritual roots, irrespective of whether a master is present or not, they will attain an awakening. However, for those whose spiritual roots are weak, a master is required, otherwise they may fall into the realm of delusion.[6]

CULTIVATING WITH GONG-ANS

The two most widely practised schools of Zen today are Cao Dong or Soto Zen and Lin Ji or Rinzai Zen. In Soto Zen, meditation is the principal means of cultivation, whereas Rinzai Zen focuses on gong-ans. It is sometimes thought, erroneously, that Rinzai Zen does not pay attention to meditation. Even Daisetz

Teitaro Suzuki, the Japanese Rinzai master who generally regards zazen as secondary to koan solving, says:

> In Zen, Dhyana or *zazen* is used as the means of reaching the solution of the *koan*. Zen does not make Dhyana an end in itself, for apart from the koan exercise, the practice of *zazen* is a secondary consideration. It is no doubt a necessary accompaniment to the mastery of Zen; even when the *koan* is understood, its deep spiritual truth will not be driven home to the mind of the Zen student if he is not thoroughly trained in *zazen*.[7]

To a large extent many people have this mistaken concept because many books on Zen, especially in the West, give interesting descriptions of koans, without explaining that they were generally addressed only to students who had spent many years in meditation.

If you wish to use gong-ans or koans as your main method of Zen cultivation, choose a gong-an you like from this book, and meditate on its hua-tou or crucial point – that is, look at it with all your might, but do not think about it or apply reason or any intellectual activity to it. As well as meditating formally on your gong-an when in the lotus position, focus on it at all other times too and regard it as the most important thing in your life.

Here are three further gong-ans for you to choose from.

One day the master, Wei Shan, told his students: One hundred years from now I shall be reborn on this mountain as a bull, with the words 'This is Wei Shan so and so' clearly written on my shoulder. If you call me Wei Shan, I am actually a bull; if you call me a bull, I am actually Wei Shan. What will you call me?

Zhan Yuan was Dao Wu's personal attendant. One day Zhan Yuan served tea to his master. Dao Wu wanted to test whether the student's mind was dualistic, so holding the cup of tea he asked, 'Is it good or bad?' Zhan Yuan rounded his eyes and stared hard at his master without replying. 'If it is good, it is good; if it is bad, it is bad,' Dao Wu said. 'I don't see it this way!' Zhan Yuan retorted; then snatching the cup of tea from his master, he asked in return, 'Is it good or bad?' The master laughed heartily and said, 'I am proud of you as my personal attendant.'

Wei Yan was meditating on a high rock. Shi Tou asked him, 'Why are you meditating here?'

'Not because of anything.'

'Then you are sitting for nothing.'

'If I say I'm sitting for nothing,' Wei Yan replied, 'there is already a motive for my sitting.'

Shi Tou asked again, 'Then what is it that you referred to as without motive?'

'Hundreds of thousands of sages also do not know what that without motive is.'

Shi Tou was very pleased with Wei Yan.

21

THE ZEN OF COMPASSION

Chanting Sutras and Mantras in Zen Cultivation

Liturgical service and meditation are the two most important activities in virtually every Zen monastery.

CULTIVATING COMPASSION IN SUTRA CHANTING

It is a common misconception that sutra chanting or any other ritual worship is absent in Zen Buddhism. Some people even think that if you practise Zen Buddhism or any form of Zen, you can scold the Buddha, disregard God, or do any of those things that most religious devotees would consider sacrilegious, and even ordinary people would consider outrageous. It is true that some Zen students shouted at or even hit their teachers (and obtained the teachers' praise), and great Zen masters did imponderable things – like Dan Xia chopping up a Buddha statue for firewood, Nan Quan cutting a cat in two, and Ju Zhi cutting off a boy's thumb – but all these unbelievable actions were extraordinary means to help their students gain enlightenment!

Despite its boisterous humour and love of freedom, Zen cultivation is a serious matter, and Zen practitioners, like all other Buddhist followers, practise the high moral values taught by the Buddha. Anyone who thinks that ritual worship is frowned at in Zen Buddhism needs only to observe a typical day in any Zen monastery. He will inevitably find that liturgical service and meditation are the two most important activities. Indeed, every day the very first thing a Zen monk, from a novice to an abbot, ever does after he has washed himself is ritual worship, and every time before he takes a meal he offers a prayer.

The striking feature of a Zen monk's prayers is that he always prays for other people and beings, and never for himself. If he ever prays for himself – if we can use the term 'pray' in this way – it is for repentance; he is not asking for favours. This is not just altruism, but is in line with Zen teaching: a Zen monk's aim is to attain enlightenment, which is the direct experience of ultimate reality where all traces of the phenomenal have dissolved into an undifferentiated, organic wholeness. Any blessings derived from prayers, or from anywhere, would therefore be a hindrance binding him to the phenomenal, because the blessings would be transformed into good karma which would bring fortune to him in the phenomenal realm. This is a perfect example of how by giving blessings to others he is doing good for others as well as for himself.

Of course a Zen monk transfers his blessings to others not because he fears that the blessings would be a hindrance to him, but because he wants others to benefit from the blessings. If he thought only of himself, he would not bother to cultivate blessings in the first place; he might just as well use the time for meditation which, in cultivating wisdom, would speed up his progress towards enlightenment. He cultivates blessings because he is dedicated to the two pillars of Mahayana Buddhism: compassion and wisdom. A Zen monk or lay practitioner does not merely talk about compassion and wisdom, but actually practises them in his life.

There are many ways in which a person can practise compassion and wisdom, such as giving money to charity, tending the sick, studying the scriptures as well as scientific and philosophical works, and learning directly from the wise. So why do Zen monks practise only liturgy and meditation, and not other forms of compassion and wisdom? In reality Zen and other Buddhist monks do practise other forms of compassion and wisdom; in fact, in some countries like Thailand and Burma, the Buddhist free school was the only form of education available to the common people for many centuries. But Buddhist monks have made sutra chanting and meditation part and parcel of their daily life because these are the best means to cultivate compassion and wisdom.

Some people may wonder how this is possible. According to the Buddha's teaching, there are three levels of charity. At the lowest level is the giving of material goods, including money;

at the second level the giving of service, religious as well as non-religious; and at the highest level the giving of teaching, especially spiritual teaching. Sutras are the direct teachings of the Buddha, the greatest of teachers. When you recite or chant a sutra, you are acting on behalf of the Buddha to benefit those who do not have the chance to listen to the Enlightened One personally. 'Those' here refers not just to humans, but to all sentient beings, including ghosts, nature spirits and gods. If you meet a ghost – and there are many around, although their vibration frequency generally falls outside the range of your limited sight – your proper attitude towards him or her should never be fear, but pity. Ghosts deserve our compassion for, being spiritually lost, they wander about hungrily and aimlessly. If you can transmit to them the Buddha's teaching, by chanting the *Khstigabha Bodhisattva Sutra*, for example, you may be giving them invaluable information on how to escape from their miserable conditions.

If you chant the *Amitabha Sutra*, you are disseminating invaluable information, as taught by the Buddha, to sentient beings, human and otherwise, on how to be reborn in heaven.[1] Even gods and other heavenly beings can benefit from your chanting. When you chant the *Heart Sutra*, which although the shortest sutra in the Buddhist canon marvellously contains the gift of Buddhism, you are acting as a medium through which the Buddha can teach gods, Bodhisattvas and all other beings how to attain the highest spiritual fulfilment. This may give you an idea of the tremendous blessings you can obtain by chanting sutras. You may keep the blessings so acquired for yourself, or transfer them to whoever you wish. (*See* page 260 for the simple way to transfer blessings.) You need not worry whether other beings can understand the language you use in your chanting; so long as you chant with sincerity, they will be able to pick out the meaning from the mental vibrations you create.

CULTIVATING WISDOM THROUGH MEDITATION

The highest form of wisdom is best acquired through meditation. According to Buddhist philosophy, wisdom can be classified into three levels: language wisdom, observed illuminated wisdom, and cosmic wisdom.

Language-wisdom is wisdom derived from the written or spoken word, for example from reading this book or listening to (and understanding) a sutra. Language-wisdom shows only an imitation of reality because not only is the knowledge derived from it second-hand, but the reader or listener interprets it through his own experience. For a person who has never been to London, no description, however detailed, can convey an exact picture of London to him, and he will visualize the description based on his experience of other cities he has visited. This does not mean that language-wisdom is not useful; in fact much of our ability to deal with everyday life is derived from language-wisdom, but when we deal with higher levels of reality its limitation becomes significant.

Observed-illuminated wisdom is wisdom derived from direct observation of reality as illuminated by a set of conditions. It may be divided into two groups: mundane and supramundane. Mundane observed-illuminated wisdom includes ordinary wisdom from direct experience as well as knowledge gained from science and technology. While such wisdom has contributed much to our well-being in the phenomenal world, it does not help us to go beyond the mundane.

Supramundane observed-illuminated wisdom may be further divided into two types: non-Buddhist and Hinayana. With the exception of their greatest masters who attained unity with the Supreme Reality, non-Buddhist religions generally teach 'eternal' life in heaven. While this teaching is supramundane, it is still within the phenomenal dimension, because heavens and hells are also creations of the mind and are not therefore ultimate reality. Moreover, whereas heavenly life in terms of thousands or millions of human years is relatively 'eternal' to humans, in cosmic scale it is transient: when the good karma which sustains that heavenly life is spent, heavenly beings die and are reborn again, but not necessarily in heaven. Nevertheless, for most people who still lack the intellectual and spiritual capability to comprehend ultimate reality, attaining 'eternal' life in heaven is probably their best choice. Hence, Buddhism shows respect to other religions. In Buddhism itself, cultivating to go to heaven is also a spiritual aim of many devotees.

Regarding Hinayana supramundane wisdom, it may surprise many people to learn that there is much information about heavens in Hinayanist scriptures. Yet ordinary Theravadin devotees are generally unaware of such information, to the extent that many people mistakenly regard Theravada Buddhism, the most important of the Hinayana schools today, as a way of life, with little or no concern for the metaphysical. This misconception is probably due to the fact that Hinayana wisdom aims at nirvana, not heaven. Nirvana, as taught in Hinayana, is the liberation of the personal self into a transcendental, blissful and cosmic state. However, according to Mahayana teaching, this Hinayana wisdom is still not complete – although it achieves liberation of self, it has not achieved liberation of dharmas because Hinayanists regard dharmas, or subatomic particles and forces, as ultimately real.

The highest wisdom, therefore, is prajna or cosmic wisdom, which is the realization that ultimate reality is devoid of both self and dharma. In other words, ultimate reality is 'void' or 'empty', known as *sunyata* in Sanskrit and *gong* (pronounced 'khung') in Chinese. Different beings, because of their different conditions, perceive the same ultimate reality as different phenomenal worlds. We humans perceive this puny 'part' of ultimate reality as the world we live in; an ant or a nature spirit would perceive the same 'space' and 'time' differently. Employing our mundane observed-illuminated wisdom, scientists perceive our moon as a dry, barren sphere; sentient beings existing on the moon would perceive it in ways beyond our imagination. But if we on our earth and the beings on the moon were enlightened, with our cosmic wisdom we would perceive the same ultimate reality as undifferentiated and void.

The acquiring of prajna, and therefore the attainment of ultimate reality, is realized through meditation. In the long process of spiritual cultivation towards this supreme aim, we will also have cosmic glimpses of observed-illuminated reality. Hence, centuries before scientists have rediscovered these facts, Buddhist masters have known that our earth is only a tiny speck in the limitless universe among trillions of other worlds, that time and space are relative, and that there are many more dimensions of existence than our ordinary eyes can see.

MANTRA AND DHARANI

Compassion and wisdom are the twin characteristics of Mahayana Buddhism, of which Zen Buddhism is a major school. If you wish your Zen cultivation to be complete, you should cultivate compassion as you cultivate wisdom. One practical way to do this is to recite or chant sutras. The terms 'recite' and 'chant' used below may be interchangeable, although 'recite' is more akin to reading and 'chant' to singing. You may recite or chant aloud, softly, or inside your heart.

The following is a short liturgical procedure which you can practise at home or in any suitable place. There are no hard and fast rules, so you may omit, add or modify any part to suit your conditions. For example, if you do not have an image of a Buddha or Bodhisattva, you can skip the first part involving prostration and start with singing praises. It is illuminating to note that the prostration is for the cultivator's benefit. Buddhas or Bodhisattvas do not mind in the least whether a person prostrates himself to them, but it is an effective way for the cultivator to eliminate his vanity or egocentricity.

Offer a joss stick, some flowers or a bowl of water to an image of a Buddha or Bodhisattva. Clasp your palms together in prayer and bow. Kneel down, place your hands, palms down, on the ground in front of you, and gently touch the ground with your forehead. Keeping your hands on the ground, turn your palms face up, and remain in this position for a second or two. Perform the prostration once or three times, after which you can continue the session standing, sitting cross-legged or in the lotus position, kneeling or in any other suitable posture.

Sing or recite praises to Buddhas and Bodhisattvas three times. The following is an example.

> Homage to Buddhas and Bodhisattvas gathered at the meeting of wisdom.

Or you may like to sing or recite the same praise in Chinese, as follows:

> Namo ban ruo hui shang Fo Bodhsat.

This chanting of praise in Chinese becomes a mantra, although some masters insist that mantras must be chanted in Sanskrit. After chanting the above mantra three times to praise Buddhas and Bodhisattvas, chant another mantra to praise and bring peace to local deities, especially the local god of the earth. This mantra, originally in Sanskrit but adapted in Romanized Chinese as follows, should also be repeated three times.

> Namo sanmantuo
> Mutuonam
> Om
> Duludulu Diwei Sahboha

After singing praises to Buddhas, Bodhisattvas and other deities, say and reaffirm your vow. You can compose your own vow; the following is the famous fourfold vow taught by the Sixth Patriarch (*see* Chapter 10):

> Infinite sentient beings I vow to save
> Infinite defilements I vow to abolish
> The infinite dharma I vow to practise
> The supreme Buddhahood I vow to accomplish.

Great masters have advised that unless you commit yourself to a task, you are unlikely to see a great result, or any result at all. Making a vow and reaffirming it every day is a practical way of commitment. If you have been telling yourself and others that you are on the path of spiritual cultivation, but cannot even bring yourself to make a vow to that effect, you have been deceiving both others and yourself.

Then recite or chant the following famous *dharani*, known as The Great Compassion Dharani, or *Da Bei Xin Tuo Luo Ni* in Chinese, popularly known as the Great Compassion Mantra, or *Da Bei Zhou*. This dharani is a long series of mantras comprising praises addressed to the numerous transformational bodies of Avalokitesvara Bodhisattva, or *Guan Yin Pu Sa* (pronounced 'Kuan Yin Bodh Satt') in Chinese. This Bodhisattva of Great Compassion, who is also my personal Bodhisattva, has vowed to answer the prayer of whoever seeks help and may be manifested as male or female according to the needs of the devotee, as in the realm of Bodhisattvas, sex is irrelevant. Guan Yin Bodhisattva is often, wrongly, associated with the Virgin Mother in Christianity, the Mother Goddess in Hinduism, and the Sacred Mother in Taoism. In Buddhist philosophy, a Bodhisattva is many levels higher than a god or goddess.

The chanting of the Great Compassion Dharani can bring

about tremendous blessings and incredible effects. Some people, especially those who need practical proof, may remain sceptical, but such chanting represents an appreciation of, or an appeal to, the numerous divine powers around us who have dedicated themselves to helping others. But in the spirit of Zen, we seek favour not for ourselves but for others in need. The Great Compassion Dharani is given below in Sanskrit:

Namo Ratnatraya Ya
Namo Arya Avalokitesvara Ya
Bodhisattva Ya, Mahasattva Ya, Mahakarunika Ya
Om Sarva Abhayah Sunadhas Ya
Namo Sukrtvemama Arya Avalokitsevara Garbha
Namo Nilakantha Sri Maha Bhadra Shrame
Sarvartha Subham Ajeyam Sarva
Sattva Namavarga Mahadhatu
Tadyatha Om Avalokelokite Kalate
Hari Maha Bodhisattva Sarva Sarva Mala Mala
Masi Maha Hrdayam Kuru Kuru Karmam
Kuru Kuru Vijayati Maha Vijayati
Dhara Dhara Dharim Suraya
Chala Chala Mama Bhramara Muktir
Ehi Ehi Chinda Chinda Harsham Prachali
Basha Basham Presaya Hulu Hulu Mala
Hulu Hulu Hilo Sara Sara Siri Siri Suru Suru
Bodhiya Dodhiya Bodhaya Bodhaya
Maitreya Nilakantha Dharshinina
Payamama Svaha Siddhaya Svaha Maha Siddhaya Svaha
Siddhayo Gesvaraya Svaha Nilakantha Svaha
Varahananaya Svaha Simha Shira Mukha Ya Svaha
Sarva Maha Siddhaya Svaha Chakra Siddhaya Svaha
Padma Hastya Svaha Nilakantha Vikaraya Svaha
Maha Sishankaraya Svaha
Namo Ratnatraya Ya
Namo Arya Avalokitesvara Ya Svaha
Om Siddhyantu Mantra Padaya Svaha.

'Svaha' is often pronounced like 'sabhoha', and means 'perfection' or 'accomplishment'. Recite or chant the above dharani once or as many times as you like. Some devotees chant it hundreds of times in each session. After chanting the Great Compassion Dharani, proceed to the *Heart Sutra*.

THE *HEART SUTRA*

Like the Great Compassion Dharani, the *Heart Sutra* is closely linked with Avalokitesvara Bodhisattva. Its full title is 'The Great Heart Sutra of Transcendental Wisdom to Reach the Other Shore', or *Maha-Prajna-Paramita-Hrdaya Sutra* in Sanskrit, and *Mo-He Ban-Ruo Bo-Luo-Mi-Tuo Xin Jing* in Chinese. It is a description of the enlightenment experience of Avalokitesvara Bodhisattva, and is recited daily in all Zen monasteries throughout the world. The original Sanskrit has been translated into Chinese many times. The English version below is my translation of the most famous Chinese version translated by the great Tang master Xuan Zang in AD 649.

Avalokitesvara Bodhisattva, coursing deeply through prajna-paramita, perceives that the five skandhas are all empty, thus overcoming all suffering and calamity.

Sariputra, form is no different from emptiness, emptiness no different from form. Form is emptiness, emptiness is form. Feeling, thought, activity, consciousness are also thus.

Sariputra, all phenomena are emptied of characteristics: non-arising, non-ceasing; non-defiled, non-pure; non-adding, non-subtracting. Thus in emptiness, there is no form, no feeling, thought, activity, consciousness. There is no eye, ear, nose, tongue, body, intellect consciousness; no form, sound, smell, taste, touch or phenomena.

There is no realm of eye consciousness till no realm of intellect consciousness; no ignorance and also no termination of ignorance till no age-death and also no termination of age-death.

There is no suffering, cause, extinction, path; no wisdom and no merit. As there is no attainment, the heart of Bodhisattvas due to prajna-paramita has no obstruction. As there is no obstruction, there is no fear, and being far from delusion and dreams, they attain perfect nirvana.

All Buddhas of the three time dimensions, due to prajna-paramita, attain anuttara-samyak-sambodhi. Therefore know that the prajna-paramita is the great divine mantra, great glorious mantra, unsurpassed mantra, and incomparable mantra. It is able to eliminate all suffering. This is really true; there is no falsehood. Therefore chant the prajna-paramita mantra; chant as gate, gate, para gate, para samgate, bodhi svaha.

If you do not understand the *Heart Sutra*, despite the clear translation above, you are in good company. It is probably the most well known but least understood of all sutras. The difficulty is twofold: the language is very concise, and the concepts very deep. The gist of the sutra is as follows.[2] In his deep meditation Avalokitesvara Bodhisattva perceived that form is emptiness, and emptiness is form. In ultimate reality there is no self, and there are no phenomena. Hence, the Doctrine of Dependent Origination, the Four Noble Truths, and the Six Paramitas – all of which are employed in the phenomenal dimension to transcend self and phenomena – are void in ultimate reality. Realizing this cosmic wisdom, all Buddhas and Bodhisattvas attain their enlightenment. The *Heart Sutra* mantra, which can speed you to enlightenment, is as follows: gate, gate, para gate, para samgate, bodhi svaha (meaning 'Arrive, arrive, already arrived, already arrived at enlightenment, perfect accomplishment').

TRANSFER OF BLESSINGS AND MANTRA CHANTING

It is a convention in Buddhism that after chanting a sutra, the cultivator transfers the blessing so acquired to others, who may be human or non-human, living now or already gone from this world to be reborn in the future, known personally or totally unknown. You may, for example, transfer the blessings to your friends in need of help, or to your parents (whether they are still living or have passed away), to people or even to ghosts whom you have never met or seen, or to all sentient beings. Do not worry whether there will be any blessings left for you, or whether your blessings are too few to go round, because blessings, like happiness, are multiplied when shared.

It is easy to give, if and when you want to give. If you want to transfer your blessings, for example, just sincerely say softly or within your heart, 'May this blessing be transferred to my mother', or 'May the unfortunate benefit by whatever blessings I have just acquired.' Or you may, like many Buddhist cultivators after chanting a sutra, exercise your transfer of blessings with a gatha or verse. An example is as follows:

> Be grateful to four types of kindness
> Overcome three realms of suffering
> Cultivate merit without tiredness
> May all beings share the blessings.

In this gatha the four types of kindness refer to the kindness of the Buddha for showing the way, of our parents for bringing us up, of our country for providing a peaceful environment in which spiritual cultivation is possible, and of all sentient beings for providing the necessary support. The three realms of suffering are the realms of hells, of ghosts, and of animals. Hence to be born a human is a rare and golden opportunity; we should therefore appreciate the opportunity to cultivate towards enlightenment with full vigour, and share whatever blessings we have acquired with all sentient beings for their well-being.

After the transfer of blessings, the liturgical service concludes with the singing of praises to Buddhas and Bodhisattvas. Sing three times

> Homage to Buddhas and Bodhisattvas gathered at the meeting of wisdom.

Or in Chinese, as follows:

> Namo ban ruo hui shang Fo Bodhsat.

Then prostrate yourself once or three times to end the session.

To recap, the liturgical service consists of the following parts:

1 Prostration, followed by singing of the mantra
2 Reaffirmation of vow
3 Chanting of the Great Compassion Dharani
4 Chanting of the *Heart Sutra*
5 Transfer of blessings
6 Singing of the mantra, followed by prostration

The above is only a suggestion: you can add, subtract or modify, or you can just chant a mantra, a dharani, a sutra, or even a part of a sutra.

Chanting a mantra is also an effective way to enter Zen, which, depending on the developmental stage of the cultivator, may be interpreted as meditation, a cosmic glimpse, or realization of ultimate reality. In other words, by chanting the *Heart Sutra* mantra (*see* page 260) or the Guan Yin Bodhisattva mantra

Namo Kwan Shi Yin Bodh Satt, meaning 'Homage to Guan Yin Bodhisattva' over and over again until no thought arises, a cultivator may enter into deep meditation, or may have a Zen awakening, or may even attain enlightenment!

22

DEVELOPMENTAL STAGES AND CRUCIAL QUESTIONS IN ZEN CULTIVATION

Ten Ox Pictures, Enlightenment and Soul

Both Mahayana and Theravada developed from the same teaching of the Buddha.

THE TEN OX PICTURES

The progress of a Zen cultivator, from first starting Zen to attaining enlightenment and then returning to society to serve others, is illustrated in the famous Ten Ox Pictures of Kuo An Shi Yuan, a Zen master of the Song dynasty in the 12th century. The Theravada master, Walpola Rahula, says:

> All the fundamental principles of Zen are already to be found in Theravada. The origin of the famous 'Ox-herding pictures' of the old Zen Masters has, for the first time, been traced back to Theravada Pali sources.[1]

These Ten Ox Pictures, each with an accompanying poem and a prose description, trace the ten developmental stages in Zen and other spiritual cultivation. But readers should bear in mind that, for various reasons, the experience of some cultivators may be different.

The ten pictures, poems and descriptions, translated from the original Chinese into English, together with my commentary, are given below. The poetry of any poem is often lost in translation; so if you do not find anything poetic about the poems below, this is because, in my translation, I have maintained the original meaning, sometimes literally, and this may appear odd when rendered into English. The original Chinese poems are of a very high literary value.

Searching for the Ox

> Spreading open long wild grasses to search;
> Streams and mountains, the road is deepening.
> Strength and spirit is spent, yet cannot find;
> Amidst some rustling hear some cicadas singing.

Accompanying description

At this stage the cultivator is full of vexation, worry and anxiety. He often finds that he has more problems now than before he started spiritual cultivation.

My commentary

The first picture shows an oxherd, with a whip and a rope in hand, searching for his ox. The ox is not in the picture, and the

Figure 22.1 Searching for the Ox

oxherd does not know where to look for him. The ox represents man's self-nature, which is Buddha nature. The man has lost his ox, symbolizing that he has lost his Buddha nature. Although he does not know where to find it, at least he has started to search. His life so far in the phenomenal world has been misguided, suggested by the wild grasses; he is tired physically and spiritually, and the path to finding his own Buddha nature is long and unknown. Yet despite the bustle of the mundane world, symbolized by the rustling sounds, the call of spiritual cultivation has been awakened in him, symbolized by his hearing the cicadas singing. In Chinese, 'cicada' is a pun for 'Zen' as they both sound alike.

Seeing Some Traces

> Beside streams beneath woods there're many traces,
> Wild grasses cannot totally hide these impressions.
> Even in deep mountains, deeper and deeper places,
> The blanket sky everywhere covers not his vision.

Figure 22.2 Seeing Some Traces

Accompanying description

After cultivating conscientiously beside streams and in woods, the cultivator's deluded heart [the mind] gradually becomes calm. He is convinced that when his deluded heart [mind] ceases, the self-nature of the ox will appear.

My commentary

Streams and woods suggest undergoing spiritual cultivation, because Zen and other Buddhist monasteries as well as cultivation centres of other religions are often built near streams and woods. Whoever cultivates, irrespective of his religion and his cultivation methods, will inevitably have inklings of the supramundane, no matter how wild his previous mundane life might be. Unlike most other forms of spiritual cultivation – such as Theravada Buddhism, Taoism, yoga and Christian mysticism – which stipulate retreat from society to concentrate on spirituality, Zen cultivation can be practised anywhere, in deep mountains or in busy cities. This is because Zen (the Supreme Reality) is everywhere; even the sky acting like a blanket cannot cover the face of Zen.

Seeing the Ox

> Yellow birds singing happily on a tree,
> Warm sun, soft breeze, and the willow green.
> There is the ox, nowhere he can hide,
> But its head is hidden, an incomplete scene.

Accompanying description

As deluded and miscellaneous thoughts become less and less, and the heart becomes calmer and calmer, clearer and clearer, the cultivator has no doubt that he has glimpses of the ox, which is his self-nature. Yet he has not seen the face of the ox clearly, and it is possible that the ox may be lost again.

Figure 22.3 Seeing the Ox

My commentary

As the cultivator progresses in his spiritual training, he feels joyful internally and externally. That is to say, he finds inner peace with himself, and beauty in the external world. He has some experiences of satori or Zen awakening which assure him that his training is correct and he is progressing. But the 'enlightenment' is not complete; in fact he has just started his spiritual training and must persist with more vigour or else his ultimate achievement will evade him. It is very important at this stage to guard against deviation and abuse; his training so far is likely to have given him some psychic powers, but if, in an unguarded moment of human weakness, he abuses them he will surely ruin himself.

Catching the Ox

> With full vigour and spirit catch the ox,
> Strong and determined it is hard to hold.
> Sometimes it goes to the mountain top,
> Sometimes into the smoke of urban fold.

Figure 22.4 Catching the Ox

Accompanying description

With full vigour and spirit to cultivate, the cultivator at last attains *kai-wu*, or awakening; he now sees his own self-nature. But the heavy burden of delusion is still on him, and is not easy to eliminate. It seems that he has climbed from the bottom of the valley of delusion right to the top of the mountain. But sometimes he is still surrounded by the smoke and cloud of delusion.

My commentary

Continuing to train with full vigour and spirit, the cultivator has deepened his awakening. He has seen his original face, that is he has had definite glimpses of ultimate reality, but because he has been deluded throughout both his present and past lives, delusion still hangs heavily over him. Although he knows that ultimate reality is void, and has experienced it, he still lives most of his life in delusion because he still considers the phenomena he meets daily as 'real'. Therefore he must continue to cultivate energetically, otherwise he may slip back into delusion.

Herding the Ox

> Carry the whip and rope at all times,
> Else the ox may enter again the realm of dust.
> Train till characteristics are pure and tame;
> Even without binding, naturally obey he must.

Accompanying description

If we do not use our disciplined and careful heart to illuminate the awakening experience that we have had, it is very possible that we will return to the delusion of the past. If we take good care of our awakened heart, then the discipline of the vinaya (monastic) rules and the effect of meditation will become daily tools in our cultivation.

My commentary

Even when we have had an awakening, we must continue to discipline ourselves, by following strictly the monastic code if we are monks, or the appropriate moral code according to our culture and community if we are lay persons. It is a mistake to

Figure 22.5 Herding the Ox

think of rules as restrictions. Buddhist monastic rules, which are varied and extensive, are there to help the monks to attain enlightenment. Sex is prohibited not because sex is considered 'dirty', but because it is probably the strongest hindrance to a monk's quest for ultimate reality. The Buddha, in fact, teaches that wholesome family life, including legitimate sex, is one of the joys of life. If we continue to train diligently for kai-wu or satori, we will find that rules and the effort to meditate are handy tools to help us attain enlightenment.

Riding the Ox Home

> Wandering on the ox, thinking of going home,
> Sounds of the flute send off the evening clouds.
> Each beat, each sound gives endless meanings of joy,
> If you appreciate the music why bother to shout.

Accompanying description

When the cultivator has reached this stage, slowly and gradually he moves along the road towards his old home of

Figure 22.6 Riding the Ox Home

non-arising non-ceasing self-nature. Along the way he can understand the existence of his own body and heart as well as of the natural surroundings. Of all these phenomena which he experiences through his five senses, not a single one can be explained satisfactorily through the use of language. Now he does not need language to describe the profound meaning of Buddhahood. Hence, it is with feeling or without feeling that the long tongue can speak; with sound or without sound is the music of the heavenly drum.

My commentary

The oxherd after taming the ox rides along leisurely on its back. He is conscious of his spiritual home, his own self-nature which is cosmic reality itself. He plays his flute or sings some songs, unbothered by mundane cares. He has personally experienced what ultimate reality is, and understands that it cannot be described through language. Thus, this ox picture illustrates two significant points that have troubled many people. One, nirvana or enlightenment can be attained here and now, and two, after experiencing nirvana the enlightened person does not necessarily vanish.

Ox Vanishes, Man Remains

> The ox rider has reached his forest home,
> The ox is not seen and the man does not arouse,
> The sun has risen high but he is still at rest,
> His whip and rope hanging in an empty house.

Accompanying description

Self-nature is originally pure and tranquil. Once deluded thoughts cease, pure and tranquil self-nature immediately appears. It is absolutely pure and tranquil, not a single thing is seen. Thus when self-nature appears, it cannot be named, because it is found everywhere, inside and outside of every-thing. It is like fish existing in water but unaware of the water,

Figure 22.7 Ox Vanishes, Man Remains

and people existing in air but unaware of the air. Thus when this ox which is devoid of any deluded thoughts is herded, the oxherd becomes one without any thoughts.

My commentary

The cultivator has reached his original home, and seen his original face. The ox, which symbolizes self-nature, is now no longer seen because the cultivator and his self-nature are the same. In cosmic dimensions he is the same as the whole universe, except that when he was deluded, he, like all other unawakened people, was unaware of this cosmic truth. Now that he is awakened, he has liberated himself from the deluded thinking that the phenomenal world is real, but he is still aware of himself as a personality. In Buddhist terms, he has liberated himself from the delusion of dharma, but not yet from the delusion of self.

Man and Ox are Lost

> Whip and rope, man and ox are all void;
> Who will believe the vast blue sky is empty?
> Upon a burning furnace snow silently melts,
> Arriving here all patriarchs you will see.

Accompanying description

This is the stage where all verbalization ceases and all thoughts and activities are extinguished. There is no use of mental impulses because there is no use of any measurement of intellectualization. Also, it is impossible to use intellectualization to define or explain it. This may be named the inexplicable realm.

My commentary

In this picture there is only an empty circle. The ox has disappeared, the ox-herd has disappeared, everything has disappeared. The ox symbolizes self-nature or cosmic reality, and the ox-herd symbolizes the aspirant seeking the ultimate of this cosmic reality. When he realizes ultimate reality, he finds

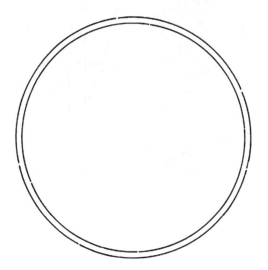

Figure 22.8 Man and Ox are Lost

that it is void; there is no seeker or that which is sought, no knower or that which is known, no defilement or holiness. Ultimate reality is tranquil and undifferentiated. Modern psychologists who try to measure the frequency of brain waves or analyse various mental states in Zen meditation, would do well to study the conclusion arrived at centuries ago in the description accompanying this picture: that effort and result are futile because in this state of no-mind any mental impulses and forms of intellectualization are useless. This is the state that all Patriarchs and Buddhas attained in their fulfilment; the state of nirvana or enlightenment where all forms of dualism have disappeared and the enlightened being and cosmos are one.

Returning to Origin

> Returning to origin appears like a waste of time.
> Tranquil all the way down as if blind and deaf.
> Inside the temple you cannot see anything in front.
> Spontaneously water flows and flowers are red.

Figure 22.9 Returning to Origin

Accompanying description

Phenomena are shown in the picture, but the observer is not. Although mountains are still mountains, and water is still water, they are not the same as the mountains and water that appeared to the person before his cultivation. Mountains and water may be the same, but the self who was sensually moved by the mountains and water no longer exists. Sound and sight can no longer cause the arising of dualistic and attached heart [mind]; hence the cultivator is as if deaf and blind. When he looks he can see, when he listens he can hear, but his heart is not moved. When he eats he knows the taste, but his heart is not moved. The red flowers and flowing water in front and at the back of his temple are merely manifestations of the spontaneous existence of spontaneous phenomena. These phenomena are not denied outside the heart, nor abide inside the heart. Faced with myriad phenomena, the heart is still unrestricted. This is what is called emancipation, spontaneity.

My commentary

In many religions or spiritual disciplines, including Theravada Buddhism, attaining enlightenment – known variously as returning to God, union with Brahman and unity with the cosmos – is the climax of spiritual cultivation. In Zen Buddhism and other schools of Mahayana Buddhism, however, this is not necessarily the end of the spiritual path. Many Mahayanists, for example, vow that after attaining enlightenment, they will come back to the phenomenal realm, in our human world or else- where, to help others. The Bodhisattva of Great Compassion, for instance, was a Buddha many aeons ago, but he returned as Avalokitesvara in India, as Guan Yin in China, and in numerous other transformational bodies elsewhere, to save other beings.

To many ordinary people, this long cultivation to attain enlightenment only to then return again to the phenomenal realm, seems a waste of time. This view, of course, is taken from a shallow, mundane perspective. To return to the phenomenal realm after having attained the transcendental, is a manifes- tation of the Mahayana ideal of compassion. If we, from an unenlightened perspective, ask why a Mahayanist wishes to be compassionate, it is like asking why he wishes to cultivate for enlightenment, or why a Christian wishes to return to God, or why a yogi wishes to attain union with Brahman. A Mahayanist cultivates compassion because it is his ideal; it is something he wants to do because he values it highly, not because of any fear or compulsion. Another valid answer is that showing compassion is doing good, which is the second step in the Buddha's practical teaching. A Zen practitioner is not interested in intellectual discussion on the ideal of compassion but instead acts on his ideal and shows compassion in his everyday life.

Once enlightened, or even just awakened, a person perceives the phenomenal world differently from how he had perceived it before. Mountains were mountains to him before he started cultivation. During his cultivation, mountains may not appear as mountains; they may, for example, appear as a huge mass of dharmas, or subatomic particles and forces. After his enlightenment, mountains are again mountains, but different. For instance, earlier the mountains moved his mind, causing myriad thoughts to arise, but now the mountains do not cause any deluded thoughts: he is aware that the mountains and all other phenomena are illusion. This is what the Sixth Patriarch meant when he advised his students to be in the midst of characteristics yet free from characteristics.

Entering the Market-Place with Helping Hands

> Entering the market-place with bare chest and feet,
> Covered with mud and dust but smiling broadly,
> There's no need for the magic of saints and gods;
> Even dried trees he can make to flower sweetly.

Accompanying description

This image depicts innocence and naturalness, elegance and spontaneity, and the application of miraculous powers that do not depend on form and shape, or rely on mundane customs. This is being free from the mundane but never detesting the mundane, entering the mundane yet not being attached to any mundane characteristics. It is full of great emancipation, great

Figure 22.10 Entering the Market-Place with Helping Hands

compassion, great wisdom and great miraculous powers. Zen Buddhism does not deal with the type of miraculous powers that are popularly mentioned. But you can liberate yourself right to the roots from the prison of delusion, freeing yourself from all attachment to people and ego, good and evil, profanity and holiness, defilement and purity, and all other dualist characteristics, to attain the heart of spontaneity. Your body too has become spontaneous, and all external phenomena are formed from your spontaneity. Thus, stones can nod their heads, dried trees can really blossom into flowers. This is not the magical powers of gods and saints, not the secrets of miraculous powers, but merely the natural happening of phenomena.

My commentary

The enlightened being returns to the phenomenal world in his present life or in future ones, in this human plane or in other phenomenal worlds, to help those in need of help, irrespective of race, culture and religion. This is the Mahayanist concept of the Bodhisattva ideal: attaining Buddhahood above, saving others below. His bare chest symbolizes that he has nothing to hide, and his bare feet that he is ready to go to the lowest levels to help. He exists in the world of defilement, symbolized by mud and dust, but he is free from defilement, symbolized by his smiling broadly not sneering at the vanity and futility of mundane life. He has tremendous miraculous powers, which he always uses for the good of others. There are no secrets to his powers; they are the natural result of his transcendentality. When you have realized that phenomena are a creation of mind, and when your mind is focused and concentrated, you can employ your mind to create phenomena.

SHALLOW UNDERSTANDING AND PERSONAL EXPERIENCE

A common and not unreasonable question many people ask is whether the supramundane experiences of Zen practitioners and other cultivators are real or merely figments of their imagination. Even Bimala Churn Law, writing on a history of Pali scriptures, comments that:

> Mrs Rhys Davids is perfectly right when she gives an idea of Nirvana by saying that it is merely the ending of the bad, and we should add, beginning of the good.[2]

As it is unlikely that this Pali scholar was unfamiliar with the Pali scripture on the Buddha's famous description of Nirvana, as quoted below, it is probable that he has missed the real significance of the Buddha's teaching.

> There is that condition where there is no earth, water, fire or air, where there are not the Spheres of Infinite Space, Infinite Consciousness, Nothingness, or the Sphere of neither Consciousness-Nor-Unconsciousness, where there is not this world, the world beyond or both together, no sun and no moon, where there is no coming to birth or going to death, no duration and hence no falling or arising. It is not something fixed, it does not move, it is based on nothing. This indeed is the end of suffering.[3]

What the Buddha says is that nirvana is where all matter and mind, all space and time, have been transcended. (Earth, water, fire and air are the four fundamentals of matter; the spheres of infinite space, infinite consciousness, nothingness, and neither consciousness-nor-unconsciousness refer to mind; worlds, suns and moons represent space; birth, death and other duration

refer to time.) In other words nirvana is the realization of ultimate reality or Zen. In such a 'state', good or bad, or any form
of dualism becomes irrelevant.

Despite having studied Zen monks for 20 years, Dr Tomio
Hirai remarks, 'I suspect religious delusions in the claims of all
Zen monks who insist that they have reached enlightenment as
an outcome of enthusiastic Zen meditation.' Who should one
believe: Dr Tomio Hirai or all the Zen monks? As the Buddha
advises, one should not accept any teaching based on faith
alone, or on the scriptures or reputation of the masters; it should
be based on one's own understanding and experience.

Some ardent Buddhist followers have asked, 'Why didn't
masters demonstrate the truth to non-believers?' While many
masters have done this through detailed explanation and commentary on relevant sutras, the characteristic attitude of
Buddhist masters in this respect is that the onus of seeking the
truth lies with the seeker. If a person tenuously clings to his
preconceived idea as the only right one, no amount of demonstration or proof can convince him otherwise. But if he is humble
enough to adopt an open attitude, Buddhist masters will point
out the way which they themselves have personally travelled
to attain awakening or enlightenment; yet they will never say,
'This is the only way; follow this way and no other.' Instead
they will ask him to find out for himself what awakening or
enlightenment is.

Unlike in some religions or disciplines where fame, glory or
even financial rewards are involved, none of this applies in
Buddhism. A Buddhist master will show you the way to truth
not because of any benefit he may get, but because of his great
compassion. This has given rise to the arrogant attitude adopted
by some Westerners who believe that because they are on a
spiritual path, or so they think, they are doing the masters
a favour, but this is both ridiculous and unreasonable. If you
want the ultimate truth, you must seek it yourself, and even if
you are lucky enough to have an enlightened person to show
you the way, it is long and arduous.

Quoted below are the personal experiences of two modern
seekers of the truth. Both quotations are taken from Professor
Holmes Welch's classic work, *The Practice of Chinese Buddhism
1900–1950.*

The first describes the Zen awakening of an unnamed Chinese

monk, reporting his experience to John Blofeld, the famous European Buddhist, while he himself was seeking the truth in China.

> ... I have discovered for myself that if I just sit perfectly still ... and open my mind to – no, not to anything – just open up my mind; though nothing happens the first time or the second, one day I begin to feel some response. My heart seems to be talking to me, revealing secrets of which I have never so much as dreamt. Afterwards I am left in a state of marvelous happiness ... What gives me hope is that, each time all this happens, the Light seems to stay with me a little longer.[4]

The second record is from the Venerable Hsu Yun, the famous abbot of Nan Hua Temple in China, describing his enlightenment experience during his meditation weeks at Kao Min Temple in 1895.

> From this point on all my thoughts suddenly cease. My work began to progress. Day and night were the same. When I moved, it was like flying. One night during the rest from meditation, I opened my eyes and suddenly there was a great radiance like broad daylight. I could see through everything, inside and out ... the attendant poured hot water according to the rule. It splashed on my hand. The tea cup fell to the ground and broke to bits with loud noise. Suddenly the roots of doubt were out. In my whole life I had never felt such joy.[5]

IS THE SOUL EXTINGUISHED IN NIRVANA?

Because Buddhism is so profound, it is often misunderstood. For example, many people (including myself in the past) are puzzled at the meaning of nirvana or enlightenment. Some mistakenly think that nirvana means total extinction – with nothing left, not even the soul. Even August Karl Reischauer, who has provided remarkable and comprehensive Buddhist knowledge to the West, and who speaks very favourably of Buddhism although he himself is Christian, is not free from certain fundamental misconceptions, as evident in the quotation below.

> And when man is enlightened and sees things as they really are,

what does he see? He sees that all things are impermanent and that all individual existence is inherently an existence of suffering, that in order to escape from this life of suffering the truly wise must give up all desires for individuality and the things that go to make up such a life. That is, the Enlightened One sees that what we ordinarily call the self is the greatest of all illusions, and hence to know this is to get free from the bondage of individual existence. Freedom from the bondage of individuality is what constitutes real salvation.[6]

The misconceptions, as explained in various parts of this book, are due to a failure to differentiate between ordinary knowledge and cosmic wisdom – the very problem that Mahayanists believe many Hinayanists face. At the phenomenal level of ordinary knowledge, it is true that 'all things are impermanent and that all individual existence is inherently an existence of suffering'; but at the transcendental level of cosmic wisdom, everything is permanent, omniscient and blissful. The supra-mundane objective of Zen is to actualize this transcendental reality.

It is also true that at the level of ordinary knowledge, the teaching of Zen and all other schools of Buddhism is 'to get free from the bondage of individual existence'. This may give the impression that salvation or nirvana means extinction of the individual. But if we have cosmic wisdom, we will realize that transcendentally there is no extinction, because there is no individual in the first place. The individual who is 'real' at our ordinary level of consciousness, is an illusion. Nirvana or enlightenment is the direct experience that the individual, any individual, is actually the cosmic reality – there is no difference whatsoever between the knower and the known.

This leads us to the inevitable question: If there is no individuality, does it mean there is no self or soul? In other words, does Zen Buddhism in particular, and Buddhism in general, believe in the existence of the self, the soul, or whatever you choose to call it? Except for Theravada or Hinayana Buddhism, there is no doubt in all other schools of Buddhism that the self or soul exists in the phenomenal realm, just as chairs and mountains exist. The modern master, the Venerable Sheng-Yen, says:

If there is existence in deep enlightenment, is there also self? Indeed there is. If self didn't exist you wouldn't be able to do anything.

What has been removed is ego, which has the sense of always being 'for oneself'. In truth, it is the attachment to self that has vanished.[7]

In his classic work, *Buddhism in China*, Kenneth K S Ch'en reports that

In Chinese Buddhism the idea of an indestructible soul was developed at an early time: this soul was forever transmigrating in the sea of misery because of its attachment to the myriad things in the world.[8]

The most authoritative statement about the self, of course, comes from the Buddha himself:

My thought has wandered in all directions throughout the world. I have never yet met with anything that was dearer to anyone than his own self. Since to others, to each one for himself, the self is dear, therefore let him who desires his own advantage not harm another.[9]

Here the Buddha is talking about the self in the phenomenal realm. All schools of Buddhism, including Theravada, accept the fact that the same self who attained perfect enlightenment as Siddharta Gautama the Buddha had existed in countless lives before.

But in ultimate reality the self or soul – like all other phenomena, including heavens and hells as well as the physical world in which we exist – is an illusion! In other words, when a self attains enlightenment he realizes that his personal self or soul is actually the Universal Self or Universal Soul. Some people call this Universal Soul, God. Buddhists call this ultimate truth by many names, such as Tathagata, Buddha, nirvana, bodhi, and void; Zen practitioners often refer to it as self-nature or original face.

Because they fail to understand this cosmic wisdom, which would enable them to differentiate the transcendental and the phenomenal, Theravadins generally believe the self or soul does not exist – which is true in the transcendental realm but not in the phenomenal. Nevertheless, it is heartening that, unlike lesser teachers who claim that the Mahayana teaching is a later adulterated form of Buddhism, great Theravada masters such as Walpola Rahula are saying that both Mahayana and Theravada developed from the same teaching of the Buddha. For example, Walpola Rahula says:

> The most important axiom in Zen is the attainment of Buddhahood by directly seeing into one's own Nature ... Here what is meant by the word 'Buddha', quite obviously, is not the same as the historical Buddha Gautama who was a *Sammasambuddha* (Perfectly and Fully Enlightened One) ... the term 'Buddha' is used in its radical meaning of 'awakened' or 'enlightened' (from the root *budd* to awake). Anyone who has realized Truth (*Nirvana*) could be called 'Buddha' in this sense, according to the Theravada tradition too.[10]

23

ZEN IN DAILY LIFE

How to be Effective and More Joyful and Alive

*When you are mentally refreshed and fully aware
that you are alive, not merely existing or
surviving, you are able to share the beauty and
wonders of life all around you.*

SIMPLE, DIRECT AND EFFECTIVE

Many people, understandably, are not ready for or interested in spiritual cultivation. But even if you are not ready or interested to cultivate Zen as a spiritual discipline, you can bring a touch of Zen into your daily life and gain much benefit from it. Zen helps us to attain the best in both the mundane and the supramundane dimensions. The most fundamental Zen practice is meditation, but you can practise Zen in an informal way by adopting some of its principles.

The three principal features of Zen are that it is simple, direct and effective. If a Zen student wants his teacher to calm his mind, for example, he does not go through various rituals, read up what mind is, then find excuses or beautiful phrases to ask his teacher in a round-about manner. He simply goes directly to his teacher and says, 'Sir, please calm my mind.' The teacher does not then analyse the student's trouble, deliver a long lecture, or measure the student's brain-wave frequency. He simply and directly says, 'Bring out your mind and I'll calm it', or if he wants to know what is troubling the student's mind, he simply asks, 'What is troubling your mind?'

These actions or statements are effective because they are directed to that specific person and situation. For instance, when Bodhidharma asked Hui Ke to bring out his mind so that the master could calm it, Hui Ke was enlightened. Later when Hui Ke told his student Seng Can to bring out his sins so that the master could help him repent, Seng Can was awakened. The masters said what was most effective for the person and situation in question. For another person or situation, their responses would have been different – perhaps closing the student's mouth to prevent him from speaking, or striking him with a stick.

We can learn a useful lesson from the simple and direct action of Zen practitioners. So the next time you want to ask someone for a date, or your boss for a pay rise, instead of wondering what to do and how, or whether you should do it at all even though you want to, simply and directly go to him or her and say – politely, or banging the table, or in whatever way seems most suitable to the situation – 'I would like to ask you for a date' or 'I want a pay rise'.

These simple, direct and effective aspects of Zen are well illustrated in Shaolin Kungfu and Shaolin Chi Kung, the two Shaolin arts that are both a preparation for and a manifestation of Zen. All Shaolin Kungfu patterns are simple, direct and effective. When a Shaolin exponent wishes to block an attack or strike an opponent, he blocks or strikes in simple, direct movements, in contrast, interestingly, to a Taijiquan exponent who first adjusts his body and leg positions and then blocks, and not directly but in a circular motion to minimize his opponent's force. Unlike the Shaolin exponent who blocks and immediately strikes, the Taijiquan exponent, after blocking in a comparatively elaborate manner, flows with the opponent's movement so as to manipulate the opponent into an unfavourable position and only then does he strike. Indeed, a comparative study of Shaolin Kungfu and Taijiquan, both of which are wonderful arts in their respective ways, illustrates the simple, direct and effective characteristics of Zen, and the flowing movements of water advocated in the famous Taoist scripture, *Tao Te Ching*.[1]

Shaolin Chi Kung is also simple, direct and effective. For example, if a Shaolin Chi Kung exponent wants to increase his stamina, instead of running a few miles and panting all the way, or sweating it out a few hours in a gym, he practises breathing exercises for about 15 minutes to clear the appropriate meridians for better energy flow and to increase his energy level by tapping it from the cosmos. When you understand that a better energy flow and an increase in energy level lead to increased stamina, which in turn is the *cause*, not the *effect*, of improved performance when running or exercising in the gym, you can appreciate how simple, direct and effective is the approach of Shaolin Chi Kung. Indeed, the Shaolin Chi Kung exercises that I have taught to literally hundreds of people to relieve diseases such as asthma, hypertension, peptic ulcers, diabetes and cancer, are bafflingly simple!

PROFUNDITY IN SIMPLICITY

To say they are simple does not mean that Shaolin Kungfu, Chi Kung and any Zen actions or statements are dull or shallow; in fact they are often very profound. For example, Bodhidharma's 'Bring out your mind' in respond to Hui Ke's 'Please calm my mind' is so profound that it is applicable only to people who have attained Bodhidharma's and Hui Ke's level of development. The same answer given to a lesser mind, despite the simple, clear language used, would be very puzzling. Many readers find gong-ans or koans incomprehensible because they are not at the same developmental stage as the monks to whom they were originally addressed.

Similarly, a simple Shaolin Kungfu block can be very profound; it is the result of centuries of Shaolin masters' efforts to find the best ways of countering a particular attack including the consideration of various combative factors such as the opponent's size and power, the space available, and the possible subsequent actions issuing from the block. Both the kungfu block and Bodhidharma's response are simple in the sense that all irrelevant movements or words are discarded, leaving only those that will bring the desired effect.

On the other hand, most people who have seen a good performance of Shaolin Kungfu are impressed by the beauty of the patterns, which are undoubtedly more complicated and elaborate than those of other martial arts like karate, taekwondo or Western boxing. How can you call those kungfu patterns simple, they may ask. The answer is that they are simple in relation to a selection of possible movements to achieve the same desired effect. Because Shaolin Kungfu has a history more than ten times longer than that of many other martial arts today, it has developed an exceedingly large repertoire of combative techniques. Where there are only two or three techniques to deal with a specific combat situation in another martial art, for example, there are 20 in Shaolin Kungfu. Hence, it is more elaborate and complicated than virtually all other martial arts, including Taijiquan.

If Shaolin Kungfu reflects the Zen characteristics of simplicity, directness and effectiveness, why then does it not use two techniques instead of 20? That would be shallowness, not simplicity as the term is used in the present discussion, and it would also undermine effectiveness. Shaolin Kungfu has a wide range of techniques to meet any one combat situation so that the exponent can choose the most appropriate technique for the occasion. Exponents of different physical stature, for example, would not use the same technique to counter the same attack; or if an exponent wants to trick his opponent into continuing his attack, the technique is again different. But no matter which technique he uses, even if it is in itself elaborate, it is trimmed of all extraneous movement. If there are, say, three different techniques that are appropriate for the occasion and will give the same desired effect, he will use the simplest and most direct.

This short description of Shaolin Kungfu is not a diversion; it is meant to illustrate the Zen characteristics of simplicity, directness and effectiveness in action. To illustrate these Zen characteristics in the use of language, the gong-an or koan is an excellent example. Just as those unfamiliar with Shaolin Kungfu will find it complex, those not yet ready for a Zen awakening will find gong-ans bewildering.

Anyone reading any of the gong-ans in this book or elsewhere must be struck by the simplicity and directness of the language used, even though he may not understand its real significance. Let us look at the language used in the gong-an below, from the famous classic, *Bi Yan Lu*, or Blue Cliff Record.

Ding the head monk asked his master, the Venerable Lin Ji, 'What is the meaning of the Buddha's teaching?' Lin Ji immediately came down from his meditation seat, and gave the head monk a slap on his ear, then pushed him away. The head monk was dazed, and stood there in amazement. Some nearby monks said, 'Head monk Ding, why don't you prostrate yourself?' At that moment his heart glowed,

and he was awakened. Immediately the head monk prostrated himself to thank the master.

It is difficult to find any other type of writing more simple and
direct in its language than the gong-an, and if you are ripe for
a Zen awakening it can be very effective. In the above gong-an,
for example, there is no description of the master, the head
monk or the other monks, or account of the emotion felt by any
of them before, during or after the slapping incident, as is
common in many other types of literature. There is not even
any mention of the time and place. All these literary frills are
unnecessary in a Zen gong-an; they are left out because they
do not in any way contribute to the desired effect.

To say the gong-an is simple does not mean of course it is
shallow or dull. The above gong-an, like all other gong-ans,
is an excellent example of profundity in simplicity. What was
the head monk awakened to, and how did the slap or the
other monks' prompting trigger off his awakening? 'What is the
meaning of the Buddha's teaching?' was in fact a rhetorical
question: everyone in the gong-an knew its literal answer. Lin
Ji's slap was to stop the head monk from listening to and, by
correlation, seeking a verbalized answer, indicating that the
Buddha's teaching – enlightenment – is inexplicable. The
prompting by the other monks worked, bringing the head monk
to a realization of the master's intended non-verbal answer, and
triggering his awakening that cosmic reality is transcendental.

Practising the Zen characteristics of simplicity, directness and
effectiveness in actions and in words can help us to make our
daily lives rewarding and meaningful, for both ourselves and
others. And it is inspiring to note that these characteristics are
found also in the works of great scientists, philosophers and
teachers. Einstein's theory of relativity, which has revolutionized
the Western world view, could not have been more simply,
directly and effectively expressed than in his famous $e = mc^2$.

Let us have a look at Lao Tzu's opening line in his *Tao Te
Ching*: 'Tao that can be named is not Tao.' Although not many
people may understand this great cosmic truth, it is expressed
most simply, directly and effectively. If you have understood
this book well, you should have no difficulty understanding
Lao Tzu's famous line. He says in Taoist terms what Zen masters
have been trying to transmit to their students in extraordinary

ways – as recorded in gong-ans – that ultimate reality is inexplicable. Once we use names to describe ultimate reality, we start the process of differentiation into the phenomenal world and what we describe is no longer ultimate reality.

If we do not understand Einstein's formula or Lao Tzu's opening line despite the simplicity, directness and effectiveness of their language, it is because we have not taken into account the profundity involved. Here is where great teachers come in: they enable deep and complex concepts to be understood. And their teachings are always simple, direct and effective. It is only mediocre teachers and writers – perhaps in an attempt to appear grandiose or because they themselves are unclear – who make simple matters difficult.

Let us see how simply, directly and effectively stated is the teaching of the greatest of teachers, the Buddha, even when translated into a language so different in vocabulary and style from its original. Its simplicity, directness and effectiveness are all the more impressive when we realize that it is a teaching on the most profound of topics – how a follower can practise to attain enlightenment:

> And what is that middle way? It is simply the noble eightfold path, that is to say, right view, right intention, right speech, right action, right livelihood, right effort, right mindfulness, right concentration. That is the middle way discovered by a Perfect One, which gives vision, which gives knowledge, and which leads to peace, to direct acquaintance, to discovery, to nibbana.[2]

DO, DON'T JUST TALK

Besides making your actions and language simple, direct and effective, another way of adding a touch of Zen to your daily life is to practise Zen principles. Two Zen principles that can enrich our own and other people's lives are 'Do, don't just talk', and 'Be mindful of the present moment'.

The first is a fundamental tenet of Buddhism. Thus, when those inclined to argument and speculation asked the Buddha questions touching on metaphysics and cosmology, the World Honoured One preferred to keep a noble silence although he possessed supreme wisdom on the subjects. This was also why

Bodhidharma asked students to burn their scriptures; he found that they had become enslaved to the words instead of practising the teaching the words conveyed. The Zen principle of doing rather than talking is also widely demonstrated in gongans, such as in Lin Ji's shout and Te Shan's staff (*see* Chapter 12). When students asked their masters what Zen was, instead of explaining to them that ultimate reality is inexplicable, Lin Ji shouted at them and Te Shan struck them. Many of their distinguished pupils attained an awakening or enlightenment in this way.

The principle is again excellently manifested in Shaolin Kungfu and Shaolin Chi Kung. The hallmark of a Shaolin Kungfu or Chi Kung master is the depth of his skill, not the extent of his knowledge, although most masters are very knowledgeable. When a Shaolin exponent has mastered the art of Golden Bell, for example, whereby he can take attacks without sustaining injury, or the art of transmitting his chi, or vital energy, to cure people of chronic illness, he can rightly be called a master, even though he may know very little kungfu or chi kung theory. The essential way to mastery is to practise the *one* technique needed to acquire the respective skill over and over again daily for many years, *not* to read extensively or learn about more techniques and skills. Inevitably the techniques required to attain these skills are simple, direct and effective.

Even though you may not have to acquire the art of Golden Bell or strike someone to trigger his awakening, the tenet of doing and not just talking can be very useful in your daily life. If, for example, you are dissatisfied with your employees' or subordinates' work, instead of scolding them futilely or complaining to your friend, take simple, direct and effective action to ensure they produce satisfactory work.

The East and the West generally have a contrasting attitude and approach to doing and talking, or practice and learning. The focus in the Eastern tradition is on doing or practice, whereas in the West it is on talking or learning. Typically, when a student in the East studies under a teacher, whether in Zen, kungfu, chi kung or any other arts, he places his complete trust in the teacher and does whatever the teacher asks. Usually he knows virtually nothing besides the little information his teacher provides.

For example, when I first took up kungfu with my first

Shaolin master, Sifu Lai Chin Wah, or Uncle Righteousness as he was better known to the public, I practised the Horse-Riding Stance, the most demanding exercise I have known in any art, for months because my teacher asked me to. Years later, when I practised chi kung and then Zen with Sifu Ho Fatt Nam, the third generation successor of the Venerable Jiang Nan of the Shaolin Monastery, I practised Cosmos Breathing and later 'sitting in a lotus position thinking of nothing and doing nothing' for years, without knowing what benefits those exercises would bring me. The thought of asking the teacher why we did what we did, never occurred to me or any of my classmates, for to do so would have been a blatant expression of distrust. It was much later that I acquired the theoretical knowledge which serves to confirm and explain what I have experienced.

Most Westerners would regard such a submissive attitude as odd or foolish, and in some ways they are right. In the first place, the Western attitude towards teachers is different from a traditionally Eastern one. To me my teachers are like my father – in the Eastern sense, authoritative and to be revered. Many Westerners regard their teachers as their peers, someone whom they can feel comfortable with, or even kick around at times. Secondly, Westerners are inquisitive: not only would they question their teachers but they would read up as much as they could on the subject.

Personally, I disagree with the first Western view but consider the second to be good, provided that the questioning is carried out respectfully and, more important, that the students 'practise' not just 'learn', in line with the Zen principle of 'do, don't just talk'.

Teachers are not your peers; they are at least a class above you, otherwise they should not, and could not, be your teachers. The need to respect teachers and their strict discipline is for the benefit of pupils, otherwise their attainment will not be high. When friends, students or strangers remarked that I was stable, full of energy and had a fresh, calm mind, I knew all these qualities were due to a large degree to the great respect I had (and still have) for my teachers. But I was very lucky; I had two of the best teachers in the world, who were not only extremely skilful in their arts but shining examples of the high moral values they held. From the way they led their lives, more than from their oral instruction, I learned the meaning of righteousness – from Uncle Righteousness, as his honourable nickname reflects – and the meaning of an impeccable conscience – from Sifu Ho Fatt Nam. They did not merely talk about righteousness and impeccable conscience, they practised them in their daily lives.

But nowadays it is extremely difficult to find teachers of such high standards. When people start teaching chi kung or meditation after only a weekend course on the art, you can gauge not only their skills but also the values they hold in life. Hence, *respectfully* questioning the teacher and his teaching is a wholesome practice, especially when many bogus instructors pose as masters. We should adopt the attitude of questioning to learn, not questioning to expose. If the teacher cannot answer basic questions satisfactorily, or cannot perform reasonably well the very skill he professes to teach, we have good reasons to be suspicious. Politely asking a teacher legitimate questions, rather than arguing with him about a subject on which he is supposed to be expert, or challenging him to give a convincing demonstration, is a simple, direct and effective way to find out if he is competent.

And if he is, it is still very useful for students to read up on the subject. But they must bear in mind that even if a teacher is not knowledgeable in theory, he can still be very skilful in his art and therefore have a lot to teach his knowledgeable students. Showing the teacher that they are more knowledgeable is not only rude and unbecoming but is certainly detrimental to their learning. Such students should take note of the 'do, don't just talk' principle; their knowledge is meant to enhance the practical attainment of whatever art they are practising, and, more significantly, they should practise that art, not just learn about it.

In Zen and all other schools of Buddhism, knowledge, while highly valued in itself, is always considered inferior to experience. A person with a PhD in building construction who cannot actually lay a brick is inferior to an uneducated mason in terms of building a house. This of course does not mean that knowledge is unimportant; knowledge serves as a map, showing not just the route to be taken but also the destination. Without knowledge most students waste a lot of time groping in the dark. But it is not enough just to hold the map; a student must walk along the route to reach his destination.

In teaching kungfu and chi kung, I have always explained the background philosophy of these arts to my students. With this knowledge they are better able to define their aims and objectives, and aware of the range of methods available, thus enabling them to achieve better results in a shorter time. In fact, many of my students could achieve in six months what I did in three years. But there is no doubt that their remarkable achievement is due not to my talking but to their doing; not because of the knowledge itself, but because the knowledge provided them with the insight and inspiration to practise regularly and diligently.

BE MINDFUL OF WHATEVER YOU DO

Even if you practise regularly and diligently, if you do not put your heart, or mind, into what you are practising, you are unlikely to get good results. Being mindful of whatever you do is a fundamental teaching in all schools of Buddhism. In Theravada temples, for example, every day monks practise walking meditation – in which they become acutely aware of the very moment when and the very spot when their feet touch or leave the ground – in order to cultivate such mindfulness.

Among the Buddha's disciples, Suddhipanthaka was said to be the most stupid; he could not remember even one line of any sutra. But his determination to gain enlightenment was so great that he renounced everything to become a monk. His brother, Mahapathaka, who was also a monk, thought Suddhipanthaka would never make any spiritual progress. Suddhipanthaka wept profusely as spiritual cultivation was the only thing important to him. The Buddha found him weeping and had great compassion for him. The Buddha asked Suddhipanthaka to sweep the temple floor, and every time he made a sweeping action to say 'sweep' and be mindful of it. Gradually Suddhipanthaka developed mindfulness of his every word and action at every moment, and nothing else. But eventually he attained enlightenment. Suddhipanthaka is a great inspiration for all of us; if a person considered to be so stupid could attain enlightenment, no one can use the excuse that enlightenment is beyond his reach.

Because, as recorded in many gong-ans, Zen masters often prevented their students from thinking or any form of verbalization, some readers may think that mindfulness is incompatible with Zen training, but that is not so. The apparent paradox is due to the inability of language to express fine shades of meaning, as well as to the failure to differentiate between the highly developed mind of the Zen monks mentioned in the gong-ans and the untrained mind of ordinary people. In fact Zen training is training in mindfulness. The mind has first to be trained to be one-pointed, then to expand. In Zen terms, we first tame the mind, then attain no-mind, illustrated in the Ten Ox Pictures by the taming of the ox, then its disappearance. In the gong-ans, because the monks' minds had already been tamed or calmed, their masters could use extraordinary methods, including giving seemingly illogical answers, shouting and hitting, to provoke them into achieving no-mind, the Zen term for all mind.

Apart from practising the many methods described in this book, you can develop mindfulness by constantly reminding yourself to be mindful of whatever you are doing. For example, as you read this sentence, be aware of the meaning of the words instead of merely going over them. Be mindful of the chair or whatever you are sitting on, and the room or whatever place you are in. When you eat your meals, be aware of the taste and texture of the food in your mouth, be aware of the contact your teeth make with the food as you chew, and be aware of the food going down your throat as you swallow. When you walk up or down a flight of steps, keep your mind on your walking up or down, not on documents in your office or someone in another town. When masters say that Zen is eating food, looking out of a window, or saying hello, they imply this mindfulness of the present moment.

Initially you may have to make considerable effort to be mindful of your present, but gradually it can become habitual. You must never force yourself to be mindful; if you do, you will become stressed. Should this happen, perform some of the chi kung exercises in this book. Be gentle in your mindfulness, as if you have no mind yet are fully aware of yourself and your surroundings and, at an advanced stage, even of what is inside you. Then you will have attained everyday Zen. Your mind will be sharp yet calm; you will be truly alive and appreciative of every moment of your life, and that of other beings.

When you are mentally refreshed and fully aware that you are alive, not merely existing or surviving, you are able to share the beauty and wonders of life all around you. If you pick a flower you can sense its fragrance and delicate texture, and if you have been practising meditation you may even sense its previous life. If you look at a grain of sand, you may see in it a whole cosmos. You may even, in an impulse of Zen, intuitively sense the interconnectedness of everything in the universe. This will fill you with inspiration and gratitude and, irrespective of your station in life, you will feel the joy of living and may, in a flash of Zen wisdom, be suddenly awakened to the fact that happiness does not depend on wealth, fame and power. You may be moved to give, to share your joy with others.

The Zen of the present moment can bring you joy which you did not know existed before. This joy is intrinsic; you are experiencing it now because of a change in your mental make up, not because of any external factors. But remember, this mental change is the third not the first step in the Buddha's teaching. The three steps are avoiding all evil, doing good, and purifying the mind. One who does evil, even if he practises all the methods explained in this book, will not attain inner joy. This is a cosmic truth: the act of contemplating evil which precedes an evil action, defiles the mind and will ineluctably ripen into suffering in this life or future ones. This does not mean that someone who does evil is beyond redemption. There is no such a thing as eternal sin in Buddhism; if a sinner sincerely repents and does good deeds, his accumulated blessings will modify his mental imprint and change bad karma into good karma. A person's destiny is in his own hands: he does not even have to pray to repent; so long as there is a change of heart, or mind, from evil to good, the mental imprint which directs the course of his future life will change. Nevertheless, for those who are not sufficiently developed in mind or spirit, praying to God, or the Buddha or any Bodhisattva, for repentance provides great spiritual support.

Zen, therefore, shows the way to a joyful life. Zen monks – who have no worldly possessions, fame or power, whose bed is a hard plank and whose meal typically consists of a few pieces of vegetable with porridge or rice (seven grains of which they daily offer to hungry ghosts whom they have never known) – are amongst the happiest people in the world. But it is not necessary to become a Zen monk to share the tremendous benefits of Zen. You can cultivate Zen as a lay person, or you can forget about formal cultivation and practise Zen informally. At the level of our everyday mundane world, Zen teaches us to be effective, calm, mentally refreshed and alive at every moment; at the spiritual level it shows us the way to the greatest attainment any being can ever aspire to.

NOTES

Chapter 1

1   Christmas Humphreys, *Zen*, Teach Yourself Books, Hodder & Stoughton, London, 1976, p 7
2   Venerable Hui Guang, *Gateway to the Study of Zen*, Da Feng Cultural Affairs Company, Taipei, 1961, pp 27–31, in Chinese
3   K Sri Dhammananada, *What Buddhists Believe*, Buddhist Missionary Society, Kuala Lumpur, 1964, p 76
4   Paravahera Vajiranana Mahathera, *Buddhist Meditation in Theory and Practice*, Buddhist Missionary Society, Kuala Lumpur, 2nd edition 1975, pp 35–42

Chapter 2

1   Daniel Goleman, *The Meditative Mind*, Jeremy P Tarcher, Los Angeles, 1977, pp 57–8
2   Quoted in Seyyed Hossein Nasir, 'The Complementarity of Contemplative and Active Lives in Islam', in Yusul Ibish and Ileana Marculescu (eds), *Contemplation and Action in World Religion*, Rothko Chapel, Houston, 1978, p 195
3   Mir Valiuddin, *Contemplative Disciplines in Sufism*, East West Publications, London, 1980, p 97
4   Swami Prabhavananda (ed), *Patanjali Yoga Sutras*, Sri Ramakrishna Math, Madras, 1953
5   Archie J Bahm, *Yoga: Union with the Ultimate* (A New Version of the Ancient Yoga Sutras of Patanjali), Arnold-Heinemann, New Delhi, 1978, p 143
6   'Golden Flower Doctrinal Instructions of Saint Lu', in Quin Ling (ed), *Annotated Selections from Ancient Chinese Chi Kung*, Guangdong Science and Technology Publishing House, 1987, p 14, in Chinese

Chapter 3

1 See my *The Art of Chi Kung*, Element Books, Shaftesbury, 1993, pp 42–3, 47–50
2 Quoted in Conrad Hyers, *Zen and the Comic Spirit*, Rider, London, 1974, p 35
3 Michael Talbot, *Beyond the Quantum*, Macmillan, New York, 1986, pp 51–2
4 Professor Edmund Jack Ambrose, *The Nature and Origin of the Biological World*, Ellis Horwood, Chichester, 1982, p 19
5 Dr Andrew Scott, *The Creation of Life: From Chemical to Animal*, Basil Blackwell, New York, 1986, p 10
6 Alastair Rae, *Quantum Physics: Illusion or Reality?*, Cambridge University Press, 1986, p 3
7 Victor Krivorotov, 'Love Therapy: A Soviet Insight', in Church and Sherr (eds), *The Heart of the Healer*, Signet Books, New York, 1987, pp 185–6

Chapter 4

1 D T Suzuki, *An Introduction to Zen Buddhism*, Grove Press, New York, 1964, p 88
2 Hubert Benoit, *Zen and the Psychology of Transformation*, Inner Traditions International, Rochester, 1990, p 51
3 Katsuki Sekida, *Zen Training: Methods and Philosophy*, Weatherhill, Tokyo, 1981, p 200
4 See my *The Quest for Cosmic Reality*
5 Ibid
6 'Mystic Experiences of Medieval Saints', quoted from Julian Johnson, *The Path of the Masters*, Radha Soami Satsang Beas, Punjab, 1985, p 332
7 Venerable Sheng Yan, *The Experience and Explanation of Zen*, Dong Chu Publications, Taipei, 1995, p 86
8 Cheng Yi Shan, *Ancient Chinese Thinking on Chi*, Hupei People's Publications, Hupei, 1986, p 111, in Chinese
9 *The Heart Sutra*, in Chinese. See my *Wisdom of the Heart Sutra* for a detailed explanation
10 See *Wisdom of the Heart Sutra*, op cit

Chapter 5

1   Edward Conze, *A Short History of Buddhism*, Unwin Paperbacks, London, 1986, p 59
2   Garma C C Chang, *The Buddhist Teaching of Totality*, Pennsylvania State University Press, 1971, pp 121–2
3   Walpola Rahula, *What the Buddha Taught*, Grove Press, New York, 2nd edition 1974, p 16
4   Ibid
5   Alastair Rae, *Quantum Physics, Illusion or Reality?*, Cambridge University Press, 1986, p 67
6   Walpola Rahula, op cit, p 51
7   Kenneth K S Ch'en, *Buddhism in China*, Princeton University Press, 1964, p 46
8   Ibid, pp 36–40, 46, 117, 138
9   Fremantle and Trungpa (trans), *The Tibetan Book of the Dead*, Shambhala, Boston, 1987, p 101
10 Rune E A Johansson, *The Dynamic Psychology of Early Buddhism*, Scandinavian Institute of Asian Studies, Curzon Press, London, 1985, p 22
11 Edward Conze, *Buddhist Thought in India*, Allen & Unwin, London, 1962, p 125
12 K N Jayatilleke, 'Buddhism and Science', in Venerable Nyanaponika Mahathera (ed), *Pathways of Buddhist Thought*, Allen & Unwin, London, 1971, p 96
13 Edward Conze, op cit, p 124

Chapter 6

1   Chogyam Trungpa, *Shambhala: the Sacred Path of the Warrior*, Shambhala, Boston, 1988, p 103
2   K N Jayatilleke, 'Buddhism and Science', in Venerable Nyanaponika Mahathera (ed), *Pathways of Buddhist Thought*, Allen & Unwin, London, 1971, pp 93–4
3   Ibid, pp 313–14
4   Mir Valiuddin, *Contemplative Disciplines in Sufism*, East West Publications, London, 1980, p 150
5   Chuang Tzu, quoted in Zhang Yong Ming, *Ancient Chinese Chi Kung and Pre-Qin Dynasty Philosophy*, Shanghai People's Publishing House, 1997, p 204, in Chinese

6 His Divine Grace Bhaktivedanta Swami Prabhupada, *Bhagavad-Gita As It Is*, Bhaktivedanta Book Trust, Los Angeles, 1986, p 583

7 Andrew Scott, *The Creation of Life: From Chemical to Animal*, Basil Blackwell, New York, 1986, p 172

8 Narada Maha Thera, *A Manual of Abhidhamma*, Buddhist Missionary Society, Kuala Lumpur, 4th edition 1979, p 281

9 Walpola Rahula, *What the Buddha Taught*, Grove Press, New York, enlarged edition 1974, p 36

10 Ibid

11 Paravahera Vajiranana Mahathera, *Buddhist Meditation in Theory and Practice*, Buddhist Missionary Society, Kuala Lumpur, 2nd edition 1975, p 472

12 Chiko Komatsu, *The Way of Peace: the Life and Teachings of the Buddha*, Japanese edition, Hozokan Publishing Co, Kyoto, 1984, trans Sekimori, 1989, p 63

13 Ibid, p 285. The original Chinese term 'fa-men' is translated as 'Law-Gate'; I think 'Spiritual Gate' is more appropriate. In a Buddhist context 'fa' usually means 'spiritual' rather than its literal meaning 'law'

14 *The Heart Sutra*, in Chinese. See my *Wisdom of the Heart Sutra* for a detailed explanation

Chapter 7

1 Alan Watts, *The Way of Zen*, Penguin Books, Harmondsworth, 1975, p 23

2 *Discussion of Zen Awakening and Enlightenment*, Bodhi Institute, Kowloon, 1987, pp 4–5, in Chinese

3 Walpola Rahula, *Zen and the Taming of the Bull*, Gordon Fraser, 1978, pp 19–22

4 See my *The Arts of Shaolin* (Element Books, Shaftesbury, 1996) for further explanation of why Zen did not originate from Taoism

5 Studies of Ming Confucian Scholars, quoted in Zhang Rong Ming, *Ancient Chinese Chi Kung and Philosophy of Early Qin*, Shanghai People's Publishing House, 1987, p 242, in Chinese

6 Wing-Tsit Chang, *Platform Scripture*, St John's University Press, New York, 1963, p 187

7 Ibid, p 139

8 Venerable Hui Guang, *Gateway to the Study of Zen*, Tai Feng Cultural Matters Co, Taipei, 1961, p 13, in Chinese

9   Junjiro Takakusu, *Essentials of Buddhist Philosophy*, Greenwood Press, Westport, 1975, p 159

10 From *Transmission of the Lamp*, quoted in Venerable Yue Qi, 'Cultivation Methods in Zen Buddhism', in Xu Zhao Ren (ed), *Guide to Meditation*, People's University Publishing House, Beijing, 1992, p 141, in Chinese

Chapter 8

1   This story is derived from numerous sources, especially from Su Xing, 'Hui Ke Seeking the Dharma', in Wang Hong Jun, *Folk Tales of Shaolin Monastery*, Henan People's Publishing House, 1981, pp 11–14, and from *Transmission of the Lamp*, both in Chinese

2   See my *The Arts of Shaolin* (Element Books, Shaftesbury, 1996) for a detailed presentation of the three Shaolin arts

3   Wing-Tsit Chan, *Platform Scripture*, St John's University Press, New York, 1963, p 17

Chapter 9

1   Wing-Tsit Chan, *Platform Scripture*, St John's University Press, New York, 1963

2   A F Price and Wong Mou-Lam, *The Diamond Sutra and The Sutra of Hui Neng*, Shambhala, Berkeley, 1969

3   Wing-Tsit Chan, op cit, p 45

4   Wong Mou-Lam, op cit, p 42

Chapter 10

1   See my *The Quest for Cosmic Reality*

2   Michael Talbot, *Beyond the Quantum*, Macmillan, New York, 1986, p 45

3   Sir Arthur Stanley Eddington, 'The Nature of the Physical World', in Commins and Linscot (eds), *The World's Great Thinkers – Man and the Universe*, Random House, New York, 1947, p 414

4   Paul Davies, *God and the New Physics*, Penguin Books, Harmondsworth, 1990, p 163

5   John Gribbin, *In Search of Schrodinger's Cat*, Black Swan, 1992, p 2

Chapter 11

1 See my *Sukhavati, The Western Paradise: How to Go to Heaven as Taught by the Buddha* which gives a detailed account of the philosophy and practice of the Amitabha School

Chapter 12

1 Cai Rong Ting, *Methods of Awakening Realization by Zen Masters,* Manjusri Publications, Taipei, 1986, in Chinese
2 *Enlighten the Mind and See Reality in Zen Buddhism,* Bodhi Institute, Kowloon, 1982, pp 31–2, in Chinese
3 Ibid, pp 170–1
4 Ibid, p 170

Chapter 13

1 Junjiro Takakusu, *Essentials of Buddhist Philosophy,* Greenwood Press, Westport, 1975, p 160
2 Quoted in Theodore de Bary (ed), *The Buddhist Tradition in India, China and Japan,* Vintage Books, New York, 1972, pp 263–4
3 From *Takuan, Osho Zenshu,* quoted in de Bary, ibid, p 378
4 Quoted in de Bary, op cit, p 369
5 Daisetz Teitaro Suzuki, *The Awakening of Zen* (ed Christmas Humphreys), Prajna Press, London, 1980
6 Daisetz Teitaro Suzuki, *An Introduction to Zen Buddhism,* Evergreen Black Cat, New York, 1964, p 116
7 Alan Watts, *The Way of Zen,* Penguin Books, Harmondsworth, 1975, p 187
8 See Giei Sato and Eshin Nishimura, *Unsui: A Diary of Zen Monastic Life,* East-West Centre Books, University of Hawaii, Honolulu, 1973
9 Daisetz Teitaro Suzuki, *An Introduction to Zen Buddhism,* op cit, p 34
10 Katsuki Sekida, *Zen Training: Methods and Philosophy,* Weatherhill, New York, 1981, p 100
11 T P Kasulis, *Zen Action Zen Person,* University of Hawaii, Honolulu, 1981, p 85
12 Katsuki Sekida, op cit, pp 66–82

Chapter 14

1 Thich Thien-An, *Buddhism and Zen in Vietnam*, ed Carol Smith, Charles Tuttle, Rutland, Vermont, 1975

2 Jerrold Sesaki, *The New Face of Buddha*, Coward-McCann, New York, 1967, p 164; quoted in Thich Thien-An, op cit, p 213

3 Thich Thien-An, op cit, p 27

4 According to Thich Thien-An's system of denotation, the founder of the sect is referred to as the Founding Patriarch, and his successor as the First Patriarch. Hence, Vinitaruci is the Founding Patriarch, and Phap-Hien the First Patriarch. But, for consistency, throughout this book, here and elsewhere, the Chinese system is used, whereby the Founding Patriarch is regarded as the First Patriarch

5 La K'uan Y'u (ed and trans), *Ch'an and Zen Teaching*, Rider, London, 1961, p 58; quoted in Thich Thien-An, op cit, p 54

6 Holmes Welch, *The Practice of Chinese Buddhism*, quoted in Thich Thien-An, op cit, p 101

7 Quoted in Thich Thien-An, op cit, pp 79–80

8 Thich Thien-An, op cit, pp 103–4

9 Nguyen-Dang-Thuc, quoted in Thich Thien-An, op cit, p 121

10 Quoted in Thich Thien-An, op cit, pp 206–8

11 Thich Thien-An, op cit, p 111

12 Ibid, p 130

13 Ibid, pp 155–6

14 Ibid, p 150

15 Ibid, p 166

Chapter 15

1 Venerable Jin Ming, *Buddhism and Chinese Culture*, in Chinese and English, Malaysian Buddhist Association, Penang, 1993. The version I have quoted is my translation from the original Chinese, because in my opinion the poetic beauty as well as part of the meaning is lost in the English version provided (p 28), which is as follows: 'This is because the transcendental mind of Zen can be easily mingled with nature (the mountains and the rivers). Therefore in landscape drawing, the idea of drawing and the mind Zen [sic] combined to create a new outlook.'

2 See my *The Art of Shaolin Kung Fu* and *The Art of Chi Kung*, Element Books, Shaftesbury, 1996 and 1993

3 See my *The Complete Book of Tai Chi Chuan* (Element Books, Shaftesbury, 1996) for a detailed explanation on how this wonderful art can be used for self-defence, health and spiritual development

4 Daisetz T Suzuki, *Zen and Japanese Culture*, Princeton University Press, 1970, p 63. In Japan, Tendai, Shingon and Jodo, like Zen, are various forms of Mahayana Buddhism transmitted from China, where they were known as Tian Tai, Zhen Yen (Mantra), Jing Tu (Pure Land) and Chan respectively

5 Eugen Herrigel, *Zen in the Art of Archery*, Routledge & Kegan Paul, London, 1976, pp 89, 90

6 Quoted from Nan Haui Jin, *Discourse on Zen and Tao Concepts*, Jin Gang Publications, Taipei, 1986, p 91, in Chinese

7 Ibid, p 94

8 Quoted in Feng You Lan, *Short History of Chinese Philosophy*, Bai Lin Publications, Kowloon, n.d, p 86, in Chinese

9 Feng You Lan, op cit, pp 65–72

Chapter 16

1 Cited in Venerable Sheng-Yen, Ch'an, Dong Chu Publications, Taipei, 1986, pp 69–70

2 Sheng-Yen, op cit, pp 89–90

Chapter 17

1 See my *The Art of Shaolin Kung Fu* (Element Books, Shaftesbury, 1996) for combat and other aspects of Shaolin Kungfu

Chapter 18

1 For a deeper study of chi kung, see my *The Art of Chi Kung*, Element Books, Shaftesbury, 1993

Chapter 19

1   Venerable Sri Dhammanada, *Meditation: The Only Way*, Buddhist Missionary Society, Kuala Lumpur, 1987, p 33
2   Katsuki Sekida, *Zen Training: Methods and Philosophy*, Weatherhill, New York, 1981, p 23
3   Ibid, p 17
4   Ibid, p 33
5   Ibid, p 100
6   Lawrence LeShan, *Clairvoyant Reality: Towards a General Theory of the Paranormal*, Turnstone Press, Wellingborough, 1982, p 78
7   Ibid, p 88
8   Tomio Hirai, *Zen and the Mind: Scientific Approach to Zen Practice*, Japan Publications Inc, Tokyo, 1978, preface
9   Ibid, p 33
10 Philip Kapleau, *The Three Pillars of Zen*, 1980, p 13
11 Satipatthana Sutta, in *Bhikkhu Nanamoli and Bhikkhu Bodhi, the Middle Length Discourses of the Buddha: A New Translation of the Majjhima Nikaya*, Buddhist Publication Society, Kandy, Sri Lanka, 1995, pp 145–55
12 Daito Kokushi (1281–1337), 'The Original Face', in Trevor Legget (ed), *A First Zen Reader*, Charles Tuttle, Rutland, Vermont, 1982, p 21
13 Ibid
14 Takashina Rosen, 'A Tongue-tip Taste of Zen', in Trevor Legget (ed), op cit, p 38

Chapter 20

1   Daisetz Teitaro Suzuki, *An Introduction to Zen Buddhism*, Grove Press, New York, 1964, pp 56–7
2   Ibid
3   Huang Dun Yan, *Stories of Zen Buddhism*, Yi Geng Pictures and Books Company, Taipei, 1994, p 96, in Chinese
4   Chuang Tzu, *The World*, section 7 (ancient Chinese text)
5   Da Hui Zong Guo (1089–1163), quoted in Venerable Sheng-Yen, *The Experience and Explanation of Zen*, Dong Chu Publications, Taipei, 1984, p 67
6   Venerable Sheng-Yen, op cit, p 112
7   Daisetz Teitaro Suzuki, op cit, p 101

Chapter 21

1 See my *Sukhavati: the Western Paradise – How to Go to Heaven as Taught by the Buddha*

2 For a detailed explanation of the *Heart Sutra*, see my *Wisdom of the Heart Sutra*

Chapter 22

1 Walpola Rahula, *Zen and the Taming of the Bull (Towards the Definition of Buddhist Thought)*, Gordon Fraser, London, 1978, p 11

2 Bimala Churn Law, *A History of Pali Literature*, Bhartiya Publishing House, Varanasi, 1933, n, p 117

3 Udana: 80, quoted in S Dhammika, *All About Buddhism*, The Buddha Dhamma Mandala Society, Singapore, 1990, p 52

4 John Blofeld, *Wheel of Life*, p 172; quoted in Professor Holmes Welch, *The Practice of Chinese Buddhism 1900–1950*, Harvard University Press, 1973, pp 81–2

5 Ibid, pp 82–3

6 August Karl Reischauer, *Studies in Japanese Buddhism*, Arms Press, New York, 1970, p 32

7 Venerable Sheng-Yen, *Getting the Buddha Mind*, Dharma Drum Publications, New York, 1982, p 47

8 Kenneth K S Ch'en, *Buddhism in China*, Princeton University Press, 1964, p 63

9 The Buddha, Udana, quoted in Edward Conze, *Buddhism: Its Essence and Development*, Bruno Cassirer, Oxford, 1957, p 61

10 Walpola Rahula, op cit, p 21

Chapter 23

1 For a comprehensive study of Shaolin Kungfu and Taijiquan, see my *The Art of Shaolin Kung Fu* and *The Complete Book of Tai Chi Chuan*, Element Books, Shaftesbury, 1996

2 Dhamma-cakka-ppavattana-sutta, quoted in *Three Cardinal Discourses of the Buddha*, trans Nanamoli Thera, Buddhist Publication Society, Kandy, Sri Lanka, 1972, p 6

APPENDIX

Dragon in Zen

Following is the complete sequence of moves for Dragon in Zen. Please see Chapter 17, Zen of Strength and Movement, for a description of how to perform each move.

No-Ego Stance (17.10)

Dragon and Tiger Appear (17.11)

Two Tigers at the Ready (17.12)

White Snake Shoots Out Energy
(17.13)

Precious Duck Swims Through Lotus
(17.14)

Black Tiger Steals the Heart (17.15)

White Snake Shoots Out Energy
(17.16)

Precious Duck Swims Through Lotus
(17.17)

Black Tiger Steals the Heart (17.18)

Beauty Looks at Mirror (17.19)

False-Leg Hand Sweep (17.20)

Green Dragon Shooting Across a Stream (17.21)

Golden Dragon Plays with Water (17.22)

Yellow Oriole Drinks Water (17.23)

Happy Bird Hops up a Branch (17.24)

Reverse Hanging of the Golden Lotus (17.25)

Beauty Looks at Mirror (17.26)

False-Leg Hand Sweep (17.27)

Green Dragon Shooting Across a
Stream (17.28)

Golden Dragon Plays with Water
(17.29)

Yellow Oriole Drinks Water (17.30)

Happy Bird Hops up a Branch (17.31)

Reverse Hanging of the Golden
Lotus (17.32)

Single Dragon Emerges from the Sea
(17.33)

Tranquillity of One-Finger Zen in the
Whole Cosmos (17.34)

Dragon and Tiger Appear (17.35)

Two Tigers at the Ready (17.36)

Standing Meditation (17.37)

FURTHER READING

Ambrose, Edmund Jack, *The Nature and Origin of the Biological World*, Ellis Horwood, Chichester, 1982

Bahm, Archie J, *Yoga: Union with the Ultimate* (A New Version of the Ancient Yoga Sutras of Patanjali), Arnold-Heinemann, New Delhi, 1978

Benoit, Hubert, *Zen and the Psychology of Transformation*, Inner Traditions International, Rochester, 1990

Bhaktivedanta Swami Prabhupada, His Divine Grace, *Bhagavad-Gita As It Is*, Bhaktivedanta Book Trust, Los Angeles, 1986

Ch'en, Kenneth K S, *Buddhism in China*, Princeton University Press, 1964

Conze, Edward, *A Short History of Buddhism*, Unwin Paperbacks, London, 1986

Conze, Edward, *Buddhism: Its Essence and Development*, Bruno Cassirer, Oxford, 1957

Conze, Edward, *Buddhist Thought in India*, Allen & Unwin, London, 1962

Davies, Paul, *God and the New Physics*, Penguin Books, Harmondsworth, 1990

de Bary, Theodore (ed), *The Buddhist Tradition in India, China and Japan*, Vintage Books, New York, 1972

Eddington, Sir Arthur Stanley, 'The Nature of the Physical World', in Commins and Linscot (eds), *The World's Great Thinkers – Man and the Universe*, Random House, New York, 1947

Fremantle and Trungpa (trans), *The Tibetan Book of the Dead*, Shambhala, Boston, 1987

Garma C C Chang, *The Buddhist Teaching of Totality*, Pennsylvania State University Press, 1971

Goleman, David, *The Meditative Mind*, Jeremy P Tarcher, Los Angeles, 1977

Gribbin, John, *In Search of Schrodinger's Cat*, Black Swan, 1992

Herrigel, Eugen, *Zen in the Art of Archery*, Routledge & Kegan Paul, London, 1976

Holmes Welch, Professor, *The Practice of Chinese Buddhism 1900–1950*, Harvard University Press, 1973

Humphreys, Christmas, *Zen*, Teach Yourself Books, Hodder & Stoughton, London, 1976

Hyers, Conrad, *Zen and the Comic Spirit*, Rider, London, 1974

Jayatilleke, K N, 'Buddhism and Science', in Venerable Nyanaponika Mahathera (ed), *Pathways of Buddhist Thought*, Allen & Unwin, London, 1971

Johansson, Rune E A, *The Dynamic Psychology of Early Buddhism*, Scandinavian Institute of Asian Studies, Curzon Press, London, 1985

Kasulis, T P, *Zen Action Zen Person*, University of Hawaii, Honolulu, 1981

Krivorotov, Victor, 'Love Therapy: A Soviet Insight', in Church and Sherr (eds), *The Heart of the Healer*, Signet Books, New York, 1987

La K'uan Y'u (ed and trans), *Ch'an and Zen Teaching*, Rider, London, 1961

Legget, Trevor (ed), *A First Zen Reader*, Charles Tuttle, Rutland, Vermont, 1982

LeShan, Lawrence, *Clairvoyant Reality: Towards a General Theory of the Paranormal*, Turnstone Press, Wellingborough, 1982

Price, A F and Wong Mou-Lam, *The Diamond Sutra and The Sutra of Hui Neng*, Shambhala, Berkeley, 1969

Rae, Alastair, *Quantum Physics: Illusion or Reality?*, Cambridge University Press, 1986

Rahula, Walpola, *What the Buddha Taught*, Grove Press, New York, 1974

Rahula, Walpola, *Zen and the Taming of the Bull*, Gordon Fraser, 1978

Reischauer, August Karl, *Studies in Japanese Buddhism*, Arms Press, New York, 1970

Sato, Giei and Eshin Nishimura, *Unsui: A Diary of Zen Monastic Life*, East-West Centre Books, University of Hawaii, Honolulu, 1973

Scott, Andrew, *The Creation of Life: From Chemical to Animal*, Basil Blackwell, New York, 1986

Sekida, Katsuki, *Zen Training: Methods and Philosophy*, Weatherhill, New York, 1981

Sekida, Katsuki, *Zen Training: Methods and Philosophy*, Weatherhill, Tokyo, 1981

Sesaki, Jerrold, *The New Face of Buddha*, Coward-McCann, New York, 1967

Sheng-Yen, Venerable, *Getting the Buddha Mind*, Dharma Drum Publications, New York, 1982

Suzuki, Daisetz Teitaro, *An Introduction to Zen Buddhism*, Grove Press, New York, 1964

Suzuki, Daisetz Teitaro, *The Awakening of Zen* (ed Christmas Humphreys), Prajna Press, London, 1980

Suzuki, Daisetz Teitaro, *Zen and Japanese Culture*, Princeton University Press, 1970

Takakusu, Junjiro, *Essentials of Buddhist Philosophy*, Greenwood Press, Westport, 1975

Talbot, Michael, *Beyond the Quantum*, Macmillan, New York, 1986

Thich Thien-An, *Buddhism and Zen in Vietnam*, ed Carol Smith, Charles Tuttle, Rutland, Vermont, 1975

Tomio Hirai, *Zen and the Mind: Scientific Approach to Zen Practice*, Japan Publications Inc, Tokyo, 1978

Trungpa, Chogyam, *Shambhala: the Sacred Path of the Warrior*, Shambhala, Boston, 1988

Valiuddin, Mir, *Contemplative Disciplines in Sufism*, East West Publications, London, 1980

Watts, Alan, *The Way of Zen*, Penguin Books, Harmondsworth, 1975

Wing-Tsit Chang, *Platform Scripture*, St John's University Press, New York, 1963

Wong Kiew Kit, *The Art of Chi Kung*, Element Books, Shaftesbury, 1993

Wong Kiew Kit, *The Art of Shaolin Kung Fu*, Element Books, Shaftesbury, 1996

Wong Kiew Kit, *The Complete Book of Tai Chi Chuan*, Element Books, Shaftesbury, 1996

INDEX